TALES FROM THE
GERONIMOO

SCOTT FRANK

TALES FROM THE
GERONIMO

my **seduction** by **junk** and **desert dreams**

Q

Quartet Books

First published in Great Britain by Quartet Books Ltd, 1996
A member of the Namara Group
27 Goodge Street London W1P 2LD

First published in the United States by Grove Press 1995

A catalogue reference for this book is available from the British Library

ISBN 0 7043 0246 2

Printed and bound in Finland by WSOY

This book is dedicated to my mother

acknowledgements

Thanks to my agent, Oscar Collier, for providing encouragement to write this book when I thought I wasn't ready. His response to my first two chapters made me realize it was time to relate these tales.

My editor at Grove Press, Anton Mueller, and the copy editor, Susan Brown, have shown sensitivity and sureness with their sharp suggestions and corrections. I'm grateful for Anton's warm willingness to consult me during the book's evolution from raw manuscript to final product.

Katie Killary was essential for early edits and for hard and worthy criticisms. She was my reliable, secret sounding board when I dared not show the first drafts to anyone else.

contents

drifting off

1 The junkies gathered in a circle on the night lawn. After midnight, flat on our backs, we sighed with genuine relief at temporarily escaping the vicious heat of this desert. Hugging the cool ground, hidden from cruising cops, we lay safely behind aged walls and ancient columns of the Geronimo Hotel.

I gazed up past a canopy of dim yellow light. Dirty floodlights, too weak even to reach the treetops. Scanning up past the sound of wind through unseen palm fronds to the stars that spun around my little world. Then over to the tower, just a silhouette whose black mass blocked the stars in that part of the sky.

It was the tallest structure on the property. Somewhere inside of it an old man kept a secret watch over the once glorious hotel, modestly commanding from the highest point in the yard a silent, unjudging vigil on us, the trash below.

Closing my eyes, I felt a light, rocking motion as the cool night mixed with opium. I dreamed: ships sailing gently away to a cottony horizon, their masts disappearing last.

"I'm misting."

Junk wasn't really a very big part of my life when I first moved into the Geronimo. I didn't like to pay to get high, and since most of my dealings, and therefore freebies, were in weed, most of my intoxication also came from weed. That and alcohol. I led a carefree existence and generally held my liquor and weed well.

While I met a wide range of people in my tradings, I retained a nucleus of longtime friends, some of whom had done quite well in the pot business. These people demanded secrecy, for self-protection, so I always had a well-monied, private clientele. As they began to use heroin, my dealings naturally turned to that. I could then take my profits in junk if I wished. The initial effects were very pleasant, so I took advantage of my trade in it.

The Geronimo was a beaten, crumbling hotel, but it had obviously seen some great days. I found it quite romantic, really. The telephones were still the old, dialless, black ones, run from a central switchboard downstairs. Even the toilets held a grotesque romance for me. With no top covers, they flushed violently, removing the contents in an instant when I pressed a silver handle. I was amused, as only youth could be, by sounds from a chronic alkie next door, heaving for an hour and rapidly whooshing anything that came up down that efficient fixture. On the other side lived a fireman, home for forty-eight hours then gone the next forty-eight. When he was there he usually boozed it up with a friend who called him Captain.

The management had the cooling process down to a science. Just as the first thin coating of sweat began to form over my drowsy body, the system would switch on. Throughout the day it hummed a current of air that wasn't cool, wasn't hot, but at least it was moving. And then at night, just as the desert began to release its heat and the first sighs of relief sounded, well, that's when they'd turn it off. That was about 9:30 P.M., and not a moment's extra cooling was wasted. Tenants would have to wait sometimes until past midnight to feel any real relief. This process contributed to my habit of sleeping during summer days and moving around at night. Most business took place at night anyway.

Tucson really emptied out when the university stopped for the summer. The postmidnight streets were quiet. Neighborhood cats would lie on still-warm asphalt, usually getting out of the way of rare oncoming cars. And at night the Geronimo took on an ethereal hibernation, revealing memories and scenes as reverie might grace a reflective soul. Long, dusky hallways led to mysterious outside passages lined with weathered columns casting discarnate shadows—great for dreamy strolls to decades past. I could imagine elegant women, tuxedoed men effecting secret rendezvous in the maze of paths between the lodges. And within the hotel proper, old fireplaces and plush emerald leather furniture (now covered with strips of gray tape) whispered comforts of a happier, more carefree time. Now, junkies nodded through the evening, and, peaceful as such a bewitching scene might've appeared, always there lurked an undercurrent of dread that life among a pack of dogs brings.

This current coursed through the silence of the coolest, darkest hours. Whether I joined the group that gathered to snooze and smoke out on the courtyard lawn or I chose to nod my time away in the privacy of my room, I could always feel a subtle, ever-tightening thread of fear. All of us felt it, knowing that the merciless sun would rise again, that supplies were dwindling and needed to be replenished. I staved off this horror with shots, followed by hours of serene euphoria. My body, released from the aches and pains of everyday existence, let my mind exalt in long, satisfying flights of fancy.

Alone in my room, I sought and found utter physical and mental joy. Sitting at my window, I stared out at a red light atop a nearby radio tower. I hoped that if I stared long enough my body would somehow learn to associate ecstasy with that slowly blinking lamp. Then I wouldn't need dope anymore. And I knew in my heart that there couldn't possibly be anything wrong with feeling so good.

Little puffs on hand-rolled cigarettes helped me fall into a hundred little sleeps, little nods, with an endless series of funny, curious dreams. Once I entered a Swiss village during a colorful festival; the townspeople were deliriously happy to see me. Toward morning, just as the sky would begin to glow, I'd hear conversations babbling in my ears. As present as the real thing, they'd stop the instant that I focused my mind. My internal dialogue went on a rampage as I drifted into shadow sleeps. Indulging this pleasure until I simply couldn't stay awake any longer, I'd flop into bed. Though I had no trouble falling asleep after these sessions, I always felt a bit like I had had to leave a fantastic, lively party with only my shabby little room to return to.

I'd drift into real sleep. Sometime later hissing sounds filled my ears, followed by a creeping bodily paralysis. Voices lurked on the other side of the hissing, but the clearer they became the stronger the paralysis would get. Alarmingly quickly I found that I couldn't move at all! I heard footsteps—just out of sight. Yes, out of sight, for I'd managed to get my eyelids halfway open. And the torrent of sound! Like the banging of huge pots from a mob whose fervent babbling rose and fell in waves. I tried to rise, but a hand pushed me back down. A hand, right on my chest. A deep, full, black voice was yelling, "No! No! *No! No!*" Straining with every ounce of strength that I could muster, I pushed, tugged, and finally snapped awake!

A thin coating of sweat covered me. The sun was almost blinding, barging in my window. No cooler on yet. I'd been having another Heat Dream, yet to my immediate regret I realized that I again hadn't managed to sleep very late.

Like most of the others, I tried to sleep through the heat of the day, but I was usually the first one up. I hated awakening with that thin coating of sweat and the sun bursting in. At least, I consoled myself, it was past my windows by the time it reached its hottest, brightest zenith. By noon I was already anticipating more cool night hours.

It was an active anticipation. I had to score, often a long, laborious procedure, to have that pleasant evening. How I was able to wring anything nice out of the Geronimo existence is, I guess, the basis of this tale.

The Geronimo offered cheap lodgings (special summer rates), and it was right in the university neighborhood. Having a part-time prof for a father, I was aware of it from an early age. Viewed from afar it seemed to be the last stop for a sad collection of pensioners and postwar alcoholics, sprinkled with a dash of indignant, feisty old men resentful at finding their last years spent in such a fleabag. It wasn't until I actually moved in that I became aware that it also functioned as Junkies, Inc.

Like most everyone there, I'd planned on only a temporary stay. Who wants to call a seventy-dollar-a-month flophouse "home"? Everyone was "just passing through." Some had been passing through for a decade. Some would die there, and not just of old age. Just passing through.

Like Nazi Paul.

"I really didn't think I'd be here this long." He scraped his spoon against a dented pink bowl. All the bananas were gone; he was probably ingesting bits of pink metal.

"Hell, I had a real rosy future in front of me. Just got out of the federal pen, up in Denver. Armed robbery. Knocked off a bank a few days after I got out, bought me a beater, and drove it down here." He grinned shyly. His young face became an impish skull.

"Pulled into town pretty late at night. Got me a motel near the freeway. Boy, was I glad to be here after six years in the can. Had me a car and six grand. Parked in front of my room, went in to take a leak—didn't even close the door to the room. When I got back out, someone had broken into my car and stolen my bags! Just like that! All the money was in 'em. I wasn't even gone a fucking minute!"

He shrugged, like someone had just pulled puppet strings. "Boy," he mused. "Some thief got lucky that night. . . ."

Paul was the only Nazi/junkie/bank robber I knew personally. Months of heroin indulgence had formed the figure of an Auschwitz survivor, his shirt hanging on his shoulder blades, wrists and elbows the widest parts of his arms. Smacking his lips, he grinned a horrible, satisfied leer.

"Ahh, those bananas and honey do the trick. Gotta have something to keep body and soul together." He spent virtually every cent on drugs, and malnutrition caused food to hit him like amphetamine. Nodding brightly, he bent back the handle of the spoon to make it balance on the table. It was the same spoon he used to cook up his dope. "It's a shame, really. You know, man can *almost* live by heroin alone." He looked around absently. "Man, I gotta get outta this place. . . ."

So, these were the types of secrets languishing inside the Geronimo. When I first arrived I had also had some money, about $1,600. Where did it come from? Well, it's hard to piece it all together now, it was so long ago. I think I middled some pot deal. That was most of it. And I occasionally made money by packing large loads of weed for cross-country shipment. Fifty cents a pound. Good work when I could get it. But that type of money always has a hidden tax. I got very stressed out, though I didn't recognize it, and I suffered unusual effects. Unable to center myself adequately to rent a house, or even pick up the classifieds and look for one, I actually spent years sleeping on one couch after another. Offering people $25 or $30 when I had it, I'd convince them to let me stay at their house for a week or four days or whatever.

When I didn't have any money, I'd just sleep in an alley or someplace like that. More than once I was stopped for vagrancy but was always able to display the minimum $10. Sometimes I'd sleep outside with $600 in my pocket, so I guess my arrangements didn't always have to do with being broke. I just preferred to rent a week's worth of couch time from someone. Those who had phones and kitchens were the best, especially if they worked during the day. I was always running around trying to set up little deals, and the phone made it that much easier. And I enjoyed tapping into that "lived in," homey feeling. The police must've heard of my activities from time to time, but I figured I moved around so much that they could never get a fix on me. That was one benefit of my lifestyle.

I'd tell myself and other people that I wanted to be able to leave town if the opportunity came up and that there was no use paying rent on houses in two towns. My passport always peeked out of my back pocket. But these were just excuses. The truth was that I couldn't get centered enough to settle down in one place. As if that's an achievement. Well, if it is, I'd finally achieved something when I walked in and rented that room at the Geronimo. Even then I started out paying the twenty-eight-dollar-a-week rate for a few weeks before I admitted to myself that I might be there for months.

I'd dabbled in junk a couple years before I got there. Nixon's Operation Intercept, a few years earlier, and other police operations had helped countless pot smokers get introduced to it, and not just in border towns like mine. While Border Patrol was frisking carloads of nuns for weed, the channels that brought it over realized that there was money to be made with smaller, harder to find, more valuable packages. Sometimes junk actually became more common than weed. If you had to see a secret connection to buy bootleg booze and there wasn't any around this summer, would you sample something else available from the same source? From the looks of our enforcement results, some people obviously would.

Actually, Tucson is a caldron for only five months of the year, from about May through September. The other seven months provide some of the most beautiful weather in the nation. Often a feeling of glee filled me when I heard of people freezing to death in Ohio while we were parading around here without shirts on. And all of my time at the Geronimo wasn't spent baking and sweating. I'd first moved in during September or October, near the last of the hot weather, and the desert, with a grace of autumn rain, was soon in full bloom.

Most out-of-towners are shocked when they see just how green our desert gets. When spring and fall rains arrive on time, the land becomes a captivating array of color. Cacti and bushes bloom, wildflowers and grasses cover the land. Newcomers usually don't realize that the desert has more life per square mile than any other environment. These same novices end up getting caught out there later in the year without water, suffering or even dying from exposure and dehydration.

Desert life is deceptive because so much of it remains unseen, underground, is nocturnal, or even changes colors to match surroundings. Of course, desert junkies aren't the only species to sleep during the day and come out at night. Darkness is filled with a lulling chirp of crickets, hoots of hidden owls, and howlings of coyote packs, screaming like madwomen as they thread their way between hills, luring out neighborhood dogs. Far from town, coyotes scurry to make way for human "mule" trains of smugglers and wetbacks crossing the border under cover of night. Small reception committees gather in covert spots, straining for the sound of airplane engines, hoping they don't get hit with the bales of pot tumbling from above.

As a child I roamed my desert, digging up pottery shards of ancient Indian pueblos. I camouflaged my tree houses so that other kids wouldn't tear them down. When I grew older I learned the secrets of cultivating crops on a land that produces some of the world's strongest poppies and marijuana. Tucson is only an hour's drive from the border, and I've often reflected on the influence that's had on my life.

When I moved into the Geronimo, in late summer of '74, the hotel walls were exploding with bougainvillea vines, the grounds covered with roses and African daisies. The sun, still a bit oppressive, marked the hours by passing through rows of flame trees whose shadows met with those cast by the weathered columns and stucco arches. I was enthralled by the simple odor of antique stucco dust drifting through passageways and hypnotized by sunlight flickering in the bushes. In short, I allowed myself to indulge in the carefree existence that a pile of twenty-dollar bills offered a young man in a hometown flophouse.

I put down twenty-eight dollars and moved into a small room on the third floor, the top floor. It overlooked a large, private courtyard lined with individual lodges and accented at one end by an odd tower of single little rooms. Every so often I tried to rent one of the lodges but was never successful in that. Paul lived in one of the lodges.

Nazi Paul, my first acquaintance at the Geronimo, got his name for the sympathies he expressed for the losers of World War II. When I first saw him he was barefoot, wearing a secondhand long-sleeved shirt and a baggy pair of khaki pants. Sporting that POW look. I made him for junk right away. Likewise, he didn't seem to have any trouble distinguishing me from the police. Of course, I didn't let him or anyone else know that I had a pile of twenties. I didn't view them as money, really, more as tickets, each allowing me entrance to a couple full days of entertainment. Grabbing a few, I made my way through a maze of stairs and worn paths down to Paul's lodge.

Motioning me in as soon as I knocked, he flopped listlessly back onto his bed. All he wore that day was a baggy pair of boxer shorts, pale against his Germanic bronze skin. His ribs rose inches above his stomach. But I could never tell if he was sick or not until he actually spoke.

"Hey, Paul!" I ventured. "How's it going?"

"Could be better. Could be a helluva lot better." He stayed on his back and shrugged his palms into the dim light, letting them fall back onto the bed. As he continued to stare passively at the ceiling, I realized that he was junk-sick. This did not bode well for my opportunities.

I stammered on. "So—ahh—can you get anything?" Mysteries of heroin procurement were, at this time, still largely unfathomed by me, but I sensed Paul had some leads. The needle marks on his arms said so.

"I can always get it." He sighed. "I just don't have any money."

I saw my in. "Well, how about if I introduce me to who you get it from if I give you a couple of dimes?"

That perked him up a bit. "I think we can work something along those lines. Hell, yes!" Laboriously, Paul pulled up to a sitting position on the side of the bed. "How much were you thinking of buying, anyway?"

"Oh, maybe five dimes. You know, fifty dollars' worth. Think they'll give me a break at fifty bucks? Six for five?"

Paul got philosophical, tilting his head. "Well-l-l. It never hurts to ask."

He was apparently so sick that the mere thought of getting some stuff pulsed energy into his veins. I myself would experience this strange effect later on, after I developed my habit. Withdrawal feelings would temporarily subside as I would buy something after a long search or as I was preparing to shoot it. Out of curiosity I'd sometimes wait before I took the shot, just to see how long that pseudorelief lasted, but it wouldn't last very long.

Not wanting to appear pushy or anxious, I paused before venturing to speak again. "So . . . you feel like going?"

It was like the sound of Allied artillery in the ears of a concentration camp victim. Nazi Paul jumped up, threw on khaki pants and a wrinkled long-sleeved shirt, then rapidly ran his fingers through stringy blond hair in front of the mirror.

"Let's go!" he trumpeted, practically walking through me to the door.

I drove while Paul gave directions. The place was in a mixed neighborhood, past some railroad tracks. Paul was relieved that we didn't catch a train.

"Many's the time I've had to endure twenty extra minutes of being sick watching the train," he commented. "Jim's really the guy that runs the place we're going. Today we'll probably have to go through his roommate, Bill. But try to get to Yaqui Jim if you can."

The house stood at a small bend in the road, making it visible to neighbors down both ends of the street. With all the traffic coming and going, they must've known what was happening, but nobody had complained yet. A blend of Mexicans, blacks, and cracker whites stood in the various yards. Next door was an abandoned house with large pieces of plywood haphazardly covering the windows. Paul knocked at the door of a house in slightly better condition; the door opened a crack, then a bit more, a sign of recognition. A short, roly-poly guy let us squeeze in, swiftly closing the door behind us. He nodded to Paul, then faced me.

Paul made introductions. "Bill, this is Scott. Scott here wants to give you some business."

Bill made a pretense of evaluating me, but there really wasn't much going on under that blond burr haircut. He looked remarkably like a young Jean Genet, which I found appropriate.

"Well," he quickly surmised. "I guess if you're with Paul you're probably all right."

He motioned us toward a ratty old couch. My knees went up to my chest when I sat down; getting up would mean climbing out. Bill picked an upright chair. His feet didn't touch the floor, swinging childishly as he broke the ice.

"So, how much do you want, anyway?"

"Can I get six dimes for fifty dollars?"

Bill rolled that around in his round head for a minute, then shrugged.

"Wait here a second." He disappeared into one of the bedrooms. From another room farther down the hall a young, redhaired woman briefly peered out at us, predatory curiosity on her face. Bill returned.

"That's Marty. She'll give you a hand job for ten dollars." He took my lack of response for disbelief, declaring, "She will!"

"Well, maybe another time," I murmured shyly.

Then a husky, serious Indian youth entered the room. His evaluation of me seemed to carry more weight.

"That's Jim." Bill motioned. Jim's eyes didn't seem to hold the cloudiness of the other occupants'. I met his stare long enough to try to indicate that I wasn't afraid (i.e., of being discovered that I might be a cop) but not so long as to be challenging. That meant looking away first. Jim made a soft growl and went into the kitchen.

"Come in here," he ordered.

When we were all seated at a cheap, gray Formica table, Jim pulled out a half dozen tiny paper packets and placed them before me, along with a syringe. His dark eyes glistened at me from a deep red face, all lurking behind long, straight, black hair.

"If you turn out to be a narc, I'll kill you." He smiled. Yaqui Jim seemed like the kind of guy you could have a good laugh with before he'd slice your face off.

"Don't worry." I grinned. It seemed a rather lame response.

Bill piped up. "Jim here doesn't do any himself. He just sells it."

I silently accepted what turned out to be true. In all the time that I did junk, Yaqui Jim was the only dealer I ever met who fulfilled the old stereotype of the pusher who doesn't mix business with pleasure. "That's right. I don't do it myself," Jim said. "But that doesn't mean I don't want to see you do some." He shoved the dirty syringe into my face.

Back then entrapment was still a respected legal concept; seeing someone do dope was considered a surefire test of whether he was a cop. Of course, that didn't weed out informers, but a person had to have been busted to do something that low, if he did it at all. AIDS hadn't been invented yet, but serum hepatitis was a real fear, and the filthy needle Jim proffered looked like a good way to get it. Paul tucked his head into his shoulders and grinned like a skull.

"Ahh—I don't really like to use other people's needles," I hedged. Jim glared. "But I'll snort some here if that'll make you happy. I can't be a cop and snort it."

Jim accepted that after some legal reflection. He pushed the little packets toward me. They were quite tiny, and I was glad that my hands didn't shake as I gently pried open the delicate corners on one. Inside was a small amount of a dark, almost black substance, strong Mexican heroin resting in a bit of white powder, like sugar or lactose. That was the cut. The absurdity of using a cut that was a completely different color than the drug didn't seem to bother these people. Pouring a bit onto the table, I crushed it into a fine powder with a guitar pick that I carried. I then used the pick to separate the now brownish powder into some little lines, rolled up a ten-dollar bill, and efficiently inhaled the stuff up my nose.

"Well." I raised my brow facetiously. "That wasn't too painful."

Bill was the only one to take me up on my offer of the lines still on the table. Then he started talking, hoping I'd forget to take my ten-dollar bill back. As I pinched it, Paul and I packed up to leave.

"Come back anytime," offered Bill, letting us squeeze out a crack in the door.

It was a relief to return to Paul's cool, dark lodge. We cooked up the stuff. I let him do me up; the guy had the touch of a Florence Nightingale. Paul flopped back onto his bed.

"Ahh," he sighed. "I didn't expect this day would turn out so well."

Myself, I laid on my back on the red concrete floor, contentedly regarding the wooden beams that crossed the ceiling in southwestern style. The heat and glare were kept at bay by a thick wooden door and heavy, water-stained curtains. In the midday blue-gray dusk of Paul's lodge, I felt soothing warmth pulse through my body. When the shot first hit me, I had been surprised to feel the sensation of knots I didn't know were there loosening in my stomach, but now, as I lay on the floor, the borders between physical and mental euphoria were becoming increasingly hazy. Taking a deep breath, my back pressed on cold concrete, I closed my eyes and let my mind drift. Away from the stress, the pointless boredom and body aches, back to my traveling days. Back to the Café de la Renaissance in the imperial city of Fez. Sipping chilled lemon sodas, leaning on cold marble slabs that lined the booths. The whole café empty but for me and a greasy Moroccan waiter in wrinkled black-and-whites, never looking up but immediately responsive to my every gesture. Lighting from an old black-and-white movie, hashish swimming in my head, as we both hid from Africa's sweltering sun. Leaning on a cool stone. Only now it was heroin instead of hashish. The Arab waiter changed into a Nazi junkie.

Paul sighed.

"Göring wasn't that bad, really. He just had his own ways, that's all. . . ."

After leaving Paul's lodge, I tried to carry those pleasurable feelings into the cool morning hours. Gradually I learned a number of ways to extend my high—smoking weed, taking pills, nursing cigarettes, small booster shots—trial and error experiments to help me nod until dawn. I would generally spend these hours on a weather-beaten third-story porch overlooking University Blvd. These were the hours of my haven.

I would usually arrive after midnight, fall into an old wooden armchair, brush flecks of chipped gray paint from my arms, and perch my feet up on the warped wooden rail. Lighting the first of a collection of hand-rolled tobaccos I'd previously prepared in my room, I began to work on an endlessly evolving brew of quick dreams, audio hallucinations, rushes of physical pleasure, and personal reflections. These last included keeping a lid on poorly suppressed anxieties threatening to boil over.

"My God, what's going to happen to me?" was either a common worried refrain or part of a blissful exhalation. Biting my bottom lip, surveying the dark, empty street, I'd smoke a cigarette. I wasn't a regular smoker, and I felt each puff; the medicines enhanced it and vice versa. It calmed me to feel tobacco poisons spreading through my limbs. Too much made me dizzy, but each breath helped dispel terrors of oncoming addiction, fears of legal apprehension, and other pressures of my situation, quelling them before they stampeded. And the unanswerable question was finally suppressed again.

The university area was usually quiet after midnight, and it was utterly desolate at those hours during summer. From my perch I could watch with impunity as patrol cars went cruising by. Footfalls would announce rare strollers a block before they appeared. Generally, I saw only the tops of their passing heads, and I enjoyed having this private look. But sometimes the walker would suddenly look up right at me, as if hailed. These nocturnal wanderers, with animal awareness, met my gaze with relief that it was only me, followed by a subtle flicker of mutual understanding. I wasn't a threat to them; it didn't matter if I knew their game. Their game was theft.

For when the deepest hours of the morning enclose the desert, before the first glows of dawn, secret armies ooze over the valley floor. Burglars burst from cover to hit dwellings they've staked out; smugglers hoist knapsacks, form their lines, and course silent paths across the border; low-flying planes aim for rendezvous with shivering, huddled ground groups, who pray that they don't get walloped by some hundred-pound flying duffel bag of weed. And a huge cat-and-mouse game again begins between the cops and their prey. The mice know that the odds are always with them.

Taking puffs on my cigarette, I dreamed of my desert: awash in green, filled with the bountiful smell of freshly fallen rain upon the creosote, bathed in moonlight like a sleek, bright snow across the land. The adrenaline of risking your life against the penalties of the law can make these things so dear. Letting my lids fall, I saw the desert from above, drenched in moonlight. Humorous conversations filled my ears, so audible, only to disappear as soon as I paid attention. I woke up almost giggling. They were so funny, yet I couldn't remember more than the last line I'd heard.

Sometimes I'd reach such a state of relaxation—a trancelike state—that I could actually direct conscious attention without stopping these exchanges. More often, though, I'd just jerk awake without even realizing that I'd fallen asleep. It felt so snug and alluring knowing that I could do it again, and I'd try to pay attention to the actual point of passing out. But I'd jump awake and realize that I'd been fooled once more.

Of course, if I was too awake I'd remember where I was—in a desolate land of contradiction and cruelty, surrounded by a threatening, suspicious population of junkies and junkie-killing crackers; the latter, straight, hard-nosed characters who celebrated John Birch Day and ignored daylight saving time. They'd taken my beautiful desert and turned its glimmering mirages into manmade lakes. I took a deep breath and closed my eyes. Mirages of silver lakes shimmered across a sunlit plain. And off in the distance, shivering through the haze, London Bridge, transported piece by piece to an inglorious end at manmade Lake Havasu. It was traversed by a noisy procession of retired stroke victims. I jumped awake.

"My God, what's going to happen to me?"

Anytime a troop of cops, with deputized crackers bringing up the rear, could swarm through the Geronimo, making room-to-room searches, knifing open mattresses, throwing hard-won stashes to the floor, and snapping on cuffs to cart off the collected residents of Junkies, Inc. Surely, I mused, they must know what's going on here. And I'd heard of other sizable raids of boardinghouses and apartments that were known hangouts of drug users and criminals. Why, one only had to stand on the street corner to pick out the users, the "fiends," as Nazi Paul called us. The junkies were the ones who wore long-sleeved shirts in the 105-degree weather, to cover up lines of festering, oozing tracks running up their arms, residue of persistent hypodermic jabs. During my year at the Geronimo, I never did shake the fear of sudden, massive police intrusion. I had to light another cigarette to calm down.

It worked. A tranquilizing effect spread through my arms. Taking a deep breath, I noticed the eastern sky. My eyes were heavy, and I was thankful to be able to count on sleep through at least part of the oppressive heat beyond the horizon's yellow fringe. Outlines appeared of windows and aerials that hadn't been visible earlier. Marveling at the permanent riot on the edge of my consciousness, I closed my eyes and summoned one more pleasant taste of nodding dreams. I moved the cigarette so it wouldn't burn me if I dropped it. My night's pleasure was drawing to a close. The medicinal feelings weren't as strong. Images of lines of smugglers, troops of burglars filled my mind, rushing back to safe houses, loathing the dawn glow. Low-flying planes scurried back to hidden hangars. A whole secret army fleeing before a huge rising sun. The desert opened up in front of me, dawn, deceptive, dangerous. A malevolent black tornado rose over the land and spun right at me. I awoke suddenly, a voice still ringing in my ears: "Sleeper is safer."

Rising from my chair, brushing off more paint flakes, I stretched and exhaled. Blood rushed to my head. I was sorry to have to go to bed. After all, hadn't I been enjoying myself?

2 Lest you get the misimpression that I was purely a nocturnal creature, let me explain that I spent many pleasant daylight hours pursuing my obsessions. And it wasn't always torturously hot. When I first took up Geronimo lodgings it was almost fall, and I looked forward to seven months of great weather.

I still owned a beat-up car, which never took less than five minutes to start, no matter how much I beat on the steering wheel. I had money when I took my third-floor room and spent many an autumn day experimenting with junk. Still snorting it at that point, I followed up with a smoke of high-quality weed, the kind that smells and tastes like a lush pine forest. Expenses for these items were next to nil, for I had my private clientele. They knew I'd keep their locations and phone numbers confidential, keeping them lucrative contacts who paid me in whatever combination of weed and cash I wished. The weed was so good that I could trade it for more junk, with which I'd supply my special customers, and so on.

A typical fall day started with a snort of heroin and a joint for breakfast. I found the combination very invigorating; it sharpened my appetite instead of dulling it, like it did later on. After a pleasurable meal—the most mundane selections became absolutely delicious—I rolled another joint and took a drive into the blooming desert countryside. The stuff I'd snorted in the morning lasted well into the afternoon and seemed to take a few hours to reach full potency. I was still new to junk and would occasionally find myself on the verge of vomiting inside a nice restaurant, or subject to loud, unrelenting hiccups. Waitresses gave me a dubious eye. Vomiting on junk isn't always accompanied by nausea, and it takes experience to recognize that you're about to do it. I've seen a few beginners sitting with embarrassed, shocked grins on their faces, trying to deal demurely with the contents of their stomachs suddenly appearing on their laps. Car travel seems to exacerbate this, and it wasn't uncommon to give someone a lift only to find the next day that he'd quietly upchucked on the back floor, something I've been guilty of once or twice myself.

These bodily functions weren't that shocking in those days, what with experimentation with hallucinogenic mushrooms and peyote cactus, the latter including vomiting as part of the ritual. Trying a new drug and having this reaction didn't strike me as unusual. Especially with so many youngsters barfing on booze. As time went on my stomach got stronger, but there were always some who, no matter how experienced, could be counted on to waste a good meal.

This aside, the autumn beauties of the hotel grounds greatly enhanced my indulgences. I was often quite content in my serene euphoria to view the brilliant vines of queen's wreath that climbed the flame trees and old plumbing of the Geronimo. Especially intoxicating was the odor of crumbling stucco dust, similar to the smell of the windy desert driven before oncoming rain. And of course the normally invigorating fall rains were positively romantic when combined with the all-encompassing seductions of opiates. Listening to thunder roll, lightning and showers glistening on my windows, I smugly held myself as having a greater than average appreciation of these beauties. I felt superior in my choice of paths that had led me to this combination of freedom, drugs, and twenty-dollar bills. The drive for self-preservation, a by-product of my outlaw ways, kept me from vocally extolling the wonders and joys of what I took to be my elevated philosophy. Still, in looking back I realize that there were times that I was flippant, moments that I was overbearing and uninhibited in my posturings and passings, and I often wonder how I and the other lowlifes were viewed by the older, more world-weary residents of the hotel.

For junkies and alkies made up only half the tenancy there; the other half were pensioners, aged men and women whiling away last years on social security or small savings. This included a collection of taciturn old men, crotchety codgers who knew the bum's rush by heart. They moved laboriously, some with canes, refused to be hurried, and didn't fight the slow flow of their hours. The junkies fit right into the time frame. These oldsters didn't seem to harbor any illusions about what was taking place there. Unlike the younger desperadoes who roamed the halls at all hours, treating the place as just one more transient experience, older tenants accepted, albeit sullenly and resentfully, the permanence of their position. They steadfastly ignored the unlawful disorder around them. Even the old lady who operated the hotel switchboard part-time held herself aloof. Spending her golden years beneath the dusty windows of the little phone room, she entertained herself with what she thought was surreptitious eavesdropping on our phone calls. Little clicks indicated that she was listening in on dime conspiracies, two-bit setups, accusations of rip-offs and informing, the random despairs and exhilarations of the lowest levels of the drug world. These things kept her occupied for hours each day. Bless her. With all the incriminating things she must've heard, she never did call the police.

There was one old fellow who did manage to carve out a niche of privacy for himself. Stegman was his name. He occupied the highest point on the property, atop the tower of single rooms overlooking the courtyard lawn. A set of concrete steps led up to his place, steps with corners filled by black widow webs. You can tell the widow webs because they're never symmetrical like other spiderwebs. A black widow can spin a mesh of sticky, haphazard threads two or three feet long in a matter of hours. They're generally in out-of-the-way spots but sometimes at face level across a nighttime path. Their presence on the tower steps indicated how little traffic passed that way.

Quixotic hints of mystery beckoning through cloisters, and poorly lit halls were potentiated by that old tower. With its peach pastels glowing in the sunset and the weathered gray bordering, it sort of embodied the faded glory of the once genteel hotel. It did for me, anyway. I felt that if the legends, the ghosts and visions of the place had somehow been stored, they'd lay hidden in the tower waiting for the right person to rediscover them. If so, I had no doubt that the right person was me.

Stegman looked appropriate as the keeper of the tower but hadn't the spiritual tone of anything more than a guardian. Rather taciturn, really, certainly not gregarious, he bore a demeanor that appeared friendly, even jolly. It must've been his short, round body, his thick, wavy, gray hair and scraggly beard. Or maybe his protruding gut, matching a round, red nose to make him look like a character displaced to the desert from a Currier & Ives Christmas card. More approachable than the other oldsters, he was introduced to me as Steggy by a flippant young deviant. I could tell that he didn't like the name, but his age and frailty left him powerless to do anything about it. "My name is Stegman," he corrected, frowning.

Index cards and pens stuck out of his shirt pocket, and he rambled on about geometry, Pythagoras, some bit about trisecting an angle. I wasn't astute at geometry, but, maybe because I addressed him as Stegman, he invited me to climb the tower steps and visit sometime. A lad whose head was in the clouds anyway, I knew I'd take up the invitation. Really, it was more than I could resist.

With some anticipation, a few days later I made my way up the steps angling about that square structure. After a series of sharp left turns, I was suddenly faced with a cracked and peeling blue door. I knocked on the yielding, shredded surface.

"Come in, come in! I was just working on my math."

The old guy was surprised and happy to see me, motioning me in with a sweep of his arm. After two steps I could go no farther; the rest of the tiny cubicle was packed tight with his bed, a large desk, and some bookshelves. And Stegman.

"Well, this is it," he explained with a flip of his pudgy, aged hand, simultaneously falling to a sitting position on his bed.

When I closed the door behind me, I found that I'd entered an ethereal blue-gray cave, a sharp contrast to the bright sunlight I'd just left. Though large windows made up fully two of the walls, outside light was dispersed by overhangs.

"Yep." He nodded to me. "This is where it happened."

Papers and index cards strewn across his desk were covered with hard to discern gray pencil lines—curves and angles and tiny notations—the same color as the twilight in there, as the gray hairs extending defiantly from his nose and ears. A strong, salty, unwashed odor filled my mouth and nose. Stegman wore the same chartreuse shirt I'd seen him in earlier and the only one I ever saw him wear. The pens and index cards never seemed to change either. I tried to ignore the smell and participate in the conversation, though I had no idea yet what it was about. I was pleasantly distracted by a breathtaking view through his huge windows. Tucson's basically a one-story town, and anytime you command a vista above that, you're pretty much the tallest thing around. My morning's medicines were coming on strong, and I reveled in the billows of white clouds scanning usually unseen rooftops, floating to the northern Catalina Mountains.

"This is fantastic up here," I finally murmured. A disappointment that I had to share it with Stegman involuntarily filled me.

"Well, yes, it is," he absentmindedly agreed, taking a brief glance outside. "It's not too bad. A little cramped, but we have to make do with the plate life hands us. Don't you want to know *what* happened up here?"

My head and attention snapped back to him. "Why, yes, of course, of course. What happened?"

"Ahh." He sat erect on the bed, which was also his desk chair, and laid his palm flat on the papers. "This . . . is where I trisected an angle!" And he looked me right in the eye.

Sudden ignorance, I realized, is a lot like awakening from a dream.

"They say it's impossible," he continued. "Nobody in history has done it since Pythagoras climbed out of his cave with a right angle. Until now. I"—he placed his hand on his chest and bowed—"am the first person in three thousand years to find a new way to do it, using only the basic tools of geometry, that is." He held up a piece of string. "They said it couldn't be done but"—he snorted—"since when do *they* know anything?" A brief rummage in the confusion of his desk. "Now, if I could just find the card I did it on. . . ."

My frown held in a laugh. It figured. I could easily imagine Stegman on the verge of world recognition, doomed to anonymous exile in the Geronimo for want of a simple index card.

He sighed and gave up his search. "It's only the biggest thing to happen in the history of geometry! I was so amazed when I finally did it that I guess I wasn't myself. I *had* to tell somebody, so I went downstairs to visit Mrs. Nutting at the switchboard, and when I came back, wouldn't you know it? I just couldn't find that card anywhere. Somewhere between here and there . . . anyway, you can imagine how that made me feel. For the last year I've been trying to duplicate it, but, for the life of me, I can't remember exactly what it was I did."

Pythagoras and Stegman, I reflected, each in his cave. It was by watching shadows in his cave that Pythagoras first decided that the Earth was really a sphere. Then Ptolemy watched the shadows in his own cave and proclaimed that the sun revolved around this sphere. Visions of Old Stegman striding manfully along the docks of Alexandria, enjoying his rightful place in lands traveled by the ancient Greeks. He and Pythagoras, beards in the wind, sharing the implications of seeing a ship's masts disappearing last as it moved over the horizon. I felt myself being hypnotized by those beautiful clouds. The distinct feeling of a breeze passed through my skull.

I forced speech. "You'll get it back sometime. Don't worry about it. I bet one day it'll just pop right up again, probably when you least expect it."

"Ahhh—" He gave a jaded snort of disgust. "Science and math have been co-opted. All the needless politics. Funding and tenure, experimentalists and all that bullshit. Science *used* to be deduced by thought. Science was *once* the realm of mystics, son."

Indeed, I reasoned. People with such contempt for the real

world that they'd just go live in a cave and invent geometry. Now that was a view that I could sympathize with. The clouds continued to sail. And Stegman vented spleen. "Why, before all that you could just be a merchant and call yourself a scientist. The mystics hated that. Their contempt for the real world removed science and math from the merchants. The merchant-scientist!" he sputtered derisively. "Nowadays science and academia are so damn stultified that we've come full circle: the goddamned merchant-scientist is coming back into his own!"

I was surprised that I could feel a sense of boredom amidst such raving. It wasn't that I disagreed with him. It was the way he kept interrupting my contemplations of the sky. And he held such a commanding view. Had he seen us, heard us? Old people have funny sleeping habits. Surely he must've witnessed some of the postmidnight scenes down on the lawn. Yet he seemed so unjudging of me, of the young fiends who stopped to chat with him. Could it simply be a lack of comprehension?

He kept up a muttering conversation without me. ". . . caliphs revived Euclid . . . dark and crumbling structures . . . Europe roused from a slumber. . . ."

I harbored my own secret, a luscious, special bit of knowledge. Opium. It distracted me from his worldly concerns. Index cards. Trisected angles. What did I care for them when I had at my command a most serene euphoria?

"Ptolemy!" he burst out. "Those were the days! He made a whole career out of thinking the sun circled round the Earth. Hell, he'd fit right in today!"

Stegman did not find my grunts and head shaking suspicious in the least. A talkative bore can usually hold up both ends of a conversation. And I had my secret. Which I knew I could never tell him.

"From Ptolemy till now," he proclaimed. "There's nothing new under that sun!"

My secret allowed me to weather his storm of pompous outrage. It made it humorous and him a harmless fool. I was distanced from his concerns. Not yet distanced from the whole world—just the sections and times of my choosing. I was not yet so far gone that I could view myself. Otherwise I might've stopped. My secret had not yet branded me or gotten a stranglehold on me. It had not yet *become me*. I got up to leave.

"Come on back up. Anytime!" offered Stegman. His round face flushed red with appreciation. The old man, guardian of the tower, obviously enjoyed visitors.

"Thanks! See you later."

Making my way down the series of right angles that were stairs, across the circle of our night lawn, I passed through the Geronimo lobby and out onto Euclid Ave.

Postmidnight. Treading deliciously cool air, piercing dark archways, I pushed through some bushes and emerged onto the night lawn. Others already sat in twos and threes or sprawled on their backs, watching the stars flicker in and out of wispy clouds. My entrance went almost unnoticed, just a nod from a couple of familiar faces, and I let out a weary breath as I lowered myself onto the grass. Remembering the afternoon's bright heat produced fatigue, and as soon as I was on my back I was panting slightly at the recollection.

Tall palms punctuated each corner of the yard, suggesting a square within the round lawn. Floodlights covered with years of dirt and rain spots were too dim to reach the treetops. The soft light cast tranquility over the area, accented by a mild breeze. Most of the surrounding lodges were darkened, their residents asleep, and the tower's silhouette was easily missed if one didn't know it was there. I wondered if Stegman was awake and watching.

Other weary junkies arrived after me, flopping onto the grass oasis. Soon there was almost a complete circle of sitting and prostrate drug fiends. Talk remained at low level—private conversations, little setups, plans for future break-ins, dreams about drugstore robberies. Packages of cheap Bugler rolling tobacco appeared and were passed around. I produced a joint but, as usual, didn't have many takers. A lot of junk users didn't like the feelings of anxiety it produced in them. Some, like me, enjoyed the way it made opiates stronger and the increased capacity for the smoke that opiates provided. A low stucco wall blocked the view of this idyllic scene from the street; no fear of the law suddenly appearing.

Every once in a while a drunk would wander in, loud, boisterous, and unappreciated. I was amused as they'd gradually become aware of an uncomfortable feeling, the obscure sense that something wasn't quite right. We didn't make them feel welcome, shunning drunks with the same repulsion that the addict has for alcohol. Eventually, wanting to escape that vague sense of not fitting in, the drunks would stumble off into the night. Use of alcohol and heroin together was rare, for it produced unpleasant results in most of us—painful vomiting, headaches, dizziness, death. The combination is highly poisonous, and after a hard night's drinking many a lush has accidentally done himself in with a morning-after shot. Just the smell of alcohol was repugnant to me when I was on dope. It reminded me of the heavy, cheerless drinking I would partake in when my supply was interrupted.

These nightly gatherings introduced me to more of Tucson's hidden junk network. Nazi Paul had been my initial contact. He, in turn, put me in touch with a few of his associates. Despite my pre-Geronimo dabblings, Paul was my first real hard-core source and gave me the sense of dealing with a different, lower, ostracized stratum of society. I began to see the junkie handshake: extending the arm at the elbow and lifting the palm up and down, as if carrying something. It was a way of silently asking, "Are you holding?" The same motion repeated by the other person meant "No." I was surprised this stuff hadn't been left back in the 1940s, but it lives on in prison systems and transient hotels. Places where time has slowed down.

Even with Paul as my conduit, I knew only one party who was a steady supplier. That was Yaqui Jim and his household. Everyone else was like me: a seller one day, a seeker the next. Demand always outstripped supply, and while solid leads to dope were kept jealously hidden, this tenuous network was usually rife with rumors about who was holding, who gave short counts, who could score or was a thief or a snitch. It was a vicious, backbiting, endlessly revolving circle of ex- and future cons, chronic liars, thieves, informers—dogs who could only be counted on to grab some change off your nightstand or weed from your drawers as soon as you stepped out to take a leak. People are dogs anyway. There's nothing you can do about it. When I was high I didn't have to think about it. But this circle of mongrels had dispensed with the civilities that most humans use to disguise their heel-snapping, groveling behavior.

The night lawn was like a small water hole where the multitude of beasts could gather to recuperate from the vicious desert heat. The food chain was suspended. I never saw any actual deals take place there, and if you were sick you weren't likely to show up, preferring to languish in the lonely agony of your room. Under black skies we gathered for the succor that every creature seeks and needs. Sometimes I would hear a tale, a reminiscence of better times or a soft recounting of somebody's past nightmare. And how often the horrible times in our lives become more bearable in the retelling.

Richard spoke.

"I went in at closing time. The keys were in the door, and I locked it behind me. There was just the pharmacist and the cash register girl. Seemed like there was some other kid in the back room, but he didn't want any part of it *at all,* which was fine with me."

Richard sat cross-legged, speaking gently into his crotch. Long, greasy brown hair hung into his face, and a sinewy build hinted at fast reflexes toned up in a prison weight room.

"I pointed my gun at the pharmacist down at the other end of the counter. Ordered him to open up the narcotics drawer. Damned if that idiot didn't reach into the drawer and start to pull out a pistol! Shit! I wasn't even thinking by then—I just grabbed the girl and held my gun to her head. He just stood there with the gun half in, half out. I told him to put it down or I'd blow her fucking head off! When he didn't move I pulled the hammer back—he put it down and got the stuff. Fuck, I don't know *what* I would've done if he had pulled that thing out!"

Only part of the circle was listening. He spoke in soft, easy tones. Lying on my side, leaning on my elbow, I nonchalantly gave a little nod, encouraging him to continue. I made a mental note that Richard liked to rob drugstores.

"Yeah," he went on. "Served my time up in State." His reference to Arizona State Prison in Florence caused a hulking dullard next to him to snort a little laugh and shake his head in agreement. Richard looked up and grinned. "You, too, huh? Were you there?"

"Yeah, sure was."

"How long were you there?"

"Three years."

"Yeah, that's what they gave me, too. Three years." The soft floodlights shone brighter in his cold, laughing eyes. "Ahh, it wasn't that bad. When I first got there I thought, Oh fuck, now I'm in fucking prison. Shit, what's gonna happen to me now? When they slam that first door behind you, that's what they want you to think, you know? But it wasn't nearly as bad as I thought. You know how it is." They both laughed in agreement. "The first year you don't have time to get bored. You know, you're running here, running there, trying to learn your way around. Takes a while to figure out what's going on, ins, outs. Then the second year you're busy using all that stuff you learned the first year. It's when that third year comes around that you start saying, 'Shit! I still have to be here?' "

"Yeah, I know where that's at."

"Sure, you know about it! And, fuck, if you're sittin' with some guy that's doin' twenty-seven years, well, you're not gonna start whining about one more lousy year. You know what I mean?" Richard regarded his crotch again, shaking his head. "Fuck, twenty-seven years. I don't know how I'd do that. Man, I don't even like to think about it."

I nodded knowingly, even though I'd never served any time. Nor did I want to imagine it. Lying all the way back down, I fired up my joint.

The tower's silhouette bore down on me. The old man's got to hear some of this. Been up there for years, drawing on his little cards, watching the clouds roll by. What's it like to be at the mercy of dozens of passing Richards, Nazi Pauls? I guessed that it tended to make him pretty unjudgmental. Out of self-preservation, if nothing else.

Soft, sensuous breezes played over me, and I closed my eyes, remembering how bright it had been the day I'd visited his cave. Viewing the clouds above as they paced our talk and below sprawled a sunny, blue harbor. Ancient sailing ships, Phoenician sloops, combing the Egyptian coast for a decent deal, a good trade. We watched, together, as they sailed away to richer lands. Their masts disappeared last.

3 "First the birds fly more rapidly and lower to the ground. Ants scurry quickly around their holes. And the trees curl their leaves to catch the moisture. These are all signs that the doctor will be writing."

Earl gazed up reflectively at gathering gray rain clouds. They matched his eyes. His jaw squared in the manner of Marlon Brando. I tolerated these indulgences because he had achieved master's status in the high art of hitting up croakers. To Earl, rain meant people would be getting sick, and so he would be getting high. ("Sick people mean active doctors.") Rain and allergy seasons made it easier for him to obtain dope prescriptions. His ability made him a favorite in many circles, and I felt fortunate to receive the benefit of his expertise. Usu-

doctor, I'm coughing up green stuff

ally, with another script granted him, he'd gravitate to more monied friends despite our running together since high school. After all, somebody had to pay. This was probably just as well; Earl was what's known in the trade as a junk-hog.

He was insatiable, utterly obsessed with pills, elixirs, powders. Cough syrups were his specialty, sometimes two or three bottles per day from different pharmacies—high-narcotic mixtures specially called in by a physician. Totally submerged in drug consumption, he would, in the absence of contraband, consume bottles of aspirins, vials of vitamins, antibiotics, antacids, anything that could indulge the hand-to-mouth action of eating medicine. He could never be trusted to divvy up a purchase between co-buyers. He'd simply split the pile and immediately consume the larger portion before anyone could say a thing. At times he literally had to be restrained from touching the stuff until someone else divided it in a more honest fashion.

Earl almost never had any money, using his croaker-milking talents to coast along from one friend's home to another. After once again exhausting everyone's patience, he'd return to his mother's until she got sick of him, too. All provided free rent, free cars, and free phones, allowing him to carry on his practice. Most often after scoring another bottle of syrup, he'd visit Mark, our richest friend, who'd pay for the script in exchange for half, throwing in a few bucks extra and maybe dinner or a movie.

"You are not to touch that until you get back here, *do you understand?* I'm paying for that, Earl, and you're not to drink a *drop* until we split it up."

Many's the time that I heard Mark admonishing Earl after giving him the medicine money, in the often vain hope that Earl would split up the stuff honestly. Still, no one could argue the fact that, of all of us, he had the greatest success by far with the doctors. And everyone knew that pharmaceutical stuff was the cleanest and the best. With Earl's coaching, some of us learned to have occasional hits using his methods. Then Earl would simply find out the name of the doctor and impersonate us to get renewals.

These questionable values ran hand in hand with his romantic self-image of poet-thief. Submerging his personality beneath a small crowd of admired writers and performers, he treated us to an amalgamation of François Villon's morals dressed in Rimbaud's velvet coat and Jim Morrison's leather pants, animated by Mick Jagger's lithe movements and Brando's pathos, all coated with a thin veneer of hip philosophers and avant-garde intellectuals. Somewhere beneath this lay hidden a very unconfident Earl, who dared to venture out for only moments at a time, usually when under the influence. He despised his southern heritage and spoke with an astute aloofness to cover it up. Betrayed by pale, paunchy, rather coarse features, dotted with a scattering of moles, he looked like a good ol' boy. At times these same traits became mysteriously charming. Once Earl's father had held up a copy of Sartre's *Being and Nothingness* and asked, "Is this all you wanna be, Earl, nothin'?" This was a source of great glee to us.

His coasting existence was just one more result of the exploding drug-dealing economy we were part of. My easygoing lifestyle owed no less to my fortunate position next to highly successful dope dealers, though I managed to generate my own funds, had moved away from Mom and Dad, and certainly hadn't stoked up the oil-burning junk habit that Earl had. Still, in retrospect, I often feel the irony offered by the successes and benefits of that great drug economy, for while it provided an illusion of freedom and fostered great individualistic ideals, it also led to our stricture. My limited local circle of friends, as they became more security conscious, retreated further and further from the world. They became casualties. Earl, Mark, myself were only a few of the enormous but invisible Reclusive Generation. Within these circumstances it was natural that Pete be attracted to us. He and Earl spent much time together. Pete, a near-total recluse, was the black sheep of his rich family, who owned a small steel company in Ohio. Pete himself lived in a corrugated steel hut, the back rooms of which were dirt floors. A cipher of a lad, he spoke too softly and despised loud noise. Circumstances didn't encourage him to break this mold; his quarterly stipend from a family trust fund was used to purchase armfuls of expensive art books and records. Inevitably he'd sell these at a loss to used stores for food money to tide him over till his next check. His parents had given him a brand-new yellow Ford, which shone incongruously outside his shack. He made extra cash with it by driving loads of weed back east. Having no ambitions, he was satisfied to spend life in front of stereo speakers, sipping tea from a teaspoon and listening to Marlene Dietrich and Edith Piaf records (at very low volume). This is exactly what he was doing when I knocked on his door.

"You may come in if you don't talk," he ordered in a gravelly, flaccid voice, gesturing to the floor for me to sit. His jaw jutted in mild offense. Conservative etiquette, well-scrubbed appearance, trimmed, curly, light brown hair all hinted at his being the product of a rich, time-honored family. Resuming a chair in front of the speakers, languidly crossing his legs, he dropped his eyelids half-closed as if I were no more than an irritating insect. I hated his French chanteuse vein, with his obnoxious insistence on absolute silence, but I'd told Earl that I'd meet him at Pete's. Some people indulge snobbery and airs even if they live in a garbage can, which is just about what Pete lived in, but he was the monied class, and it was natural that Earl would go to his place. I was relieved when I heard a knock at the door.

"Oh, perfect timing," sneered Pete, recognizing Earl's knock. He wasn't aware of our plans to meet.

Earl entered clumsily, carrying three large grocery bags that made a horrible grinding and clinking sound as he laid them down. They were each filled to the brim with empty brown glass cough syrup bottles. His files. By meditatively considering labels on these old soldiers—the dates, doctors' names, pharmacy phone numbers—Earl could determine the most auspicious moves in conjuring up a new script. Virtually all his work was done on the phone, so, with barely a word of greeting, he disappeared into Pete's back room and whispered covertly into the mouthpiece. Practically covering it with his hand as he spoke, he hunched his shoulder when I peeked in. He didn't want anyone to hear the doctor's name, afraid that they'd impersonate him and get his refills.

"And have the doctors been good to you today, Earl?" I asked him when he came back in.

"The doctors are always good to Earl," Pete sneered.

"We'll see, we'll see." Earl grinned mischievously. "Oh." He turned to Pete. "If the phone rings, let me answer it, okay?"

"All right, Earl. Of course, of course."

"*But it's all right!*" screamed Earl. He mimed holding a microphone, twisting and gyrating over to the stereo to put on some rock music. Rolling Stones blasted as he hopped and balanced precariously on one leg. Really, he made far more noise than I did, but Pete tolerated it—to a point. He was a slave to Earl's attentions and syrups. In return, Earl could crash at his house, use his phone, and surround himself with Pete's expensive books and records. Earl hooted and screamed along with the songs until Pete calmly lowered the volume.

"That will be all for now, Earl. Please sit down and tell us your prospects for the day." Pete gallantly motioned to the floor, where Earl suddenly flopped, cross-legged. "Your prospects, Earl?"

"I'm awaiting a callback from the doctor," he replied obediently.

"Ahh," I sighed. "Do you think he'll do it? Is he a good writer?"

"We'll have to wait and see." Earl shrugged, being unusually cooperative. "I can't do anything until he calls back. That probably won't be until four or five."

"What?" I exclaimed. "That's four hours from now!"

"You cannot push these things," Earl tutored in measured tones. "They will not deal with it until they're ready." He paused to light a cigarette, then blew the smoke out quickly as an afterthought. "Anyway, doctors usually don't make their callbacks until they've finished with their patients for the day. I've had to wait until seven or eight at night sometimes."

"No-o-o!" I cried. Composing myself, I faced him again. "Do you think they'll turn you down?"

"Earl turned down?" snorted Pete sarcastically. "They *never* turn Earl down."

"Oh, I don't know. It has been known to happen." Earl shrugged modestly.

We killed the afternoon listening to records, leafing through art books, discussing movies, conductors, new recordings and performances of symphonies and chamber works. I sometimes found their parochial intellectualism a bit trying, but they reveled in it. Our name-dropping recalled a term thrust on Earl and me by our high school P.E. teachers: "Hey! Pseudointellectual!"

"What do you think the odds are of some packing coming up?" I queried.

"I have no idea," Pete waffled. "Hopefully something'll develop soon." He buried his face in his teacup.

I shouldn't have bothered asking, for those with upcoming packing or driving jobs tended to keep it to themselves. All of us had lied to each other about work possibilities, which strained our relationships. And all three of us were still annoyed at another person who had kept a session to himself, packing 3,000 pounds of weed in a weekend and pocketing the entire $1,500. We all knew that we'd love to do the same thing. Of course, when it came to a driving job a person would naturally want to keep it under wraps; talking would only increase personal risks by making more people privy to it. One big giveaway would be someone's getting a haircut to improve his image on the road. No one bothered about haircuts unless he was transporting; then everyone denied it, saying that they just felt like a haircut, which none of us ever did.

We languished through the warm afternoon, Pete sipping teaspoons of tea, I smoking an occasional joint. Earl pulled out a bottle of pills, pouring out a dozen, then offering the bottle to me.

"Want some?"

"What are they?" I squinted.

"Tetracycline." Earl nodded when he saw my reluctance. "You can get a buzz from tetracycline!" he insisted.

"Ahh, no thanks." I politely refused, watching him guzzle them down with a quart of milk. Later on we'd hear that tetracycline loses its effectiveness when combined with milk, but I don't think that was the main point with him anyway. Earl always seemed to feel better as long as he took something, anything. I think he liked to feel things hit his metabolism, which demanded to be in a constant state of flux. This is addiction in its most slavish form. His body didn't feel right unless his metabolism was reacting. Earl was compulsive about it. I'd stopped taking him to other people's homes when I went visiting since he had no qualms about rifling the medicine cabinets.

He'd devour the most meaningless collections of aspirins, vitamins, and so on, right on the spot, as well as the prescription items. It had become a sore point between us, for he shamelessly invaded my mother's medicine supplies. This despite his being warned more than once; he knew that she suffered from severe arthritis and really needed the stuff. To say that he couldn't help himself would be too kind.

It was during a particularly loud and moving guitar solo that Earl's head suddenly pointed with alertness. Pete turned down the stereo, facing me with his finger to his lips. I hadn't heard the phone ring, so it took me a second to understand. But Earl had the ears of a hound for his master's call.

"Ahh," I exhaled, realizing what was happening. "The great man has called."

"Shh!" urged Pete.

I heard Earl's voice drift in. "Doctor, I'm coughing up green stuff." My stifled laughter annoyed Pete, who was overly alarmed at my impertinence.

Earl coughed into the phone for the doctor, producing a funereal, timpanilike roll. It had me in stitches, this heartrending cough that no doctor seemed able to turn down.

"My God! What a master!" I sputtered.

"Scott! Be quiet! They'll hear you." Pete's face was practically shattering with tension as Earl returned to the room, his expression serene with fulfillment. He ignored the minor sounds I'd been making, uttering one simple word: "Success."

My excitement and impatience to get to the pharmacy were mercilessly deflected by his cool demeanor. "Give them time, give them time," he urged me in a fatherly manner.

Once there Earl insisted on going in alone; he had a great horror of the pharmacist gumming things up at the last minute. Therefore he'd spend hours preening in front of a mirror, building up deflated confidence, returning repeatedly to ensure that not a hair, not an eyelash was out of place. Traveling with Earl often meant sitting in a car full of people, sometimes for a half hour, everyone groaning with impatience as we waited for him to show. And it was worse if he had to see a pharmacist.

Upon our return Earl undid the package he'd been keeping a tight grip on. Another six-ounce, brown glass bottle to be added to his collection. Hycodan this time. Unscrewing the top and tilting his head back, he made gulping sounds as he drank huge swallows. When he put it down, half of the contents were gone. The normal dose was one or two teaspoons. Earl had just taken fifteen to eighteen. There was little danger of overdose since his body had long ago raised its tolerance for this type of behavior.

Still, when I saw what was left, my mouth fell open. "Jesus, Earl! I would've made that last three days, at least!"

Earl just shrugged. "I do that all the time. It's a good dose. It works very well." He sat down in Pete's chair and lit up a cigarette. His actions were now smooth and economical, and he dreamily blew smoke from his mouth. "Boy, I love that stuff. I can feel it as soon as it goes in."

"Well, yes, Earl," agreed Pete, measuredly considering the bottle for his own smaller dose. "I imagine taking ten times the usual dose would tend to have a more profound effect on you." Pete's dry tone sent Earl into a paroxysm of laughter.

With difficulty, because he was squirming and giggling so much, I handed Earl a few bucks to cover my share—less than an ounce. I drank it immediately; it had a mild cherry flavor. I was grateful for it after the long afternoon's wait.

About twenty minutes later I went into the kitchen to make some instant coffee. Caffeine heightened the effect of the drug. I also felt stimulated now that my body was no longer a collection of minor aches and pains, the result of an afternoon on

Pete's floor. A feeling of well-being settled over me, along with images of my high school coaches repeating stern warnings in my mind: "Watch out for that feeling of well-being. It'll get you every time!" A man in blue shorts with a whistle around his neck eyed me sternly. What a set of values, I thought. Self-denial, exercise to the point of pain, constant degradation of the intellect. And when a feeling of well-being reared its capricious, ugly head, it was cause for double allotments. They tried to take the same old values and cram them down the throats of a more awake generation. The conflict between those narrow-minded, unforgiving spoon feeders and their poorly eating pupils, so hungry for other things, had spawned a backlash culture that the crackers just couldn't understand. The explosion of drug use, black-market economics, new music, riots, sarcasm, freedom had yet to be co-opted by our own vulgar traits. And though by that time signs of decay were clear, there was still a chance to exercise some weird, rugged individualisms. Like most people, these desired a better world. It's this ability to know of and see the better side of things that drives all opium users.

Secure in my secret knowledge, as afternoon passed gently into evening, I remained well satisfied lounging on Pete's hard floor. My mood rode the fine music, and my vision was titillated by collections of the masters. From Byzantine times all the way down through the Renaissance, on to Mahler and Berg, Rembrandt, van Gogh, Munch, and young Kandinsky, I did draw the line at Edith Piaf.

"Jonny, Oh Jonny!" begged a smoke-throated drunken French chanteuse. Barely ebullient, an opiated Pete nursed spoonfuls of tea in front of the speakers. I arose to polite French applause. It was getting late.

Earl muttered. "Old arcane teachings suggest opium as an ingredient to combat strength. That is, the strength that has

become a handicap because it is so great as to be unmanage-
able. . . ." His eyelids started to close, his index finger sliding
absently down a cheek. "Dionysus, the god of the irrational,
the instinctive. . . ."

I would have to walk back to the Geronimo and hoped
enough of my medicines would arrive with me. The phone tin-
kled softly in the back room. This time Earl didn't respond,
letting Pete answer his own phone. I waited for him to hang up
so I could say good night.

"Well, gentlemen," he announced when returning. "We
have been ordered to report upon the morrow."

Earl opened his eyes with delight. I still didn't understand.

"Yes," continued Pete. "Another long-awaited packing job
. . . and our team has been summoned."

4 Pot packers are the peons of the trade. It's the distributors, the employers, who top the hierarchy.

I've mentioned having a private clientele for my petty trades. These were people with whom I'd grown up around town, high school and such. The differences between these incredibly wealthy, lucky pot dealers and the dogs at the hotel never ceased to entertain me. I could, within minutes, change from scenes of two-bit squalor and petty bickering to those of decadent, self-indulgent wealth, the former tinged with tough talk and bluster, the latter guilded with a transparent coating of high culture and pretentious intellectualism. My friends had enjoyed phenomenal success in the weed business.

To grow up in Tucson was, for many, to be raised into the

burgeoning marijuana business that spread during the sixties and seventies like a laissez-faire wildfire across the nation. The few sizable border towns of the Southwest (Phoenix, Tucson, El Paso, Yuma, Douglas, Nogales) became and remain depot points for the nation. We have virtually any kind of drug. Peyote and mushrooms grow in abundance. Pills are available everywhere. And from over the border, sixty miles to the south, arrive daily deliveries of cocaine, heroin, opium, and marijuana. I've even heard of loads of weed that contained kilos of counterfeit money. Youths making a quick $20,000 or $30,000 were a fairly common story. So was armed robbery, soured deals sometimes ending in death, and legal apprehensions with subsequent jail terms for the felonies of selling, transporting, possession, and/or conspiracy.

As with virtually all drug dealing, the odds were with the offender; numerous were tales of success. The severity of a penalty is usually a good indicator of how hard it is to catch the perpetrator. Convictions could bring penalties of five, ten, or more years because most dealers never got caught. Widespread popularity of the business assured that the odds were with them. Murder has the death penalty; half of all murders go unsolved. Your odds are fifty-fifty.

It wasn't long before someone close to me (for practically everyone I knew dealt at one time or another) started to accumulate money. One group of friends did millions in trade, making cash hand over fist. They were soon literally drunk with money. Once I saw them lighting cigarettes with a C-note. But with success came the need for privacy and security. The law was a worry, but the biggest concern by far was robbery. It usually involved guns, sometimes torture, and the victims had no recourse except a slight chance of personal revenge. They couldn't call the police to complain about having lost their dope money.

So wealth demanded a separation from society. Phone numbers became classified information because of phone taps. For every five people who had the phone number, only one would know an actual address. If someone didn't abide by these rules (by giving out a phone number, for instance), he was removed from the list of the privileged. I was known as a good risk—in other words, I kept my mouth shut—so I retained a high-security status with this particular circle. And that was relatively profitable for me, because I also dealt with the outside world. When these secluded people began dabbling in heroin, they naturally turned to me.

Their abhorrence of strangers gave me almost instant buying power. They usually gave me cash on my word, so I let it be known around the Geronimo and other places that I was the one to contact if something interesting turned up. And I could sweeten the deal with the highest quality weed around.

We had yet to learn that Wisdom doesn't go hand in hand with Wealth. If the truth be known, it seems on looking back that early, easy wealth was a curse for the people I knew. But in those days we were still living the dreamy part of the experience.

I took off for Mark and Marie's in the late afternoon. They made more money from dope than anyone I ever knew. I had to call first, from a pay phone, of course. No phoning through the Geronimo switchboard to have the operator copy the number before dialing and listen in. Mark never arose before mid-afternoon. The sun was just beginning to impart warm, rich colors to the sky and trees when I arrived at their place.

At the door I was evaluated by Marie, a tall, pale, black-haired example of Italian Catholic peasant stock. Her tendency toward illusions of grandeur was horribly exacerbated by their incredible dealing success. Copious money allowed her to indulge royal airs. Catholicism and dope wove a strange braid with Marie. She'd eventually go to Leavenworth at the age of twenty-six for selling cocaine to a police officer after making him swear on the Bible that he wasn't a narc.

"Does Mark know you're coming?" she quizzed breathily, a custodial concern on her face.

"Oh, yeah. I called before I came over."

Marie switched to a pout and huffed. "Well, I don't know if he's awake yet." She remained thin-lipped and obstinate.

"Who is it, Marie?" Mark called lazily from another room.

"It's Scott, Mark," she wailed, but with nasal restraint.

"All right, tell him to come in."

Opening the door all the way for me, she smiled sweetly.

"Mark's in his room."

Marie's protective secretarial service took place in their small five-room house. It was quite typical of her behavior. Seemingly protective of Mark's privacy, she awakened him at 7:00 A.M. after his insomniac nights, instructing that it was wrong to sleep late. Keeping a firm grip on her meal ticket, she would eventually consolidate her hold by leaving town for her pregnancies until it was too late to abort. "What's that?" Mark would ask aghast, pointing to her belly. Naturally sensitive to incursions on her territory, she successfully defended her man from all comers save one: opium. Haranguing, berating, nagging him whenever he indulged, she never played anything better than a poor number two to it. Though this drove her to distraction, it didn't stop her from using the drug herself.

I encountered the object of her designs in his usual spot, sitting on a mattress laid without springs on the bedroom floor, sipping his afternoon Colombian coffee. He wore a V-neck T-shirt and boxer shorts. This mattress was where he was to spend the next decade. Mark raised his cup to me, turning down the volume on his massive stereo system. Two speakers stood like refrigerators against one wall, softly dispensing a Renaissance chorale as clear as a bell.

"Ah, Scott. So what's happening?"

"Oh, not much, not much. Just the usual. I met somebody the other day who seems like a pretty steady source for papers. I don't think they'll trade, but it's easy to get if I have the money." I spoke this offer from the depths of a plush chair. The sudden comforts of luxurious seating and refrigerated air made me struggle to stay awake.

Mark raised his brow behind gold wire rims. "And do you have the money?" he quizzed through thick lenses. He hadn't shaven for days, and his unruly brown hair showed that he'd recently awakened.

"Well, no, not exactly. But it wouldn't be any problem to get the stuff for you if you just front the cash for a couple days." I shrugged, presenting my palms upward in a posture of reasonable offering. Mark looked at me perplexed, then proceeded to roll a fat joint. It was his manner to let business decisions ride unspoken for a while, often until I was just leaving. He pulled down a large, thick volume from his bookshelf—a *PDR (Physicians' Desk Reference)*. We perused colored plates of various capsules, tablets, and injectables, filled with the enthusiasm of adolescents thumbing through a skin magazine. How'd you like some of these? What if you had some of that? It brought to mind stories I'd heard Richard tell on the night lawn.

"How'd you like to know someone who just robbed a drugstore?" I offered.

Mark let out a breath. "I'd buy everything they'd get." He waved his arms. "They wouldn't have to talk to anyone else. If you ever hear of something like that, just tell them you know someone who'll buy everything they have. I'll give them a better price than anyone. Hell, it'd be worth it."

I smiled at his enthusiasm. "Well-l-l—" I began when Marie entered the room.

"Are you guys talking about *that* again?" she admonished us as she saw the *PDR.*

"Are we talking about what, Marie?" Mark asked innocently. I shrugged.

Hand on her hip, she continued to berate us in a patronizing falsetto. "Is dope all you guys ever think about? Why don't you do something interesting?" She took a puff of the joint.

Mark began to yell. "Because there's nothing interesting to do! Do you think I'd be fucking sitting on this mattress if I had something interesting to do?"

"Well, you could do something besides just sit around," she replied, blowing out smoke.

Mark's head snapped to attention. "Marie, would you shut *up!*"

"I just thought—"

"*Get out!*" Mark's nostrils flared. Marie silently headed for the door, then edged over to the bedroom closet instead. I watched with curiosity as she stroked the sleeves of her dresses. Tracks showed on her arms. Mark looked up after a minute.

"Are you still here, Marie?" he queried. "I thought you were going out somewhere."

"Well," she purred. "I have to get ready first. I'm going to leave soon."

"Then you get ready to leave," he replied soothingly with a smirk, trying to catch my eye.

Marie began to waffle. "I wanted to . . . I mean, I need to . . ."

Mark's mouth fell open in disbelief. "Are you going to ask me for money again?"

Marie demurely ran her toe around Chinese characters sculptured in the wool rug.

"Jesus Christ!" screamed Mark. "I just gave you money yesterday! What happened to that? Huh?"

"Shhh." Marie put her finger to her lips.

"You told me you'd be able to make that money last till the

end of the week. That was four hundred dollars! I can't believe you're asking me for more already! What do you do with the money, Marie? What do you *do* with it?"

Marie sucked on her knuckle, doing little half turns at her waist.

"Well? I asked you what you spend the money on!"

"I don't remember," she finally whispered. "I can't go out if I don't have any money. We need some stuff at the store. And I'll pick up that Chinese food that you like."

"Oh, and when will that be here? At ten o'clock tonight? Every time you say you're picking up food, I end up having to get something to eat myself. Then you come home with a fortune in Chinese food when nobody's hungry! Oh, *Jesus Christ! Here!*" Mark reached into pants pockets by his mattress and pulled out a wad of money. He peeled off some hundreds. "Here's three hundred dollars for Chinese food! This is definitely all the money you're getting for the rest of the week. Don't *ask* me for *any more!*" He handed it to her with a sardonic grin on his face.

She smiled back graciously, victoriously. "Thank you. . . . You know, I was thinking—"

Mark snapped to attention. "Are you thinking again, Marie?"

"No," she whispered, her hand at her mouth.

"You know what happened the last time you thought. No more thinking, I'm warning you!"

"Hokay."

Boy, I reflected. This is really rich. Those well-sucked knuckles reap a good return for the workout they get. For three or four years now I'd watched the process of erosion that these two waged on each other. When they'd first gotten together, Mark was the dominant one. At that time Marie still lived with Mom. She'd never lived anywhere that she wasn't taken care of. Yet it was she who was now taking control of the relationship, because the more money Mark accumulated, the more unmotivated and bored he got. This easy money usually has a hidden price in terms of stress, inertia, and other hard to define residue. Mark would end up very addicted to junk from years of continual use.

As they took their long skid through a huge pile of cash, I was fascinated by parallels between the Geronimo's low-life junkies, languishing on cheap beds when supplies got low, and Mark's self-imposed despair. Immersed in deep depression, he helplessly watched funds disappear, collected unwanted kids, faded into his mattress. Once supplies run out, it doesn't matter where you park your mattress, you still feel thin until you get more. When occasionally motivated to purchase another house or some land, he'd put the deed in Marie's name. One day, in a fit of pique at Mark, she signed a $100,000 home over to her spurious brother, who never returned it. But this was down the line. At this point neither of them had even formed a physical habit. And they and other of my rich associates were critical of my heavier heroin use.

While their own use continued, they gradually ostracized me as they perceived that I was getting addicted. But they could never banish me completely because they always wanted more. This, of course, angered me. I knew that they were developing their own habits, and, when exiting their plush surroundings for the squalor of the Geronimo, I considered with morbid pleasure their upcoming problems.

Was I the cause of their addictions? Hardly. For opium comes in many varieties, from many sources, and I was but one source for one type (heroin). Many other types are available for the asking, more if you're a rich dope dealer. They got gifts of heroin and pure gum opium with their loads of bricks coming over the border. There was also the legal route: getting it prescribed by a doctor. The extensive menu of painkillers, cough syrups, antidiarrheals made great fun for those lucky enough to get them. Indeed, some people, like Earl, demonstrated a natural knack for hitting up croakers. He was always welcome in that wealthy realm. These future addicts would've formed habits whether or not I supplied them. There's only one indispensable factor in the addiction formula: the user. Once you form the habit, all other variables will seem like inevitable stops on a journey that was going to be made anyway.

"I have the arms of a fairy princess," murmured Marie as I scrounged in their kitchen for something to eat. She airily admired a long, skinny appendage covered with a sprinkling of black hair. It was as a fairy princess that Marie had consumed a pretty patch of mushrooms she'd encountered in the woods. A trip to the emergency room followed. And it was I who supplied the arms of the fairy princess. I held a diplomatic silence while I raided the refrigerator.

"Wait till Marie leaves," Mark had whispered to me when I'd again raised the topic of a real live drugstore bandit, so I took the opportunity to make a ham sandwich. The fridge was well supplied with exotic, expensive tidbits, most ruined by age or desiccated from remaining uncovered. There did, however, lurk among odd acidophilus drinks and strangely shaped Chinese royal jelly vials some simple, edible stock for the enterprising forager.

The refrigerator's style of interior design extended to the rest of the tiny house. Decorations were literally stuffed into it. Huge Maxfield Parrish prints dominated the walls. It was unclear how anyone had hung them, for practically all walking space was consumed by gargantuan pieces of old, heavy wood furniture. Many-tiered antique organs, old foot-operated harmoniums, impossibly long, dark wood dining tables, lengthy couches covered with tapestries—all these intertwined and overlapped, so tightly packed that the house seemed occupied by deposed Russian nobility. This hodgepodge included stunning wood and glass bookshelves and richly upholstered oak chairs, washed by a dazzling tide of small collectibles and curiosities. All of this rose and tumbled on the sides of narrow walkways. These trails, soothing the feet with not yet covered bits of sculptured Chinese wool rugs, wound through the house from the front to back entrance, where surplus antiques poured out onto the porches. They were shredding and peeling from exposure to our harsh environment. These paths blazed on through uncut, weedy lawn out to the street. There a nonrunning antique Corvette served as a mailbox post, the mailbox itself perched ignominiously on the edge of the car's roof. A sign in the windshield announced "Not for Sale," but it did nothing to prevent strangers from making offers on the car. These were turned down, for at this point it was more important to have a mailbox support than an extra seven or eight grand.

Incense hinted amidst the rooms, melodious vespers and sacred chorales trickled from expensive speakers, soft lighting from Tiffany lamps glimmered off a gold crucifix shining between Marie's large breasts. And at the end of a weaving, mysterious path to a bedroom sat an impatient, impetuous Mark on his mattress, yelling, "*I am so fucking bored!*"

The bored and wealthy person can never know the tortures imparted on the psyche of the creative, active mind that receives his complaints. Who can have sympathy for a person whose only obstacle to a great life is the unwillingness to enjoy it? The suggestions that I and others offered to appease Mark's incessant whining, like taking impulsive trips to foreign countries ("Well, what will I do once I get there?"), renting time in recording studios ("So, what will I record?"), starting interesting businesses ("What *kind* of business?") did absolutely nothing to motivate that wealth-cursed creature off his mattress. Junk and the stresses of his profession had immobilized him. Not always having the stability offered by my classy digs at the Geronimo, I sometimes ended up listening to Mark's self-pity when I was sleeping in cars or broke.

Boredom, however, is an elusive, wavering shade that flitters in and out of the most exhilarating circumstances. After he has experienced the surprising pleasures and gratifying fulfillments of heroin, it's not unusual for a person to be subject to an irritating, lingering boredom in its absence. An irksome, simple question keeps prodding: Why not?

"Why not use it again?" "Why not end what you thought would be an endless regime of body aches and fatigue with something that stimulates your mind and imparts exhilaration to your flesh?" Something that your body previously only dreamt about. Because the body won't be denied. Once you open the opium door to relief and euphoria, it will conjure up whatever facts or illusions make you think that you want more. That only a moron wouldn't want to feel so good is strong logic in your body's favor. Just in case you miss that point, it will, after a few doses, manufacture the most pointless boredom, always leading to the same question: Why not?

Since it takes months of daily use to form your first habit, the answer inevitably becomes There's no reason not to. Even after months you may stop and suffer no ill effects, or perhaps just the most minor sniffles and watery eyes. Most of the public and medical profession remain ignorant of just how incredibly much opium one can consume without forming any addiction at all. Stupidity in this regard has caused much needless suffering (even to the point of death) brought on the ill and recovering patients of this world by uneducated doctors and nurses. Medical personnel consistently overestimate an addictive drug's toxicity. When Dr. Brandt, one of Hitler's personal physicians, attempted to assassinate him, he injected him with a *double* dose of cocaine. Hitler claimed that he never felt better. Imagine the suffering we'd have been spared if Dr. Brandt had received a better drug education. This lack of education and purposeful withholding of information concerning narcotics cause much abuse and accidental death. The situation with drug use has gotten so poor that if the stuff was legalized and people properly educated as to its use, even for recreation, things couldn't be any worse than they are now. They'd probably be better.

It would be logical to ask, If opium's not that addictive, then how did you and all those other people get addicted? These tales I offer will go far toward an explanation. Readers may have to do additional serious thinking on their own.

I ate my ham sandwich and lounged around for a while, leafing through more large, slick art books and listening to music. I enjoyed having no pressing engagements; my only real commitments were the ones I dreamt up and imposed on myself. Today's involved some minor trading with Mark and querying him on his interest in Richard's facility at robbing pharmacies. I waited for Marie to leave before broaching the topic, patiently indulging in weed and refrigerated air as she got ready.

Marie had this front of cutesy dumbness, but she was manipulative with it, brilliantly using stupidity as a weapon like some evil Gracie Allen. So Mark was happy to get her out of the house for a while, though he never knew if she'd return in a taxicab, having again driven the car into a ditch. She had a penchant for wrecking cars without suffering injury, and after a few hair-raising rides I avoided traveling if she drove. It was with mixed relief that Mark watched her leave.

"I know this guy that robs drugstores," I mentioned after she'd gone.

"He robs drugstores?" Mark inquired myopically. "And

does he have anything now? Has he robbed any drugstores recently?"

"I'm not sure what you mean by 'recently.' Those Percodans I got a while back were through him. I was thinking it'd be worthwhile to let him know there's someone waiting with cash if he should choose to take up his hobby again."

Mark shifted his head abruptly, like a child turning down food. "I don't want to meet anyone. Anyway, I don't have any money."

I heard this from all my rich friends. The more earnestly they claimed poverty, the more money I assumed they had. "Well," I mused facetiously. "I guess if he robs a drugstore I'll just have to go to someone else to sell the stuff."

Mark snapped at the carrot. "What stuff? Is he planning to do it soon? What did he say?"

"He hasn't said anything exactly. I was just thinking that if he knew there was cash waiting he'd be willing to come to us with first pick of whatever he got. I have a feeling we could offer what he'd consider a good price and still get a great deal."

I *knew* we'd get a great deal. Some weeks before, a third party had offered me 500 Percodan pain pills for a mere $100—twenty cents apiece. He'd gotten them from Richard at ten cents apiece. I'd called Mark, who advanced $100 for 250 pills at forty cents apiece. He was ecstatic to pay it. My contact made 500 pills, I made 250, and Mark was happy with the remaining 250. They'd been the product of a recent robbery, and I figured that even if Richard doubled his prices we'd still get a ridiculously good deal. And now I dealt directly with Richard. The biggest problem would be making him understand that I'd have to see something before he got any money. Otherwise I'd end up with him robbing me and not bothering with the drugstore. This point was immediately clear to Mark, whose money would serve as the catalyst. It pulled at him from one direction while the lure of a huge, cheap supply of pharmaceutical dope tugged enticingly from another. I silently let him struggle with this for a while.

"I definitely don't want to meet anybody," he announced finally. "And I don't want to give you any money until you see that he actually, *definitely* has the stuff. There's no other way I'll do it."

"That's fine with me. I'll see what he says." I'd gotten half the commitment I sought. I wanted to be able to tell Richard that I could guarantee cash within minutes of seeing goods. Mark's reluctance to meet him made it more difficult, but that and his keeping the money also provided an insurance policy. I made ready to leave. As an afterthought I asked for a small consignment of Mark's extrastrong pot.

"See if you can get more papers," he mentioned as he weighed it out. "And make sure it's not crappy junk. Use the money from this weed if you have to."

"Shouldn't be any problem." I nodded agreeably as I rose to leave. "And I'll let you know if anything develops about the drugstore," I called through the house on my way out.

"Somebody please help me!" came Mark's plaintive cry. "I'm so fucking bored!"

5 I had been at the Geronimo a little over three months. Though middling small deals had fore-stalled it, the pile of twenty-dollar bills was finally exhausted. The holidays were approaching.

My disgust with my old car reached such a furious point that I tried to enlist Nazi Paul in a scheme to drive it to the desert, stick a fuel-soaked rag in the gas tank, and light it. I think I wanted him for a return ride and a cheering section to cele-brate my escape from the maddening grip of the car's quirky mechanics. Being carless, he quite naturally had little interest in the scheme except to wonder why I'd want to destroy a vehi-cle that still ran. I didn't see anything unusual in my irrational plans or feelings. At that point I had been using heroin on and off for close to six months and had begun shooting it more than snorting it, for economic reasons as much as anything else. I used less per dose that way.

Feeling squeamish about other people's dirty, bloody needles, I had, while I still had the money, utilized Paul to buy bags of twenty diabetic syringes. These were small, disposable plastic jobs meant to be used only once. Although initially I had adhered to that policy, it wasn't long before expense and inconvenience tempted me to use them repeatedly. I had contracted hepatitis a couple years earlier from bad food or water in Morocco, and this usually discouraged others from using my fits (syringes).

My early take it or leave it attitude toward the shots gradually changed to pleasurable anticipation. An irritating sense of boredom permeated days that I put off taking one. This restlessness was often filled with rationalizations of why I hadn't yet used it, preoccupying thoughts of how pleasant it was, and the final relief when I convinced myself that I'd be better off doing it since I'd been thinking about it all day anyway. I still suffered no physical symptoms when I didn't have any. Neither I nor the small circle of rich friends who continually badgered me to get them junk had developed a physical habit yet, though the needle tracks creeping up the insides of my arms served as an unpleasant reminder to all that continual use carried the risk of addiction. It was probably their own fears of becoming strung out that prompted their critical observations and patronizing "Better watch out" warnings. Often they'd proselytize as they handed me money to get them more or even as they consumed. Their sheer hypocrisy chafed at my well-suppressed fears.

The desert's heat and glare, still a bit oppressive when I'd first moved into the hotel, had dissipated, and pleasant daily winter weather soothed what minor stresses came my way. Even my steadily dwindling funds caused me little worry, for such was my faith and experience with the dealing business that I was sure something would turn up. Thus, when I found myself with no money at all, I wasn't surprised at being offered lodgings and a chance for extra cash by Luke, a weed-dealing friend. Plans to enlist Richard in a pharmacy project went on indefinite hold.

Luke lived on the north side of Tucson in a well-furnished house rented from his old philosophy teacher. He'd remained on good terms with him after graduation, and for $400 a month, a decent sum in those days, the doctor let Luke occupy his luxurious home for two years that he was out of country. Located in a fine, old, upper-class area, isolated from neighbors, with lots of extra rooms and storage capacity, it was perfect for conducting the day-to-day affairs in Luke's burgeoning pot business. Luke had an upper-crust veneer cultivated from his Air Force officer family background and his old fraternity days. This helped him blend into the neighborhood in spite of his youth. His short, stocky build and pugnacious manner were leftovers from his days as a state wrestling champ. As with the other rich dealers I knew, I had watched Luke do the Big Rollover from the start. Initially investing only hundreds at a time, he was now taking part in six-figure deals. When I first moved in, he was expecting a load at any time, but it proved more difficult than usual, and I spent some extra weeks there.

Waiting was pleasantly passed by going to restaurants, procuring and doing junk with Luke and friends, and playing with small alpha wave meters. The alpha meter was quite interesting, sounding a high-pitched tone that got lower as my galvanic skin conduction decreased, supposedly as alpha brain wave production went up. I spent a lot of time practicing keeping the tone low. Those days were quite leisurely for me. The house was situated on a hill, and after dark I'd hear coyotes wind their screaming way through the gullies below. Once, I awoke to tumultuous thunderclaps in the middle of the night. From behind huge glass doors I watched lightning bolts striking a couple hundred feet away and below me into those gullies. Snow capped the Catalina Mountains and the air was crisp, but we stayed warm and snug with our heroin. Luke prided himself on his record collection, and the days were filled with great music. Luke was critical of my pronunciation. "It's Moat-zart, Scott, not Moes-art," he instructed me in his Texas twang.

But Luke eventually got impatient and discouraged about the lack of weed in town. He finally ended up begging me to recall some of my old contacts. This I did, but when I introduced Luke to one of them, he whined something about having known the guy when they were fraternity brothers some years back and refused to pay my commission. Thus it was that I arranged the sale of 3,000 pounds of pot for nothing more than the chance to hold off in paying my share of the rent. I howled about this, to no avail. In that circle those who had got more and those who didn't, well, too bad. My obvious naïveté has a place in this drama, but it does little to excuse their greed. Luke went on to become a successful accountant back in Texas, and Luke isn't his real name. It's to his credit that he displayed a semblance of control in his personal drug use and never became addicted. "You have to use these things in moderation, Scott," he repeatedly counseled me, taking little snorts of junk up his pug nose.

As a fob I received the chance to make the numerous crosstown drives needed to transport the load from the west side Tucson Mountains to Luke's house up north. I was provided a truck and chose a late-night route that followed the western and northern city limits in the hope of avoiding cops. This was mainly for my own peace of mind; the city police probably wouldn't show up at these boundaries, but the county sheriffs had the entire county and city as their jurisdiction. I encountered no problems, and the hundred dollars I earned for each of the ten-minute drives I made once or twice a night soon payed off my rent with Luke and got me some pocket money. Even that I had to harangue from him, explaining that temporary poverty didn't automatically qualify me for indentured servitude. It was hard to believe that he was the same person who had been begging me for that weed just days before.

How could I be flat broke, get screwed out of thousands, constantly risk serious felony charges, and simultaneously enjoy myself? This should be an indication of my dread at having to leave that lifestyle. One should keep in mind the alternative: a two-dollar-an-hour minimum wage. I would've had to work over 100 hours to take home the same $200 I was making practically every night. After New Year's 1975, a couple weeks later, the minimum wage jumped a big ten cents. Every day I'd see newspaper headlines proclaiming a collapsed housing market while I stayed in a nicer home than any owned by my friends' parents. The stock market fell steadily, and I remember seeing Dow Jones averages in the three and four *hundreds*, proof of a major business decline. Meanwhile, the businesspeople with whom I associated were making five-figure sums in cash every month; the spillover of menial labor from their trade was enough to keep me going, certainly in the grand Geronimo style to which I was accustomed. To take part in the common, logical alternative offered by the drug world seemed like the action of a sane individual. I was no longer penniless, and I looked forward to making additional money when Pete and Earl showed up to pack for transport the ton and a half that Luke and I had collected.

Pete arrived in his yellow Ford with Earl in tow. I hopped in. The three of us were responsible for picking up necessary supplies before commencing the actual packing. Pete and Earl were both upbeat at the prospect of making easy money that evening, though Earl's joviality seemed a bit forced, as if he were preoccupied. We first hit the offices of a moving company, purchasing dozens of moving boxes, roughly three feet square. Then discount stores to buy many rolls of strapping tape, masking tape, boxes and boxes of large, green plastic garbage bags, and many pounds of baking soda. This last helped diminish odors over the days the stuff moved across country.

Pete was temperamental when I insisted on purchasing baking soda at a separate location, to avoid tipping off an alert clerk. Pot dealing in Tucson was so common that even unsympathetic citizens were often quite knowledgeable about the details of an operation. Busts rarely came about as a result of good police work; the main leads for cops came from informers and anonymous tip-offs: suspicious neighbors observing youngsters unloading hundreds of small packages, motel owners reporting odd transfers of luggage or cash, eavesdroppers noting license plates. Our sense for security kept us pretty tight-lipped. This had helped create a record of buying, selling, and transporting without mishap dozens upon dozens of tons of weed over the years. Most busts that I'd heard of, and I heard of many, seemed to spring from bad luck and/or stupidity. Good law enforcement practices ran a distant third to these.

It was sunset by the time we'd collected all the items, picked up some fast food, and returned to Luke's ready to work. A roadrunner dashed in front of the car as we pulled up. Bats swept through the rainbowed twilight. I had noticed Earl getting more distracted as the day progressed. He immediately, upon our return, found a bottle of Luke's booze and adopted a convivial, chatty attitude, smoking cigarettes and hanging out in the living room with our employers. Pete and I labored at the preliminary job of taping together moving boxes; each would hold about 70 pounds. Then, using a large old grocer's scale, we weighed all the bricks, 10 to 15 pounds at a time. Around 2,800 pounds. Pete was a phlegmatic but steady laborer. He looked sparkling when compared with Earl. As Earl got more drunk, he'd have to be continually reminded to do his share and be practically dragged into the workroom. I soon realized that he was suffering from a lapse in his syrup supply, breaking out in a sweat at the slightest exertion, fending off physical discomforts with large doses of rum. These were accompanied by the usual handfuls of aspirins, antihistamines, and vitamins, plus an occasional joint.

"I'll bet he's finally addicted," I haughtily thought.

The packing procedure was one I'd personally designed, and it had gained acceptance in other shipping circles nationwide. It was not really that complex; I'm sure many others could've independently devised something similar. But I enjoyed the fact that I had thought of it.

After we'd taped the flat cardboard boxes together and weighed the bricks, the actual packing began. A flat piece of cardboard went on the bottom of each box for extra support; then one of us grabbed a plastic garbage bag, held it high on outstretched arms, the opening down, and someone slipped another bag over it. This double bag was placed in the square box, still held open while the other two packers rapidly and methodically piled bricks compactly inside. These bricks, generally wrapped in colored construction paper, usually weighed between one and a half and two pounds. They were pressed rectangles of weed, actually shaped by an adobe brick press somewhere south of the border. Care was taken not to bunch up the garbage bags as the box was filled, and one or two bricks were cut in half to fill in small spaces left at the top.

Once the inner bag was full, we poured liberal amounts of odor-killing baking soda in the gap between the bags, where it would stay invisible for the cross-country trip. No white powders need precipitously peek out in Iowa. Someone grabbed the vacuum cleaner, and the inside bag had air sucked out of it and was taped closed. Then the same was done to the outer bag. Through trial and error we discovered this absolutely mandatory step, for once on the road it didn't take long for decomposition of the product to produce so much expanding gas that the bags would burst the boxes and stink to high heaven. The packing was so efficient that we'd have to slice excess plastic from the bags to be able to seal the box. As Earl got more tipsy, he came precariously close to slicing my thumb off with the carving knife used for trimming, and I had to warn him to concentrate on his aim. Ideally the process worked like an assembly line. The last step was to seal the box shut, then begin again.

In four or five hours, about three dozen clean, tight boxes were piled in an orderly manner in the storage room. Pete and I were winded, but Earl seemed rummily jubilant, having let us do most of the work. A few times he'd been led back to the room by Mark, who, having a major share in the load, had come up to observe.

"That's very nice, Earl," he'd explain. "Now get back to work." Earl would appear, laughing self-consciously.

"Nice of you to show up, Earl," I complimented him, and he soon disappeared again. He thought to make up for this by enthusiastically appearing with a broom, but I grabbed it from his hands. I preferred that job myself, for the shavings from cutting bricks in half amounted to over half a pound. I could garner another eighty to a hundred dollars by selling it later, compensating for shredded paper and hairs in it by adding more to each portion. Despite the garbage, I never had trouble selling it. I figured this gratuity appropriate compensation for having to listen to Earl express his resentment at our statements that he didn't do his share of the work.

Pete, Earl, and I happily collected the $465 apiece that we'd earned, fifty cents a pound being the going rate for our services. Now it was up to the drivers, who'd be given ownership papers for a used pickup truck with a camper shell. A plywood board the size of the cargo bed would be laid on the wheel wells, just high enough to cover the boxes. With the entire bed filled, it held about 1,500 pounds. Sleeping bags and other camping paraphernalia were tossed in front of the boxes and on top of the board, giving the appearance of a well-used vacation vehicle. Even on those rarest of occasions when the truck was stopped, the cops never displayed any suspicions about what might be under that piece of plywood.

Ahh, those were the days. Today a young male traveling alone, using cash, and bearing Arizona license plates can count on being stopped by the Highway Patrol.

6 I returned to the Geronimo $600 or $800 richer, enough to let me continue coasting in the manner to which I'd grown accustomed. The holidays had recently passed, a period of celebration about which I was quite blasé. The residents and daily life of the hotel hadn't changed much. Stegman still drew on little index cards, officiating from his tower; Nazi Paul continued his manic devotion to intoxication at the expense of caloric replenishment; the old woman at the switchboard still eavesdropped on our calls. The hotel itself remained essentially the same. But my perceptions of it had started to change.

Sporting a generous prescription of Percodans that I'd talked out of our family dentist—a man who had no business in the profession as he was horrified by pain—I checked into the main office, putting down a month's rent on Number 316, another third-floor room. Like the old masters, Coleridge and De Quincey, I was beginning to discover the truth in the maxim "Woe to those who use opium before retiring, for sleep will stubbornly avoid them." Thus, I began to spend more late-night and early-morning hours roaming the Geronimo's catacomb halls, loitering in the quiet, empty lobby, or nodding out in dark, little traveled niches dotting the maze of passageways through the grounds. These silent spots were developing a romantic appeal for me, wellsprings of nostalgia for my reverie-gilded, drugged soul.

The beaten hotel had memories flickering from almost every corner. Drifting into short dreams, at times I thought I heard the putt-putting of old Model Ts pulling up to the lobby, dropping off elegantly gowned women accompanied by pillars of the community in cool, white tuxedos. Opulent repose, 1920s desert style. Back in 1919, when the Geronimo was built, edges of huge desert tracts were still nearby. Horses and Model Ts pulled up to the community growing around the new University of Arizona. Founded in 1885, the school was an irritating disappointment to Tucson merchants. The prize contract, an insane asylum, had gone to Phoenix, and the Tucson representative was pelted with eggs, rotten vegetables, and a dead cat. "Whoever heard of a professor buying a drink?" yelled the mob. But alcohol was outlawed the year after they built the Geronimo, and I could easily picture student dealers and Mexican smugglers buzzing around the Prohibition neighborhood—just like they do now.

When dragging hours in the hotel corridors reached post-midnight hush, time secretly eased its pace. My eyelids would droop; then faint brown light oozing from dust-covered globes caught in my lashes. Momentarily I'd catch the glimmer of sparkling chandeliers and the bright warmth of old-time lightbulbs. They had a filament in them that you could see clearly, and it wouldn't hurt your eyes to look. Sometimes I fancied flickering on the dreamwalls, flames dancing in the lobby's old fireplace. But when I opened my eyes, all I saw was a sealed up chimney and an old black-and-white TV sitting where the logs used to burn.

With surprising alacrity I whimsically recalled days that I'd never lived, imagining the innocent peace at the beginning of the century. Men jumping from the Eiffel Tower in failed attempts to fly, people hearing their own voices for the first time from some polished oak contraption, Nikola Tesla commanding fantastic displays of light. An age of wonder, drawing upon small remnants of magic still in the world. Technology, just beginning to outstrip the species that created it, still gave the tingle of new thrill, not the shudder of horror that it does today. My footfalls gently padded along worn, threadbare carpet, dreamily echoing off thick, aged wooden doors. I roamed silently through southwestern cloisters, carefully balancing a state of half-sleep through a myriad of twinkling shadows. And through my half-closed lids, beckoning up ahead, I could almost see tall, thin Tesla in his tuxedo.

It's probably just as well that I spent my time like this, for sleep in my opiated state was most often elusive. Not until my medicines had almost worn off would I be able to snatch some solid rest. Naturally I was impatient with any early-morning interruptions breaking into my recovery period and would greet with foulmouthed rudeness any who had the gall to awaken me. It was a generous helping of this arrogance that my father received when he phoned one morning in January. He paused measuredly before informing me that my mother had taken her own life the night before.

Her suicide was not totally surprising. My mother, bedridden for years, had suffered long from severe arthritis. Every day for decades had been a losing battle with pain, physical deformity, and attempts to have a normal life. Massive doses of steroids, mostly cortisone, had had side effects, including psychosis, and she had been seeing Japanese soldiers in the bushes a few days before her death. "Ideas of reference," my social worker–father had declared, then sent her back to the psychiatric hospital. Her utter despair at the collapse of her life had frequently caused her to discuss and reflect on ending it. As is often the case when a suicide strikes, the final act was long anticipated and actually brought our family a grotesque sense of relief.

It was then that I began to question seriously the tyrannical and pompous attitudes of the medical profession. For in all the years of my mother's suffering (she actually died of chronic pain), she was never given adequate pain relief. Consuming aspirins to the point of ulcers and hearing loss, she was never prescribed anything stronger than codeine. I can speak from personal experience when I say that codeine, which does almost nothing to relieve *severe* pain, has as side effects of continual use nervousness, odd dreams, and hallucinations. Furthermore, it's just as physically addictive as many stronger narcotics. The few times that I did give Mother something decent for her pain, she begged me for more, claiming that it was the first time in years that she'd felt real relief. If they'd only give her something like this, she'd complain, she felt that she could lead a more normal life. She'd then go on to curse "the bastards in the medical profession" (she was an R.N.) as "the stupidest, most unfeeling ignoramuses," et cetera.

My father, a psychiatric social worker, kept his own private supply of addictive medicines. For decades he'd had bottles of a thousand Valium, amphetamines, opium-based diarrhea medicines lying around the house in such quantities that if I was short of money I could grab a handful, fairly confident that their absence wouldn't be discovered. My love affair with dope of many kinds wasn't really a secret from him. In fact, I was always allowed to smoke weed around the house, even to have friends over to do it. So it's always been a source of amazement to me that when I mentioned that perhaps I should've supplied Mother with some decent narcotics for her chronic pain, he replied, "That would've been a death sentence for her." The irony of his statement escaped him.

I took a melancholy visit to Palo Verde Psychiatric Hospital, which she'd entered a number of times and where she'd spent her final days. Quietly roaming the halls, I saw some of the last paintings and posters she'd seen. A thin, reserved young intern, Renny, who'd had the suicide watch the night she died, spoke to me. "Your mother was very well liked here. All of us were so shocked when it happened."

My own shock at her death prompted me to request a refund on my hotel room, and I took up lodgings at my family's home. However, after three days of this (I've mentioned before being a pretty well brewed, arrogant cup of tea), my father announced that he no longer wanted to associate with me, shouting down my suggestions for investigation into negligence by the hospital staff. "I still have to work with these people!" He told me the wrong hour for the funeral and handed me a large bottle of Valiums, ordering me to beat it. I quickly found myself back in the Geronimo's main office, asking for another room.

"Don't you have anything a little bigger?" I pressed Mrs. Gilmore, the aged proprietress of that crumbling monument. It was she more than anyone who held the place in stasis. With her clipped gray hair and silver wire-rimmed glasses, her air of conservative authority, she looked like one of the notable women whose portraits adorned the upper walls of the lobby. Those absurdly huge paintings of old women in high, frilly collars peered down in stern, disapproving manner upon the steadily descending quality of clientele nodding out over the taped furniture. I could easily imagine gray Mrs. Gilmore, upon retirement, taking her lofty place amongst that overbearing gallery. That, of course, would imply that people would want to remember the Geronimo and their time there.

After considerable hemming and hawing, Mrs. Gilmore assigned me a large room at the southern end of the hotel. It was as close to a basement room as they had to offer. Insisting that I was interested in it, I overcame all of her allusions to violent deaths that had taken place there, plus her apologies for the room's state of disrepair. This meant a portion of the floor that had never been completed, still displaying bare earth. It always filled at least part of the room with a dusty, humusy odor. She compensated for it by lowering my rent ten dollars a month. I immediately liked the room, for it was almost three times the size of my other rooms, containing an enormous wooden office desk, a bed with brass bars, and an antique clothes closet, one of those "portable" wooden affairs so large and heavy that they stay in one place for forty years. Earth from the alley outside partially blocked my two windows, and I enjoyed the subterranean feeling in that large space. There was a sink, toilet, and shower in the corner by the dirt portion of the floor. I would emerge from that shower stall barefoot and wet into a layer of the finest desert dust.

It was in this room then, in the depths of the old hotel, that I was to form my first real habit. Here I would fail to kick for the first time. I was to learn the great variety of dreams that await the adventurous, determined soul. And, in my headstrong, stubborn quest for freedom, I was about to become one with the Geronimo.

dreaming

seeing the threads

7 A day is twenty-four hours, but left to our own devices, the human cycle is twenty-five. Having no pressing commitments on my routine, I consistently went to bed and arose a couple hours later every few days. I enjoyed this natural schedule and observed with fascination how it meshed with heroin's eighteen-hour cycle. It takes eighteen hours from the time of ingestion for junk to work its way out of your body. If you are addicted, you will more markedly feel this limit approaching. The newer heroins, like China White, a more concentrated compound, have shorter cycles.* Generally, the ending of the brown Mexi-

---

*China White's cycle is six hours. This can surprise users who are accustomed to longer European and Mexican heroin cycles. They may attribute to

can heroin cycle would announce itself by a throbbing in a rather deep dental filling, followed by a dull ache at the base of my neck. Then the tracks on my arms hurt. These things passed quickly. Minor aftereffects, they were simply the result of the deanesthetizing of my body when junk left it. I still hadn't formed a real physical habit; no actual physical symptoms plagued me in the absence of dope. But psychologically I found day-to-day life ever more bearable and entertaining when I used the stuff, and quite pointless, flat, and boring when I didn't. And I saw no point in spending a day or two thinking about it when I could just do it. Despite what poorly informed "drug specialists" claim, there are light-years between a psychological junk habit and a physical one. I was, however, brewing up my first real habit.

Why does one continue to indulge when physical addiction clearly lies ahead? Casting aside those few who really didn't know that their actions were leading to addiction, be assured that the answer is quite simple. It is junk meeting with an element of personal pain that it handily eases. Some had pain before they tried it and found that it helped. Others, like myself, were dabbling in it when something bad happened. And many have denied bodily pleasure to such an extent that when they encounter opium their bodies simply *will not* take no for an answer. Those who scoff at the idea of such needs are usually the very ones who prompt them in others.

"I know," said Nazi Paul, soothingly. "You were feeling bad and it made you feel better."

---

psychological reasons their growing physical needs. Could the producers also lengthen the cycle or even get rid of it? *Nonaddictive heroin?* That they do the opposite shows the kind of market they really want. Volumes have been written about heroin bosses and how their influence overlaps with the law enforcement industry.

What if nonaddictive opiates gained wide market and the question of addiction suddenly disappeared? We would probably still see many of the same critics vehemently opposing junk use, regarding with unbridled horror a specter of unlimited personal pleasure. Is denial good? How much should those who shape morality be allowed to deny you? When does morality become self-consuming? The Tibetans call it "the disease afflicting the world—Morality Without Wisdom."

I grappled with these philosophical premises as I lounged around my new basement room. My mental review, however, was nothing more than an extension of a rationalization process taking place within me. Suppressing fears of addiction and dismissing as unimportant the growing tracks of painful needle marks had already established a ready process by which I could bury my worries. I practiced by pushing back anger and remorse over my mother's suicide and my father's distasteful actions before and after. Except for some brief tears at the family home immediately following her death, I steadfastly refused to dwell on my feelings and made remarkable outward progress in supposedly healing from the disaster. My friends were reluctant to bring the subject up, and I think they regarded my matter-of-fact attitude as curious. But I held other resentments toward them, over their greed and unfair business practices. Pressures of my sorrows pushed in a number of ways, and though I had thus far managed to keep from getting addicted by sometimes giving myself time off from dope, I no longer considered a physical habit a matter of any importance, especially compared with the emotional benefits of the drug. In other words, I no longer gave a shit.

This, combined with my growing junk trade market, led me to find newer contacts. Many turned out to be a bit shady. Most displayed poor judgment, were crass and unappealing. They would've set off alarm bells in any rational person because they were clearly headed for trouble. But I held reduced concerns for my welfare and felt an odd fascination observing at close hand the callous recklessness of these fiends.

One particularly nefarious person lived by a downtown underpass; he was known for generous, high-quality papers. For some reason that I couldn't fathom he'd refuse to sell to me, though he knew well that I was a user. If his good side existed, I could never get on it. One day as I was standing with some other people in the hall of his boardinghouse, he turned his back to me and farted, much to everyone's entertainment. The next day I heard that hours later that cocky son of a bitch had shoved a .38 revolver into his belt, causing it to discharge and shoot off one of his nuts. This news I greeted with sheer delight.

I was now a familiar customer at Yaqui Jim's household, warmly welcomed because my appearance heralded fifty dollars cash. I suspected that Jim and Little Bill were merely turning five papers into six when I asked for a break, but I tolerated it because I appreciated the steady supply. It was rare that they didn't have something to sell. Sometimes I'd find myself there for most of an afternoon while they awaited delivery, but they didn't mind me and other customers gathering. It meant ready sales. Marty, the redheaded woman who also lived there, worked at a local massage parlor, supplementing her growing habit by giving her ten-dollar hand jobs to a private clientele. Periodically, the pimp who ran the massage place (The Gentle Touch) would pop in to try to confirm his suspicions that she was moonlighting, but he never caught her in the act. A thin, high-strung, unpleasant character, he figured he owned *all* the girls' services, wherever they took place.

"Boy," muttered Yaqui Jim. "She's got a habit that won't quit. She better get a handle on it soon. And now the bitch is pregnant."

A P.E. coach's face appeared in my mind, explaining

through a severe telepathy how pregnant addicts give birth to junkie babies. I grimaced with the rest of the class. Down the hallway I saw some tall, tattooed biker-robot lying on Marty's bedroom floor, his head propped up on a pillow as he awaited her ministrations. She murmured something and smiled as she kneeled beside him, catching my eye a second before she closed her door.

We waited in the living room, the "older" junkies enviously eyeing the clean, healthy veins on the arms of the beginners. Conversation was pretty repetitive.

"How long did you have to do?"

"Five years." A tall, light-skinned black I'd seen there before nodded. "Got out in three and a half."

"Yeah, Lenny," said Bill, rapidly rubbing his burr haircut. "That must've been a pisser, being so close to really doing it."

Lenny got very animated, pushing his pale prison-issue glasses up his nose as he paced and chattered. "Yeah, still makes my mouth water. What really gets me is we *had* what we wanted; all we had to do was *leave*. But this guy I was with just couldn't quit grabbing stuff. All he could see was Eli Lilly, Eli Lilly. He wouldn't fucking quit! And, man, it was quality stuff, too! Blocks of pure morphine marked .999, bottles of thousands of injectables. . . ." The speaker just shook his head sadly as his openmouthed audience absorbed the picture. "I kept saying, 'Let's go! Let's go!' but the other guy just couldn't help himself. Kept throwing stuff in the van. 'Just this. Lemme get this!' Man, when I saw those headlights come around the corner and hit that fence, boy, I knew it was over! We was only there about twenty minutes, but it was five minutes too long. Man, for twenty minutes I was as rich as any king! My mouth still waters when I think about it. You 'spect that stuff to show up pretty soon, Jim? All this talkin's makin' me hungry."

Jim's blood ties to the Yaqui villages on Tucson's west side made him a natural to grab and hold the position of dealer. Those Yaqui pueblos remain a well-known source of good Tucson junk. (Except during Easter festivities, which attract visitors from throughout the nation. There are lots of resentful junkie eyes peering from dark doorways during the Easter procession.)

As steady a supplier as Jim proved to be, I continually searched for someone who'd give me a better count. I began to frequent a ramshackle apartment complex on North Sixth Avenue at Fifth Street. This huge place was on the verge of being condemned. It looked more like a drawing of an old house in a children's book; some rooms seemed like they were about to fall off the main structure. It was the kind of place that if you dreamt about it you'd get lost in it. A neon sign flashing "Junk!" might've been helpful to an out-of-towner, but for cops and locals it was patently clear what took place at that crumbling vortex.

Manny was my contact there. In his late thirties, tall, thin, with a grossly protruding stomach, he resembled a grown-up version of those starving kids who eat too much starch and form fat tummies. He had that long, straight, black hair common to Indians. "I'm a full-blooded Cherokee," he told me once, but it looked like there were some other genes mixed in there, maybe some white trash or something. His bulging stomach was dappled with this horrible red-and-white discoloration but, fortunately, he slipped on a wrinkled black shirt as he answered my knock. Some Mexican slut appeared behind him, trying to squeeze her way out. "How 'bout a good-bye kiss for me, baby?" Manny leered, sticking his acned, greasy face into hers.

The woman was totally repulsed. "You've got to be kidding." She pushed his chest, a wave of disgust twisting her smeared, garish lipstick. I smiled as she passed, but she ignored me. She couldn't get out fast enough.

"That was my girlfriend." Manny glinted mischievously as he ushered me in. This involved a brief choreography for both of us, as his tiny place was filled by a bed, an armchair, and a refrigerator. By walking in sideways past him, then sidling along the sink and cabinets that made up one wall, I was able to advance to the end of the bed and a chair where I had no choice but to sit down.

"You believe that was my girlfriend?" Manny tilted his head pixieishly at me. It was frightening.

"Sure," I answered diplomatically.

Recalling the whore, he gave a derisive snort. "She was cute. Had a nice pair of tits."

I smiled again. A familiar odor attacked my senses—a combination of sweat, farts, old food, cigarettes, heroin vapors, burnt sulfur from lighting entire matchbooks to cook up spoons of dope. It was a smell that I was learning to identify instantly, the smell of a homey, lived-in junk room. Years later in another town I'd walk into an apartment, encounter that same odor, and involuntarily announce "Heroin" to the surprise and discomfort of everyone there. Now I tried to breathe normally for the half dozen breaths it took to adapt to that thick scent.

"So, how'd your friends like those last dimes?" asked Manny. He deftly produced an old mayonnaise jar from a hiding place. Years of sharing prison cells had made him quite good at this. Though it always happened in front of me, I never actually saw from where that jar came. It was half full of little folded papers. "Good enough to send you back for more, huh?"

"Oh, yeah," I agreed, trying not to sound overly enthusiastic. "They were real happy with that stuff. Is this the same? I wouldn't mind getting another ten of those."

Manny's shoulders gave the easy shrug of a seller's market. "Ah, it's not exactly the same, but I think you'll like it. Haven't had any complaints yet." Then he looked straight at me, frowning under his cynical brow. "You got all the money, don't you?"

"Oh, yeah," I replied easily. "Money's not a problem with these people. They just want quality."

He turned away. "Yeah? Well, I told you it's good." He unscrewed the mayonnaise jar. "What'd you want? Ten?"

After conducting our business, Manny pocketed the cash with a satisfied air. "I like people like you that always have the bread." He read his tattoos a little too nonchalantly. I could see his mind working. I stifled my dread. ". . . his eyes moved . . . and his soul penetrated the meaning without his uttering a word" (St. Augustine).

"You got a lot of money to spend on this stuff?" he queried from beneath the oily shelf he called his forehead.

I was used to walking a tightrope when doing my dealings: offering ready cash without giving the impression that I was a ready mark. A relaxed attitude and knowledge of protocol and terms let me maintain a precarious balance. Mark, Luke, and Co. had begun giving me orders for thirty or more papers at a time. They'd make wry remarks as they handed me the $300, concerning my growing tracks and the risk to their money. Naturally I felt resentment. They didn't want to associate with the people who did this small-time, high-risk dealing, so they sent me to take the heat. And they expected the refined manners they thought due them as rich dope dealers. Going from places like Yaqui Jim's and Manny's to Mark's and Luke's necessitated my presenting two faces, two fronts. I was Mr. Wonderful, a streetwise, savvy, cultured intellectual—the man of many faces. While I found these masquerades stimulating and challenging, they were also draining on my nerves.

Manny reached over and turned on his radio so low that I

couldn't even distinguish what station it was. As a parting gesture before leaving I pulled out a joint.

"Yeah, why not? I'll take a little." Manny inhaled the smoke, holding it in his lungs as he spoke. "Shit, I ain't got nothing pressing to do anyway."

"Well, I know about that. I just try to take it easy myself. No sense in rushing through the day."

Manny handed me the joint. "Yeah, I hear ya. I just don't like people to fuck with me. When they're fuckin' with me they don't know who they're fuckin' with." He hunched his shoulders and considered his "In the wind" tattoo. "I ain't afraid to blow 'em away."

"Yeah, well, uh, they shouldn't fuck with you," I stated agreeably. I don't think he heard me. His head just kept bobbing up and down, sinking lower into his shoulders. The smoke produced a tingling in my scalp and fingers.

"I've done it before. Man, I'm wanted for murder in thirteen states. But they'll never take *me* alive. Just remember that, man." He turned and glared at me. "There ain't *nobody* takin' me alive."

I raised my brow and nodded seriously at him. What would you do? When the joint got low enough to call it quits, I rose to leave. This meant that Manny had to stand up and let me out, something I was involuntarily relieved at seeing. Again I felt myself walking a tightrope: wishing to continue business with this madman while trying to avoid falling victim to his regional homicidal tendencies.

"I'll let you know how my friends like this stuff," I said chummily.

"No one takes me alive." Manny nodded, closing the door.

I became quite reflective while walking back through the shabby student neighborhoods to the Geronimo. Often I experienced this distant self-observation following the completion of actions based on instinct. My faith in personal instinct was getting me through more tight spots. Or, more accurately, I was getting into more stressful, seat-of-the-pants situations. But my faith was based on deeper abilities.

To skirt the gamut of threats encountered when one habitually breaks the law, often with strangers, one needs instantaneous judgment. For years I had to judge just who the stranger in front of me was—are they a cop? Would they uphold their end of the bargain? Will they rob me or kill me? After this I next tackled the question of whether or not they'd inform if a bust occurred. I found that I had an infallible sense as to whether someone had been in or was headed to prison. Some people were just too easy for me to imagine in jail clothes. This was a sure personal tip-off. When I saw it, it was a 99 percent chance that the person had some association with the law: they had spent or would spend time in jail or they were a cop. Affectionately, I called this handy talent Seeing the Threads. Seeing the Threads of what? The Threads of Perception? Of Reality? Of clothes? Well, it sounds good, anyway.

To survive I had to have some extra intuitive sense. Those with these abilities know what I mean, even if they don't break the law. Those who don't experience them, well, no amount of talk will make it clear. It's like trying to explain dreaming to someone who doesn't dream. What you take as natural he may refuse to believe even exists. It's frustrating to watch some blockhead persist in dull, parochial, depressing habits, stubbornly and proudly insisting that he owns a firm grasp on reality as he plods on with blinders. Such people are oblivious to the possibilities of seeing more than what's in front of them. Place these innocents among the pack of dogs that I found myself running with, and they will be eaten alive. Dogs don't argue the niceties of spiritual perception—either you have eyes in the back of your head or they'll take a bite of your ass.

I returned to my room, eagerly anticipating a meaningful dose of the dark, powerful stuff I'd just acquired from Manny. I gratefully appreciated being able to indulge in this now routine pleasure. I'd been shooting heroin off and on for almost six months and had largely abandoned the off part of the equation. The drug's effectiveness at masking irritations and the angers and sorrows at the turns my life had recently taken combined well with my natural ability to rationalize. I no longer even thought about this efficient process; when something bothered me too much, I simply utilized my secret potion and wiped the slate clean. It buoyed my spirits that I was once again free to enjoy utter physical and mental pleasure. I considered my plan that of a superior, intelligent man who could overcome the rigors of whimsical emotion. With the subterfuge complete, I contemplated the rewards of a job well done.

There was, however, a little gadfly buzzing about the streamers of my romping jubilee. It harkened subtly as I sat down at my huge desk and removed one paper from my purchase. I placed the small bag with Mark and Luke's stuff in a hidden corner of a drawer. Like a mosquito when you're half awake, my gadfly lighted in the back of my mind without drawing attention. Then I gathered the implements of my habit and prepared for a well-anticipated shot. My spirits rose high as I rinsed off my shooting spoon, its handle bent back so it could balance without tipping the contents. I gathered my fit, my matches, a glass of water, a small piece of cotton, and a blue stretch sock with which to tie myself off.

So I wouldn't have to deal with the mechanics of it after I was high, I paused to roll a joint. Then I poured the contents of the paper into the spoon, observing with satisfaction both its rich coffee color and the generous amount—at least twice what I'd been getting from Yaqui Jim. Pulling up about half a syringe full of water from the glass, I carefully squirted it onto the powder in the spoon. It dissolved readily, a good sign. I opened and bent back the matchbook, making the matches stand up. When I lit the whole book at once, a sudden cloud of smelly bluish smoke rose to the ceiling; then the matches began burning steadily for the ten or fifteen seconds needed to boil the fluid in the spoon. Not too much or it would all boil away, just enough to sterilize it. Black filaments floated in the air from the burning matches, which I tried to keep out of the spoon.

I rolled the tiny piece of cotton into a ball between my finger and thumb, and deftly dropped it into the fluid. It would act as a strainer when I put the point of the needle to it and pulled up the cooked medicine. The cottons themselves were worth saving. A few boiled up in the same manner would provide a decent shot. One had to be careful, though, not to pull any cotton fibers up into the fit. This could lead to a dose of "cotton fever," an unpleasant attack of chills and shakes. Straining the dark brown liquid into the fit—it filled it up about one third—I lovingly set it on the desk.

A deep breath released some of the tension built up from this fine, detailed work. More work lay ahead, as well as the rush of pleasure I knew would follow, and I took more deep breaths until I felt the quivering pass from my stomach muscles. It was a vibrating similar to what I'd feel before initiating some exciting sex. A combination of an unsettling feeling and a pressing thought crossed my mind, but I pushed it away before it had a chance to congeal.

Pumping my left fist open and closed to raise the veins inside my elbow, I simultaneously grabbed the stretch sock and tied it around my upper arm, not too tight but enough to restrict the blood and raise my veins. I didn't tie a full knot, just some affair that slipped under the band to provide tension, with one end sticking up toward my face. That let me pull it with my teeth when my hands were occupied and I wanted to let blood flow again. It needed to be undone gently so I wouldn't lose touch with the inside of my vein, and it had to be undone when I desired so my blood vessel wouldn't explode with too much liquid.

The knot done, I wiped off sweat glistening in the bend of my arm. In my concentration I saw little reflections of white light from the windows, glimmering like pearls on sand at the spot I planned to inject. This severe concentration brought back shocking reality. There were actually three lines of tracks at that junction on my arm—three veins in one little area that had already been probed, jabbed, and prodded to the point of pain and swollen redness. I had to keep them hidden since they were a sure giveaway of my habit, and I'd developed a whole set of graceful movements to disguise them when reaching for things. Hardly anyone saw these welts but me.

I swallowed my amazement as I regarded the length of the track on my best vein. It had been less than a day since I'd really looked at it last, yet I still felt shock at what I was doing to myself. The longest track, on the best vein, was a line of deep, red, moist elevations. Some had little pinpoint scabs at their tops where the needle had entered. One was a particularly annoying sight, its bulging discoloration a reminder of a day I couldn't hit the vein and accidentally shot the stuff into the skin beside it. The junk had to dissolve slowly before I felt it. The whole track was so tender that I didn't dare try hitting it that day. And in this pause, this offhand evaluation, I felt a definite, absolute, yet totally unfamiliar feeling: the thought condensed that, as sure as I breathed, if I took *that* shot I would be strung out. I suddenly *knew* that this would be the shot to addict me. It was not a question but a fact. Moving my eyes a couple millimeters, I considered the promise held by the rich, dark fluid in the syringe, and in the time that it took to shift my gaze from my battered arm to that dependable panacea, my mind was made up.

The whole sight couldn't have taken more than two or three seconds, yet it remains fixed in my mind's eye as a slow-motion wealth of detail. An image as clear as yesterday. This vivid personal moment is a common experience among those who have gotten addicted to heroin; many can remember saying the same things to themselves that I said that day. Addiction is a metabolic change to the physical body. It is a shift in the speeds and chemistries of your life. When a change like this occurs, you can *feel it*. I knew.

My pause, my thoughts, however, were just gestures. My fate was a foregone conclusion. And at that moment the advantages outweighed the disadvantages.

I moved my attention on to the vein next to the best but sore vessel, placed the point of the syringe lightly against my skin, and hammered it softly to let it grab flesh. I needed an angle that wouldn't let the vein move when I pressed all the way through the wall. I aimed and pushed. The pain was minimal, though this always surprised me. Pulling up the plunger, I registered a little flower of red within the dark solution. The Inside Touch. I loved it. Then, barely breathing, I eased the plunger down—not too fast. Jamming the stuff in could lead to anxiety later on. As the vein filled with solution, I pulled gently with my teeth at the tie in the stretch sock around my arm. In.

Now the tricky part. As the shot began to send tingles of excitement through me, I pulled the plunger back again, to boot it. This meant filling the fit with blood and shooting it back in for a quick rinse of the residue. Losing touch with the vein isn't uncommon at this point. Done. I had to fight an urge to sit back and let the stunning wave of loving warmth overtake me. Reaching out, I sucked up some water from the glass with the syringe to rinse it before blood clogged it up. This last operation I performed with one hand.

Finally I could sit back and relax. I looked down at my left arm. A crimson droplet had run all the way from the inside of my elbow to my wrist. It could wait. I was free again. Issues were settled. The slate was clean. I did not have to think about anything but my pleasure for the rest of the afternoon and evening. My heart, my head, my limbs were filled with a magnanimous swell of elation as medicines pulsed through my bloodstream. Yet my body felt lightened, buoyant from the sudden absence of dozens of irritating aches and pains. An odd, tranquil alertness keyed me now that gravity and time no longer pulled at me. Lighting the joint, I reveled in the large hits I could take without feeling the sting of hot smoke in my throat. Faint prisms of color pulsated from the walls. I dabbed the blood droplets from my arm.

A fascinating image of a checkerboard Geronimo filled my mind. Long rows of tiny rooms sitting next to and on top of one another, dwellings of alkies alternating with those of junkies. The alkies never squealed on the junkies, for doing so would mean having to reveal their own nightmarish lives. Stretching my arms high above my head, I took a deep breath, leaned back, and closed my eyes. Clear greens and reds appeared on my lids as I watched. They became brighter, more complex, and I let myself fall into them. Strange, flickering Geronimo midnight halls, somehow no longer an orderly structure but an endless series of ramshackle rooms, like Manny's dilapidated place. Though I knew that it was still afternoon in my own room and that my room actually sat at the end of the hotel, I was surprised to find other, larger rooms attached to it. I wandered, intrigued upon entering the bowling room, elated on encountering the rolling fields room, profoundly impressed at finding the open seas room. And I awoke in a gentle frame of mind, eyes half open, a bemused smile on my lips, pleased with my fate.

I knew that my time was my own: I had bought it.

on parade

8 First my mind awoke. Then my eyes opened a crease. Morning light filled the room. Lying on my left side, trying to turn over, I realized that *I couldn't move.* And my eyes wouldn't open more than halfway. Fighting growing terror at this somehow familiar situation, I forced myself to relax. But whenever I really started to relax and fall back to sleep, a heated hissing filled my ears, punctuated by the sound of soft footsteps warily walking around the room. Just out of sight.

I knew it was morning; I could see light on the walls and bed. But I could move nothing but my eyes. And they refused to open more than halfway. I couldn't see behind me, and I knew someone was there. I was paralyzed, and my mind was almost arrested with fear. My head felt hot—I hated to sleep with the sun on my head, and here I'd let it happen again. I tried to get some foothold, some sort of traction *somewhere* to make my muscles move. Faint murmuring and careful footsteps behind me. When I tried to relax, hissing filled my ears. Suddenly I felt something on my right thigh. I heard my breathing—shallow, rapid from my mouth. A mental spasm of total fear: *There was a hand on my thigh.*

I gratefully, finally jerked awake covered in sweat. I'd been having another Heat Dream. While lying there bathed in relief, I fought to dispel a heavy, hot cloudiness lingering in my head. Though awake, whenever I relaxed I'd feel myself falling asleep and the hissing would again fill my ears, the stiffness would start to creep over me, accompanied by physical shocks of fear that *it was all starting again.* And I'd shake myself awake. I swallowed, forcing my eyes to focus on the wall. A large, black mass of flies covered the spot I gazed at. They faded as I woke all the way up. Rising to a sitting position, I blew exhales of sheer thanks. Turning around to adjust the pillow, I realized that there was no way for the sun to hit my head from where the window was located.

I initially called them Heat Dreams because I thought they occurred when I was too hot or had sun on my sleeping head. But to my consternation, I soon realized that hot feelings were just another symptom of the dream and not caused by an outside source. The only correlation I could make was that when Heat Dreams started happening, I was feeling more nervous in my waking life. Yet whenever they were happening it seemed so real, the incidents so familiar and clear. I shook my head, telling myself that I'd better calm down during the days. That usually put the dreams on hold.

It's not that I didn't find these episodes worth investigating. I just had trouble dealing with the fear when a Heat Dream actually started. I guess that there are many types of dreams, and since I was making dreaming a profession of sorts, I dismissed Heat Dreams as simply one more species to explore.

And I easily understood growing feelings of personal pressure. After all, my priorities had changed over the last couple of weeks. When supplies got low, an involuntary tension brewed up inside me. Waiting too long to replenish them or finding nothing available, I'd feel my body getting achy and stiff. Sniffles would develop, along with watery eyes. An occasional unheralded, single, loud sneeze would spontaneously burst from me. My tracks, my teeth, my head all began to hurt, sometimes with a throb, other times a dull, constant pain, reminding me that I hadn't had a shot for a while. Nervousness would precede or follow these symptoms. I'd seen other addicts get edgy and snappish, but I didn't have that reaction. Still, I didn't consider it unpleasant to have to ingest opiates to quell these withdrawal symptoms. Hell, I figured, what better way could I spend the time anyhow? Upon taking my medicine all symptoms would disappear.

Mark, Luke, and Marie all looked with growing suspicion at my lengthening tracks as they handed me money to get them dope.

"Those are getting really long, Scott," Marie nasally intoned. "You'd better watch out. . . ."

"Scott, you have to do these things in moderation," urged Luke as he crushed his junk and snorted it off the table. He always did some before visiting the dermatologist and claimed the doctor was amazed that he never flinched an iota while he sliced open masses of zits on Luke's back.

"Don't get strung out," warned Mark. "Can't you get us a better price on these papers?"

I naturally avoided letting them know that I'd already developed a habit. Certainly, I resented their two-faced attitudes.

It may be said for my acquaintances at the Geronimo that

they never troubled me with such epistles. Most of them had been through numerous habits. They gritted their teeth and bore prison time and withdrawals, and when times were good they knew how to appreciate them.

"Make hay while the sun shines!" advised Nazi Paul, pulling on a yellow, hand-rolled cigarette, smiling a yellow smile.

"I know that, I do," I answered, still feeling a bit down in the mouth. "It's just having to hear these people criticize me for what they're doing themselves—it, you know—I just can't stand—"

"Ahh, you mean you're having trouble coping with it." Paul nodded, presenting his best counselor's face.

"Yeah, sure! Of course I'm having trouble coping with it!"

"Well." Paul nodded, frowning and scratching his chin. "You should just follow my policy."

"Oh, yeah? And what's that?"

"You know: Don't cope—get even!" He shrugged and smiled a little skull smile.

"Yeah, well," I mused. "There is something to be said for that philosophy. Yes, indeed, yes, indeed. . . ."

And so, smoking out on the porch or nodding out in my room, I anticipated the upcoming time when my rich friends would find themselves in a situation similar to mine. That would shut them up.

Of course, one of the illusions of friendship is how it functions on seemingly opposing levels, so it wasn't long before Mark and I were again discussing ways to expand our sources of supply. These brainstorming sessions usually took place as he sat on his mattress in a pair of blue gym shorts, with a ready thermos of hot tea and symphonies draining from the speakers.

"Whatever happened to that guy that likes to rob drugstores?" he asked, like it had just popped back into his mind. I realized he'd been thinking about it for a while.

"Shit." I shook my head. "Anyone who thinks they can rob more than one drugstore a year is gonna get caught. That guy's going to prison—I can tell by looking at him. Whenever he robs a place, he sells the stuff for so cheap that he's back where he started from in no time. Of course," I added enticingly, "if we're around after he does it, we can get some good prices."

Marie entered the room. Something was on her mind. "I'm going out now, Mark," she breathed. She glanced down at my arms. "Hitting that stuff kinda heavy, huh, Scott?"

Mark adopted a daddy-to-baby voice. "All right," he cooed. "Get me some green corn tamales."

"Hokay. But—uh—first I—that is—"

Mark snapped to roaring posture. "Are you telling me that you're out of money again, Marie?" he yelled.

"Mmmm." Marie smiled sweetly.

"Oh, Jesus Christ! Here!" He reached into pants lying by the bed, pulled out a fistful of bills, and threw them at her. The mass fluttered apart in midair, like a punch that turns to cotton in a dream. Much of it landed in front of me. Avoiding temptation, I scanned the ceiling. "And get me some green corn tamales!" Mark ordered sternly.

"All right," hummed Marie. We waited while she took a full minute to pick up the money bill by bill. When she was done she stood up, put her hand on her hip, and let out a sigh. Apparently it was heavy work caring for Mark. He would have none of it.

"Marie, would you get *out*!"

I sat with my chin resting in my hand. My face felt like Jack Benny's as he gave that quizzical, blank expression to his audience. I pursed my lips like he did, but no one laughed. Mark stopped glaring when Marie left the room.

"Anyway," I continued. "There's a good chance that we could convince this guy—"

"*Haven't you left yet?*" screamed Mark, making me jump. Marie stopped halfway into the room.

"I'm leaving now. I'm going, I'm going. . . . Now, Scott, I don't want you getting Mark any more of that nasty heroin."

I shrugged innocence. Mark rescued me.

"Oh, shut up, Marie. You do it, too, don't you? Well, *don't you?*"

Marie remained mute, showing injured concern. This evolved into obstinate innocence. Behind her rose explosively colorful Lautrec posters—women on swings at the raucous Moulin Rouge, laughingly showing garters to the crowd below. Vivaciousness sparked from the eyes of girls named Greedy Guts and Sewer Trap.

"That doesn't make it right." Marie finally sighed. "Anyway, I don't do it nearly as much as you."

"Green corn! Green corn! Green corn!" Mark chanted at her, bouncing on his mattress in his shorts. He did this until she left the room. Though I knew it was true, I still found it amazing that this was the man who masterminded much of the Northeast United States's marijuana supply. "And you'd better not drive the car into a ditch!" he bellowed as she was leaving. I prudently waited until the front door closed and Marie's car pulled away.

Then Mark turned to me, a portrait of concerned reasonableness. "Now, what was it you were saying before we were so rudely interrupted?"

Exasperation impulsively gasped from me. "I was saying that if we let the guy know that there's money waiting for him ten minutes away—"

"I *don't* want to meet *anyone!*" Mark pouted.

"You don't have to meet anyone. You just have to let me call you—"

"I don't want to *talk* to anyone!"

I threw up my hands. "See? This is how you always are! You're never forthcoming with details, then when something happens you have a shit fit because you weren't part of it."

Mark began pounding his mattress with his palms, like a spoiled child. He shook his head back and forth at the same time. "What am I going to do? What am I going to do? I am so fucking bored!" He flopped onto his back and flailed epileptically. "Somebody help me! Somebody give me something to *do*!"

Thus are great crimes planned.

We were back at square one. I hated it when things deteriorated like that. Against my better judgment I remained reasonable. "Well," I heard myself say. "Why don't you just grab a handful of money, go down to the airport, and buy a ticket for Spain? Then, when you get there you can figure out something to do." This went against my grain, for it meant having one of my main income sources disappear. But I needn't have worried. Mark just shook his head and whined "What am I going to do?" the entire time I was talking. I tried to fit in suggestions between his outbursts.

"There's a million things you can do when you have money. Go build a recording studio. Start a business—"

He perked up. "That's what I'd like. I need some kind of front. Some sort of legal business. But I can't think of anything."

I knew better than to start suggesting businesses to him. "What will that do for you? All you'll do is make more money, and then your problems will be bigger." Try telling someone that money won't solve his problems. Then try telling it to an insatiably greedy man.

Mark chanted, "I need a front! I need a front! I need a front!" Finally, he shut up.

In silence we listened to music. Everywhere my eyes fell I

saw suggestions of wealth. Imported tapestries, well-framed original paintings. The furniture had cost thousands, as had the stereo. A closet was bursting with clothes. Chinese wool rugs covered the floors. Expensive collectibles were falling off shelves, lying hidden amidst newspapers and magazines on the floor. Jade statues, antique brass boxes, daguerreotypes, Edward Curtis prints under books, expensive guitars, crystal balls—and new things appearing weekly. It's hard to listen to someone complain about his circumstances in such surroundings. After some time Mark finally spoke.

"Well, okay," he announced. "If the guy's really going to do it, you can tell him that I'll buy everything I'm interested in right away. Tell him that there's cash waiting, that it can be over in five minutes. I just don't want to see anyone. And I definitely don't want anyone over here."

"Right, right, I assumed that. That's always a given."

"When you've *actually seen the stuff*, you can give me a call and not before. I am not interested in anything until it actually happens!"

"I understand. Keep in mind, though, that the reason he's probably going to do it is because of me telling him I have a cash buyer."

"Yes, yes, *yes*, I understand." Mark shook his head at his mattress. "Just make sure that I don't meet anyone. At least until you see a suitcase full of pharmaceutical dope."

"No problem!" I shrugged agreeably. The argument went in circles: the guy's going to do it because Mark's interested, but Mark's not interested until the guy's done it. "I'm sure we can work something out." I had the type of commitment that I could use. Mark was devoted to the idea, and the thing probably wouldn't go down without me having some warning. I hoped.

We smoked some heroin. Using an impromptu paper tube,

we pulled in clouds of white smoke as the junk sizzled on some aluminum foil. Opium and heroin aren't smoked with direct flame but instead are cooked until the oily, tarry substance starts boiling and releasing smoke. A heat source is held under the smoking surface. The residue, called yen pox, can be crushed and eaten. Few people in the United States can afford to smoke their heroin. It was pleasant feeling the extra boost provided by this smoke mixing with my earlier shot.

I left with a plastic bag of a few ounces of weed, a front from Mark.

As usual, it was dark and cool in Nazi Paul's lodge. Thick curtains covered with brown water stains ensured that the room kept its timeless quality. Paul disappeared into his bathroom after letting me in. Richard, the robber, was visiting, along with a couple other guys. I could tell that they were high as I sat down on the end of the bed. Richard sat apart from us on the floor, cleaning weed on a newspaper, getting seeds out of it. Carefully I chose my opening words.

"I have a good friend who will buy every bit of good pharmaceutical dope he likes, all at once, if you come to me first after doing a drugstore."

A brief glint of angry surprise flickered in Richard's eyes; then he nonchalantly returned to his pot cleaning. "Ye-e-s, I've been thinking about that. It ain't so easy to rob a drugstore." He looked at me. "You can go to jail for that, you know," he added somberly. The others laughed.

"Yeah." I grinned. "I've heard you can!"

"These things take a little planning. Shit"—he shook his head—"sometimes I think it's more trouble than it's worth."

I shrugged. "Well, I'm not telling you to do it. I'm just saying that if you do it, come to me first and I'll get you the best price, plus you can sell most of the stuff right away."

"I really like junk," said Paul, emerging from the bathroom. "I just wish it didn't make it so hard to piss."

Richard sat cross-legged on the red concrete floor. He gave a little snakelike weave with his body as he worked and talked. "Yeah. We-l-l-l, how much money you think this guy can come up with, hmmm?"

I paused for effect. "He can come up with three thousand right away."

Richard frowned and nodded, obviously impressed with the sum. The rest of the room was quiet while we spoke. All I could hear was weed sliding along the newspaper, seeds rolling down to a picture of a gymnast on some parallel bars.

Finally Richard spoke again. "We'd have to get a car."

"That shouldn't be too hard," I answered.

Nazi Paul interjected. "I don't think he understands."

"Maybe not." Richard raised his head. "You really need two cars for an operation like this. The first one you dump about two minutes from the store; then you hop into the getaway car. That first car can't be traceable."

Paul agreed. "Some stolen license plates will do nicely for that."

"A stolen *car* is what you need." Richard snorted. "Boy, I'd sure feel better knowing that three thousand bucks was waiting right here for me."

"It'll be ten minutes away," I replied. "Really, even closer than that if you give me some kind of warning."

"Yeah, but ten minutes away and right here are a lot different. I'd sure feel a lot better if I saw the three thousand."

"Well," I lied. "I wouldn't mind doing it like that. But there's no way the guy will front me the money. He doesn't want to meet anyone, and he won't give up the bread until I see the stuff."

"Mmmm, I don't know. . . ." Richard's eyes closed to

creases. He seemed to see a problem where I couldn't see one. "Sure would hate to do the job and find out I did it for nothing. I wouldn't like that at all." Vague threat lingered in his manner.

"Look," I answered firmly. "I've known this guy for years. I know he has the bread. Three grand is no problem for him, believe me."

"'Believe me.' Famous last words." The other guys snickered.

"If you show me the stuff, he will absolutely take my word that I've seen it. He doesn't even live ten minutes away."

"Well, I'd just *feel* better if I could *see* the money."

"Hey! I would if I could. But I don't see how that's going to happen."

With that the discussion puttered to an end. We lit up a joint that Richard had rolled. Paul, Richard, and the other two boys looked like they'd all come out of the same mold. They were tan and wiry, with naturally taut muscles. All seemed like they'd be quick to anger; their eyes were alert, but they were at ease. In a society of cheap little hotel rooms and tiny, crappy houses, we all appreciated the simple luxury of Paul's dim, well-built private lodge. A salty, sweaty smell wafted through the air. There was a sense of crime at rest.

"Naw," one of the guys was saying. "I gave up that house-breaking shit. But when I see people shut their windows and give it that little tug to tighten it up—shit! I still hate when I see that shit!"

I could tell that Richard had interest in my idea. I remembered the image of him holding a gun to the head of a young female cashier. When my own head appeared in place of hers, I forced the picture from my mind.

After they all left and it was just Paul and me in his lodge, Paul spoke. "I wouldn't go fronting any three thousand bucks to that guy Richard if I were you. Nope, I sure don't know about that."

"Ahh, there's no way I'm fronting anything to him," I snapped, feeling exasperated at the unproductive negotiations and at still having to talk about it. "Why bother robbing a drugstore if you've got three grand? Anyway, the guy won't front it to me, so I don't have to worry about fronting it to Richard."

"Good." Paul nodded. "I'm glad to hear you say that. No need for harm to come to those that don't deserve it." Paul gazed off thoughtfully. "Maybe I oughta take you up on this deal and just do the thing myself. . . ."

I yawned. "Yeah, well, the money's there. First come, first served."

"I don't know. Something about drugstores make me nervous. Man, they really come down on you heavy for that shit. They don't dig that stuff *at all.*"

My left arm was so sore, the tracks on it so lengthy, that I'd started shooting into my right arm. Being normally right handed, I found it a bit awkward at first. I hated producing extra welts because of trouble hitting the vein. Now that I was shooting every day, sometimes twice a day, these marks were adding up. I'd seen addicts who no longer had any veins in their arms left to speak of. They'd hit other places: the backs of hands (a favorite for parolees because it's harder to detect) and hard to find veins in their legs. I heard stories of prisoners injecting stuff into their necks using primitive tools made from broken lightbulbs. And rare references to veins under the tongue. While I still stuck with the disposable, plastic diabetic syringes, everyone seemed to have his own preference in this matter. Nazi Paul was very attached to his old glass hypo with round wire finger grips. Others swore that the traditional eyedropper and fit technique was really the only way to go (the fit is the little piece of paper which firmly holds the needle point to the dropper). Squeeze the dropper once, and it registers blood to show proper vein placement. Squeeze it again, and the stuff flows smoothly in. Using physics to improve daily life. I now had my own real live habit, which I was a few weeks into. Though I noticed that I often awoke feeling sore, especially in my lower back, and that sniffles and miscellaneous throbbing pains asserted themselves when I hadn't had a shot for a while, I hadn't suffered any real break in my supply. I hadn't experienced what a true lack of junk was like. Despite awareness of my addiction, I assured myself that being merely a few weeks into it wasn't that serious. In fact, I was still interested in asserting my independence from the drug, and one day I decided I would just stop using it for a while. I still enjoyed getting high; I simply wanted to show myself that I could stop whenever I felt like it.

I assembled some over-the-counter analgesics and borrowed a good book. After buying a few snacks, I made up the brass bed and generally pictured myself lounging through a brief period of abstinence. This project began one pleasant, sunny winter morning.

Upon opening my eyes, I was immersed in a mental battle to keep from indulging in what had become one of my favorite pastimes: the breakfast shot. If I could get past that urge, the rest of the day wouldn't be as hard. I took some aspirins. It was irritating having to wait for them to relieve the collection of backaches and neck pains that I'd become accustomed to erasing each morning. After an hour I realized that aspirin did virtually nothing for these annoyances. The thought of eating breakfast was unappealing; my appetite was nonexistent.

Groaning, I forced myself over to the bathroom. Constantly wet nose and eyes forced me to stockpile toilet tissue by the bed. Getting my tissue, stamping raw earth from my feet, I fell back with a moan onto the mattress. My eyes drifted to the window high on the wall. It was warm outside; gently swaying bushes showed that the pleasant temperature was enhanced by a breeze. The idea of ruining a lovely day added to my torment. Wistfully I recalled how much I'd enjoyed the previous days, satisfying good appetites, moving fluidly through gentle winds and cottony air. Whenever I started to read, I became too impatient to cover more than a couple paragraphs.

Somehow I made it to early afternoon. The doldrums lay in these hours. Nighttime and sleep seemed a minor eternity away. I listened to weekday traffic wisp by on Euclid Avenue. Sometimes a car swept past the alley window, and I watched the dust settle until I couldn't see it move anymore.

I decided to smoke a joint. Urging myself to the desk, I fell into the chair and listlessly regarded rolling papers and a little bag of pot. "Why am I doing this to myself?" I asked aloud. Ignoring the question, I manfully went about rolling up the joint. When I took the first puff, I felt the only real relief I'd experienced all day. It lasted about five seconds. Then the weed seemed to magnify all my unpleasant symptoms.

Suddenly I had a rare illumination, a glimmer of forthright logic that appears in only isolated moments of a lifetime. This gem of intuition, this simple clarity of thought must've been what Ptolemy felt as he watched shadows progress inexorably over the walls of his cave. Then he suddenly realized that the sun circled the Earth! Feeling the thrill of briefly being in real touch with the music of the spheres, I verily quivered with excitement as a single, simple thought boosted its profound message into the desperate hollows of my mind: "Why suffer?"

A eurekalike laugh fluttered at what could have only been my previous obtuseness. An old joke prodded me, the one about the man who hit himself in the head with a hammer because it felt *so good* when he stopped. The simple answer to my problem had surfaced to rib-tickling reality! Gasping thankful breaths at finally being allowed to come up for air, I haphazardly dug into desk drawers and gleefully piled shooting implements in front of me. In my fervor I fought to keep my shaking hands from sending things flying onto the floor.

Never was the smell of boiling heroin so sweet! Never had the sizzling, noxious cloud of blue smoke from lighting a whole book of matches been so irrelevant! The quick, sharp pain of the needle breaking skin had never bothered me less. And, yes, the utter relief at having that stupid, self-inflicted torture *finally end* had never been so welcome.

With the medicine in, I sat back and panted with pleasure as it pulsed through my limbs and trunk—a most exquisite, rolling sensuality. Tears of joy flowed from my grateful psyche. Passing a hand over my forehead, I became aware of beads of sweat formed there. So intent was I that I didn't even care if the needle clogged up with blood.

And, as I felt an appetite returning, I stepped outside to tread those balmy desert breezes; through cotton dusk I resumed my noble path. I caught echoes on my now calmed pond as it gently rippled to the skipping of my philosophers' stone: "Why suffer?"

That evening I sat out on the third-story porch, now becoming a favored place. The few extra hours I'd forestalled my daily shot let me feel it that much more, and I was lolling in a languid, well-medicated state. Though I didn't wish to dwell on my failed attempt at stopping, the implications of this defeat would not stay buried. I wasn't bothered that I'd again have to see that madman Manny; I knew that Yaqui Jim's quaint little household couldn't supply me forever, but neither did that worry me; the monies from in-town drives and packing sessions already needed replenishment, but I dismissed that as a problem that would, as usual, somehow take care of itself. In the face of my failure to stop the first time I tried, my adept rationalization abilities came to the forefront, allowing me to pursue a pleasant set of nods and dreams, bathed in soft, charitable postmidnight air.

There is a quality of wind so gentle, so cottony, that it titillates with its stroke; so perfect in temperature that it doesn't even register in the tactile range, and so sweet that beautiful music would interrupt its melodious play upon our ears and skin. In this sympathetic, pastoral setting, I let my mind wander the structure of illusions that I insisted remain standing. Heroin was indeed, I reticently acknowledged, a greater force than I'd originally given it credit for being. I thought about how boring and flat things were without it—I didn't remember things always being like that. True, there had often been for me a lack of satisfactory mental occupation, the sense that I owned powers that were thirsting for use, and often I found myself discouraged from trying to cross the enormous chasm between ability and opportunity. But it wasn't until I found the incredible mental stimulation of junk, until it had actually joined the senses of physical and mental euphoria, that I perceived life as stale in the absence of these beauties.

Listening to lulling winds sweep through the old maple trees grazing my perch, I realized that no one, not even a Superman, could resist the kryptonitelike powers lying hidden beneath junk's seductions. So many have tried, yet in the end almost all have gladly given in to its sirenlike lure. It's a shame, I mused, that this real-life kryptonite is illegal. Half its power drain is from feeling pressure to keep its use secret or from having breaks in one's supply. Why are the most stimulating, best-feeling things always withheld from us?

My first experiment with altered states: nine years old,

inner-city Philadelphia. I found that by getting as close as possible to traffic on six-lane Broad Street I could feel a pleasant dizziness as the cars sped by. Wistfully I remembered Superman comics (kryptonite) and old sci-fi mags of my 1950s childhood. Dated, stylized cartoon frames filtered through my mind: post–nuclear war worlds, evolution mutated by radioactive genes, the entire midwest population beside themselves with terror on encountering a new breed of human—strange children with abilities beyond the five senses, routinely Seeing the Threads. A line of thin youths without hair and with tall foreheads weave an orderly march through the rubble of some demolished city, sending hidden, bearded, ragged *normal* citizens into paroxysms of fear. Cries rend the air, warnings of "The PSI's," "The Espers!" And finally, with a face so panicked, so spasmed with horror, so desperate to escape that it can't even be contained by the frame of the comic book, one bearded cracker screams, *"Good Lord!"*

First science facts: eight years old, and I stand under gray, inner-city smog. A 1958 *Weekly Reader* shows a double-pointed green arrow between the sun and Earth, labeled "93,000,000 miles." Even then I realized that the span is sometimes greater, sometimes less than that exact number of miles. So great is this distance, I read, that it takes light from the sun eight and a half minutes to reach us, and I shuddered at imagining the sun suddenly blacking out. We'd have only minutes of warning before all life here stopped abruptly. I filled many hours by replaying these last few minutes of consciousness, trying to grasp the enormity of being frozen in place, in blackness, for eternity. It made me dizzy.

My second- and third-grade teachers provided encouragement through repeated calls to bolster our country's ranks of scientists and engineers. I wanted to cooperate. What lad wouldn't want to grow up wearing a white lab coat and holding test tubes or spend his days running trains? The hard streets of Philly faded behind old black-and-white World War II newsreels on TV. My young impression of the 1940s was that everything stood in long, neat rows. "American Industry on the Firing Line!" yells the announcer; satisfied, happy squares of civilian tradespeople parade on the TV screen. "Plumbers on parade!" Formations of plumbers, huge wrenches riding their shoulders like rifles. "Milkmen on parade!" Battalions of milkmen effortlessly carry metal baskets of glass bottles, all smiling, dressed in white, black visors tipped jauntily on their heads. "White Blondes on parade!"—

I snapped to.

Hadn't realized that I'd fallen asleep. A voice still rang in my ears: "Fighting for a decent world!" It contrasted with the deep, neutral silence of University Blvd. A gentle wind rustled the leaves above my head; sighs escaped me as it stroked my skin. A subtle, blue glow had grown on the horizon, but the street lay dark and empty below me. One of those moments when time takes a breather. I needed a breather. These were my hours. Why did they seem so well earned? How could I command such pleasure yet have such a sense of slipping control? Why did I see flies on the wall so clearly when I awoke in the mornings?

"My God! What's going to happen to me?"

I lit a cigarette, making a mental note not to shove the contents of syringes so rapidly into my arm. It seemed to lead to anxiety. I reviewed my stock of supplies. I had the upcoming day's doses, and, with my old cottons, I could probably scratch enough together for the following day. I had a little money left so, if push came to shove, I'd simply buy some more. It was preferable, however, to supply myself through dealing profits instead of spending what little cash I had. But after I took these stronger, more generous papers to Mark and Luke, I knew that they wouldn't be needing anything for a while. Of course, there was always the possibility of setting up that drugstore deal with Richard. I told myself that it could happen anytime, easing back on a dream of a rich supply of free pharmaceutical dope. With all these possibilities, I soon soothed myself into expertly barricaded comfort. Since I had tomorrow's stuff, I reasoned, I really didn't have any problems at all.

9

I awoke in the middle of the night feeling very light. Not light-headed, but actually almost weightless. So lucid was my vision and thought that I didn't try to ascertain if I was actually awake, I simply assumed it. Having a weightless body was pleasant, but the stimulating sensation within my skull was better. It was similar to the way my head felt when I dreamt about flying or when in my dreams I could move objects without touching them. I stared at a note I'd taped up on the wall across the room, beyond the foot of the bed. Safe in the depths of silent night, secure in the privacy of my bed, I determined to try to move the paper from the wall without touching it.

Though unfamiliar with a successful method, I concentrated on this action. This caused the pleasant, stimulating sensation in my head to expand through my limbs. It was punctuated by delicious jolts of pleasure, which I brought on at will. In fact, I felt it best when I tapped my will to move the paper, and, to my delight, I saw the paper on the wall getting closer to me! *It* wasn't moving. *I* seemed to be advancing toward it! Yes, I distinctly felt myself rise from the bed, effortlessly, head first, then trunk, and I realized that I was viewing the room from two angles!

This lasted briefly, for the shock of realization instantly returned perspective to my prostrate form. I rose and, leaning on an elbow, gave my head a good shake. I was indeed awake. A woman's voice addressed me. It seemed to be coming from above and to the side, perhaps from the antique closet by my bed. That I was awake there could be no doubt.

"Yes?" I answered hesitantly. "Yes, I can hear you."

The voice continued a soothing murmuring. "It's all right, Scott. It's okay" was about all I could make out. The rest of it was garbled, seeming to stress tone rather than words. The way you might address a dog when trying to make friends or reassure.

"What?" I whispered back. "What did you say?"

This exchange of pleasantries soon ceased. The whole time I'd been leaning on my elbow, wide awake. I again shook my disbelieving head. Falling back, I tried to grasp the enormity of what had taken place. I wasn't frightened, I was surprised. Memories resurfaced: the hotel manager's hesitancy to rent me the basement room; her allusions to violent death there. Someone named Scott had rented it previously.

In the depths of the night, I understood that my dreams and the Geronimo's lingering memories were merging.

I decided to give kicking another try.

"Some days are better than others for starting *that*," advised

Paul, and I realized that I could feel which days were best to start a kick on. Beginning on the wrong day can cause needless discomfort, even contribute to failure. "No use trying to do the right thing at the wrong time," Paul instructed. "All you're doing is sucking up to Fate." Later on I'd learn that a reduction program is also helpful. Discipline, however, can weaken when trying to follow it. Those idiots who insist that cold turkey is the only way to quit don't know what they're talking about. There're many ways to skin a cat. Skinning it alive is usually the hardest.

I took the precaution of begging a strong barbiturate from Luke. He usually stashed stuff like that, and, since his own use was so controlled, it would lie around his house for months. He reluctantly parted with one Tuinal. I knew from my previous failure that if I could get to sleep I could get over a major hurdle.

"Well, I wish you luck with that, Scott," Luke offered.

I must've picked the right day to start; the first two days were surprisingly easy. Avoiding smoking weed, which I'd learned magnified unpleasant symptoms, I reached the third day with a minimum of back pains, no cramps or unwieldy spasms, just a lot of sniffles. But that day the withdrawals hit with full force. Both psychological and physical stresses eked at my discipline. It started that morning, and by early afternoon I was in a worse position than the first time I'd failed. A most irritating itching plagued my legs, a maddening tingling right beneath the surface of the skin, making it impossible to scratch. Unable to ignore it, I started hitting my legs with my fists, trying to use pain to end the torment. It was practically useless. I had odd fantasies of shredding my skin to scratch the itch. A distasteful sweat coated me, unrelated to activity, simply popping out unbidden. Little chills rippled through my body. As these things got more trying, my mind wandered helplessly to the papers stored in my desk. I'd known better than to try kicking without the security of junk around, in case things got too ugly, but thus far I'd had no trouble resisting the lure. Nevertheless, I knew that in my present condition I couldn't tolerate the itching, the sweats, the aches, the chills, the tensions, and the panics. I had to make it to sleep.

I was discovering the cycles of kicking. There were a number of them. The first, third, and fifth days were usually the worst (or alternately, the second and fourth days). And within those bad days were smaller cycles, four- to six-hour periods of stress and symptoms followed by equal periods of ease. Kicking through the abstinence method was a matter of getting past one cycle to the next. On that third day I became aware that getting over that horrible, seemingly insurmountable cycle I was then in would get me through the worst of it. "Over the hump." I went to the desk and, ignoring papers and syringe in the drawer, pulled out the barbiturate I'd obtained from Luke. Water fell from the glass and over my face as I gulped the pill down.

Lying back on the bed, I determined to pass the next hour of torture until the pill hit. When I tried scanning a book, I couldn't concentrate on it. My vision was blurred. I lay motionless. Doing this seemed to keep agonizing physical sensations to a minimum. But I'd finally jerk into action, grabbing at insanely unscratchable legs or wiping snot pouring into my mouth and over my face. Pounding the bed with my fists, I gritted my teeth and waited for some undefined deliverance to well up inside of me. That idiotic pill was my last line of defense. I had heard that barbiturates hit relatively quickly, so after forty-five minutes of this torture I was feeling a lurid combination of impatience and hopelessness. It wouldn't be long before I'd spring to my desk and cook something up; I didn't relish reactions from the mixture of the useless barbiturate and intravenous heroin.

Time seemed to stop. Repeatedly I dismissed a mental image of me jumping from the bed and cooking up a shot. Each picture returned more quickly. Absolutely nothing developed from the sleeping pill, and with a sudden, angry, involuntary groan, I robotically punched the bed and rose. I had lost again.

At that very second of defeat, I was hit by a staggering wave of dark tingling. The potent barbiturate entered my bloodstream at full force. Immediate gratification that the pill had actually worked was quickly overtaken by one of the most complete and fulfilling reliefs that I've ever known. The pleasure of having itching stop, of feeling raw nerves and knotted muscles relax and become anesthetized had taken me by such surprise that I fell onto my bed and groaned in ecstasy. I wanted to indulge that feeling for hours, but I knew that I must take advantage of the opportunity for rest offered by the luxurious pill. With a gentle float rocking me into oblivion, I fell into a deep, dreamless sleep. When I awoke early the next morning, I felt that I had passed the biggest hurdle to my kicking.

There were a couple more days of minor symptoms, but they were nothing compared with that third day. Upon awakening the sixth day I was finished. I was charged with a strong appetite. Four meals a day weren't enough. I had what they call the chucks, the desire to eat everything all the time, as my digestive system awoke from a long anesthesia.

My vision also became sharper and more sensitive. Rosebushes and early spring flowers blooming around the Geronimo held me absolutely captive. Colors glowed in the absence of drugs as incredibly as they ever had when I was stoned. "These things are so beautiful!" I whispered, beholding crimson roses on the empty path. My mind was light. Sun flickering through flame trees and dancing upon walkways and arches grabbed me with a depth of feeling I didn't know was possible without dope.

These captivating emotions lasted about two or three days. A period of severe boredom followed. Everything seemed dull, flat. Time plodded through a molasses of days and nights. I felt listless, completely unmotivated. The pleasant spring weather, reading, eating, nothing interested me in the slightest. I turned down large orders for papers from Mark. I ignored offers of quality stuff from Nazi Paul when he mentioned our mutual contacts getting good shipments. With no dealing to produce income, my small stash of money shrank.

I began to drink alcohol. Though the initial feelings were pleasant, I didn't enjoy the glum, dull buzz that alcohol provided. I started drinking just occasionally. People at the bars were shallow, transparently boisterous. Soon I settled into a pattern of monotonous, cheerless drinking. The alcohol depressed me, as did the hangovers. Sometimes, late at night when I was really inebriated, that old unscratchable itching started in my legs and I'd beat them with my fists. The next day I'd see black and blue marks. I was constantly bored, not from lack of desires or ideas but from lack of any chance to put them into practice. Ideas for musical composition were pointless to dwell on—I had no outlet. I tried approaching Mark with music projects but received his usual whining over how bored he was, how he wished he had something, anything to do. I saw my life as an unrewarding, static existence that was no longer even highlighted by the mixed blessing of opiates.

After a few weeks of this pointlessness, I decided to reward my abstinence with a shot. I felt a distinct pleasure, as if cool air was blowing within my bones. There were no ill effects the next day. I shot up a couple more times. Luke frowned as he eyed the growing line of tracks on the inside of my arm. "Don't worry about it," I told him. "I know how to do it without getting strung out."

Soon I was addicted again.

* * *

Many be the dreams we are, but countless are the ways we be them.

In addition to Heat Dreams (barometer of my nerves), opium dreams, and normal nightly dreams, I was now encountering conscious visions from the depths of the Geronimo—light-bodied affairs complete with voices emanating from the antique closet. Add a few out-of-body experiences and my secret life was rapidly becoming a compendium of arcane travels. Awakening in a state of morning paralysis, struggling to move as I watched a thick patch of flies fade from the wall became commonplace. I attributed it to nervousness and financial pressures. Perhaps, I thought, I should change rooms, get something a little less dusty smelling, not so haunted.

The only thing available was one of my previous rooms, Number 316. I paid for a month. It took most of my money, leaving me with about thirty-five dollars. I had a few days of papers and cottons left and hoped that Mark and Luke would soon place another order with me. As always, I had a small supply of decent weed, and I rolled some up to survey my new surroundings.

The single bed had metal rails at each end, like the lovely old brass bed I had had downstairs, but this was just steel painted some dull, dark brown, like that of a child's crayon. The bedspread was an old, deep purple affair that somehow vaguely matched the faded brownish orange and red splotched wallpaper. My night table went with the small desk, both repeatedly varnished until they'd acquired a deep, umber, archaic shine. Today they'd be quaint and simple antiques, but at that time they were just one step from being thrown into the alley as garbage. An old, dialless black telephone sat on the desk. The number 316 on the face looked like it'd been there for fifty years. Frayed, once white curtains hung on black metal rings across a wrought-iron curtain rod. They looked like one good pull would shred them. As they let in more light than I liked, I fought every morning with the eastern sun to stay asleep. It was usually a losing battle. The room was narrow and about twice as long as the bed. A collapsed, torn chair sat by the windows. Its upholstery had turned gray with age, emitting a cloud of dust when someone sat down. The small bathroom was done in old black-and-white tiling, with a topless, violently flushing porcelain toilet. The bathroom looked like an easy and devastating place to lose my footing. In the medicine cabinet I found one item: a black-bottomed spoon for cooking dope. I have found these spoons in medicine cabinets of all strata of hotels.

Since I didn't want anyone nosing around my business, I had avoided asking residents about how they made a living or, more accurately, fended for themselves. Nazi Paul brought up the topic of money during one of our afternoon shooting sessions. Though he'd initially offered encouragement for my kicking, he seemed disappointed at the loss of business it implied for him. Now that I was back on schedule, it was just like old times, almost. It soon became clear to him, however, that my cash situation wasn't as vibrant as it had once been. Of course, I'd never pressed him about where he got his funds and, judging from his emaciated physical state (which by this point was shocking to outsiders), there didn't seem to be a whole lot of funds. Displaying the houndlike nose of a true survivor, Paul delicately sniffed the question with me.

"They haven't seen you around as much at Yaqui Jim's," he began, peering sideways through sly slits in his eyes. "You been trying to cut down?"

I snorted in disgust. "No, no. I just don't have that much money."

"Hmmm." Paul pensively rubbed his chin. "I know the feeling. Fortunately, there's an abundance of opportunity awaiting an enterprising young man around the neighborhood."

"Oh, really?" I raised my brow in disbelief. "And where might that be?"

Paul raised his palms to indicate obvious manna lying within the simple reach of those who would but see. "Why, I'm surprised you even have to ask. When I walk down the street sometimes I'm overcome by the wealth of possibilities that I see going by me. Sometimes I have to hold myself back from going overboard." He nodded, wide-eyed and knowingly, his neck springing in too large a collar. "That's the trick. You have to stay balanced in these things. Going overboard can dump the whole pretty picture."

"Paul." I looked at him squarely. "What are you talking about?"

"Shee-it!" He hooted. "I would've thought you'd get it by now! When I need money for food or dope I just go into someone's house and help myself!"

"Ooohh, you mean robbery."

He stiffened proudly. "Not *robbery*, man. Burglary. There's a difference. *People* shoot. Houses don't shoot."

"Burglary, huh? Well. . . ." I nodded, staring out the window. I saw many run-down houses with unlockable, warped windows and easily forced doors. My window, I noticed, was far enough away from the porch to prevent outside access. The glare out there was unpleasant. "That's what you do, eh? Why don't you talk to Yaqui Jim? He seems like he'd do that. He's got that hard attitude that wouldn't care too much about other people's stuff." I felt immediately embarrassed after making that last statement, but it didn't bother Paul in the least. He did express shock, though.

"Jim? Fuck, that guy ain't no burglar! *Jim?*" A look of horror crossed his face. "Shit, that guy'd be a nightmare to break into a house with. He'd make some god-awful racket. Have you seen the size of that Indian? I can just see him getting stuck in some window, then crashing to the floor. Man, I don't even like to think about it!"

Paul then considered me in a fatherly sort of way. "It's the guys that are wiry, the thin guys that make good burglars. I mean, think of it, when you see some muscular, skinny junkie, that's the kind of guy that can slip through a small opening." He waved a hand at me. "Now you look like you're in pretty good shape. You're certainly not carrying excess weight. Shit, that's what I made you for a long time ago. I thought you were into all that stuff. With all that money you seemed to be getting, I figured you must have some angle on the houses around here."

"Me?" I laughed. "Naw, I never went into anyone's house for money. The bread just came from some pot deals that I put together."

"Well, you know, if you're interested, the two of us could probably make some pretty good hauls. Shit, some of the houses I've been in around here aren't as poor as they look. These students have money! Some of the stuff I've had to leave just because I only have two arms. . . ." (a longing, wistful look) "You know"—Paul got more conspiratorial—"I've been scoping out a place just a few steps from here. I'm almost positive that the people there work at night. Their place is always dark in the evenings. Man, if you're interested, I know it'd be really easy. Just in and out, that's all it takes. I'd be really surprised if it wasn't worth our time. Fuck, if you want to, man, we could do it tonight!"

A small shock riddled me. I'd grown up to despise burglars, although now that I was living among them I'd softened my attitude. I knew that some of my associates combed the university for a living, pouncing on forgotten purses, open cars, school books. Eight-hundred-dollar bicycles would be turned over for twenty or thirty bucks. Still, a distasteful uneasiness filled me when I imagined Paul and me sharing the stressful situation he had outlined. To be quite honest, I was more worried about his talking if we were caught than I was about some anonymous person's house goods. He already had a prison record.

I shook my head. "No, thanks anyway. It's not really my style."

"Whatever," Paul stated nonchalantly. "I just thought I'd make the offer. You wouldn't mind, then, if I borrowed this—" He stood up and walked over to the window, laying his hand on an eighteen-inch brass rod, part of a rickety old mechanism used to open it. "These things make great burglary tools. This hotel's full of good tools! Gotta make use of what the environment offers you." He smiled a proud scoutmaster's smile.

"Yeah, sure, go ahead." I didn't care.

"Yeah, I've been eyeing this thing since I came in." He juggled it a bit until it detached from the window mechanism. "It'll fit nice and snug down my pant leg."

I laughed. "Why bother keeping it down there? Shit, there's nothing illegal about carrying some metal bar around!"

Paul leaned back as if I'd just insulted his craft.

"I wouldn't be so sure about that, if I were you," he admonished me. "The last time I checked, possession of burglary tools was a felony in this state." He paused to let it sink in, then gazed out the window, shaking his head. "Man, that's one of my greatest fears, getting stopped at dawn by some overly ambitious cop and having him find something like this"—he waved the brass bar—"down my pants. Shit, that's all I need, a seventy-two-hour stay in the county jail. Fuck, I don't think I could handle that."

With that I knew immediately what he meant. We both sported habits that would brook no large interruption. Always the danger lurked of being detained for possession of hypodermics, for weed; even something as simple but inescapable as tracks on our arms could get us incarcerated without charges for up to seventy-two hours. If a cop saw my tracks, he could pull me in and let me cool off for a while, simply to see if I got sick. Just another risk for me to have to consider.

I shook my head imagining it, speaking almost to myself. "Yeah, that's about all I need at this point."

"Yeah, you and about half of this hotel!" Nazi Paul rose to leave. He waved the bar one more time. "I'll be sure to bring this back when I'm done with it," he called agreeably, as if borrowing a measuring cup. "Let me know if you change your mind about doing one of those houses with me."

The reader now warmly assured that all junkies aren't thieves or burglars, let me briefly expand. At this point it should be clear that the mechanics of addiction can allow some people to indulge without forging an inescapable path to crime. I knew many addicts who worked nine-to-five jobs; this gave them the funds to deal, if they wished. Their schedules caused the junk business to get into real gear only around sunset. For many customers also kept working hours. Many junkies are Ph.D.'s, teachers, well-respected parents, businesspeople, steady workers, homeowners, and so on. The list is endless. Junkies abound in all strata of American life. Being addicted doesn't automatically imply failure and disaster. Many junkies are enlightened enough to utilize the powers of opium without it overcoming their lives. It should be stressed that most in this category don't inject their dope.

I'm sure that this information comes as a surprise to many, but most people's understanding, indeed most experts' understanding of the opium user derives from poor examples found in detox clinics, isolated shots from TV and movies, junkies squirming and thrashing in jail cells. They bear an attitude as poorly informed as that of the victims of drug abuse themselves. For it's lack of education that causes most "abusers." They are sensationalized to the rest of us. Most uninformed critics and moral indignants would find it totally absurd to base their opinions and understandings of alcohol users on the narrow cross section found in detox clinics or lying in the streets. The most uninformed actually believe that a person magically increases the chance of getting AIDS because of smoking a joint. And after one has used illegal drugs, as I have, with drug counselors, legislators, and cops in uniform, it's not hard to reach the conclusion that drug laws in this country are purposeless, archaic, and ignorant.

Combine pressures of avoiding getting caught with anxieties created by poverty and intravenous injection of adulterated street drugs, and one often sees judgment fly out the window. When money becomes short under these circumstances, the lure of easing one's burden through theft, burglary, prostitution, armed robbery becomes greater.

The thirty-five dollars I'd had upon moving to the new room was dripping steadily away. I became more conservative in the amounts I shot; I cooked up my cottons more often. I talked Mark out of another small front of weed to sell. When visiting I would impress upon him the importance of ordering more papers from me. Never explaining myself, I assumed that the idea that I was in need of a shot could somehow become both clear and unspoken. The fact that I'd turned down Nazi Paul's burglary offer gave me some bit of reassurance that I wasn't completely at the mercy of circumstances. Actually, almost the opposite was true.

After a week or ten days of this nonsense, I received the

hopeful possibility, through my brother and sister, that a small inheritance awaited me. Not daring yet to believe it fully, I phoned my father, who reluctantly gave me the details. My mother had saved up $1,200, which he had decided to disperse among the three children. That this was her expressed wish seemed beside the point. He, in fact, confiscated everything else that she wished us to have, but I avoided that issue at the time, deciding first to collect this timely $400 windfall.

I put on a long-sleeved shirt to cover my tracks when at the bank. The weather was getting warmer, though, and I disliked the stinging sweat gathering on my needle marks. Really, I had started to count on the easing of my burden from the money, and I falsely believed that the bank officer could withhold it if he saw tracks. To complete my disguise I adopted a suitably glum attitude, presenting a rather convincing picture of despondency. The guy bought it all.

Deftly I reached to sign the seemingly endless collection of necessary papers, turning arms this way and that, throwing up verbal camouflages, expertly drawing attention to various parts of the desk when there was danger of his noticing marks during a reach. He seemed as glad to be finished with me as I was with him. I was in a state of disbelief at my good fortune, even as they counted out the $400 at the teller's window.

I rushed first back to the Geronimo to hide most of it, then on to Yaqui Jim's, where I purchased a full gram of heroin. I was glad to leave my parents' old neighborhood and all the unpleasant associations it held for me. I figured that I could sell enough of my eighty-five-dollar gram to replace the cost and still keep myself supplied for a few days, when I could do it again.

What did I think about spending my mother's bequest on dope? I had some minor twinges of guilt at the time. These have completely disappeared now that I look back on this period with more distance and objectivity. My mother died of chronic pain. Had she been able, she would herself have spent the money on narcotic relief in a logical attempt to lead a more normal life. She certainly didn't reject this solution in favor of suicide; suicide had been the last resort. Without putting words into her mouth, I can't imagine that she would've thought that there was anything better to spend the cash on. The irony couldn't have been more appropriate—here I was killing myself with the very stuff that would've helped her live.

10 As spring progressed the weather got warmer. Blossoms and greenery gradually fizzled away. The spring rains had passed, and I felt distaste for these intimations of summer's heat.

I spent a week reading the complete Sherlock Holmes mysteries, reveling in the simplicity of crime and drug use during the Victorian years. Holmes himself had a lively taste for the needle. I longed fondly for 1890s London, seeing it as modern civilization's equivalent to Greece's Golden Age. At week's end I was, like Holmes, studiously puffing a pipe of tobacco (into which I dropped an occasional pinch of weed).*

---

*When Queen Victoria, her household, and guests lived at Balmoral they stayed well supplied thanks to A. R. Clark's pharmacy in the Deeside village

This was May, a time I'd learned to associate with drug shortages and the resultant short counts and robberies. Those lucky enough still to have something to sell refused to give any kind of break, no matter how large the purchase. One contact with whom I briefly dealt was the beneficiary of some large paper orders that I got from Mark and Luke. Though I purchased as much as $300 worth at a time, he never sold them for less than ten bucks each since he knew that I had nowhere else to go. The last deal with him was for fifty papers—$500. Each paper contained a small amount of dope cut with an unusual substance, creating an unhealthy grayish color.

"I wouldn't shoot that stuff up. Just snort it," he cautioned. He was a young Mexican kid in a white T-shirt, greasy black hair combed like that of some fifties hood, who was clearly growing an awesome habit for himself. I never saw him again. The next time I heard of him someone had found his three-day-old body in the front seat of a pickup, sitting too long by a northside park. There were bullet holes in his head and fifty of those crappy papers on him.

This was a common story every year in Tucson, starting in late spring and carrying on through most of the summer. Rip-offs, busts, kidnappings of rich dealers for ransom, armed rob-

---

of Braemar. According to old store records, they were granted a royal warrant to supply medicines in 1897. From that year through 1914 they provided the royals copious amounts of cocaine and heroin solutions, sleeping pills, bromides, chloroform, belladonna, adrenaline, and opium. Winston Churchill, when visiting, preferred cocaine solution, as did Princess Louise, the Princess Royal. Members of the Rothschild family were steady users of heroin, cocaine, and opium. The Master of Peterhouse used a mixture of belladonna and chloroform. In those times opium was sold at the grocer's and was cheaper than booze. Those Highland nights and mornings can get quite chilly. Cocaine lozenges, opium pipes, and heroin reefers were the order of the day. (Source: London *Times*, August 28, 1993) beries of out-of-towners looking for weed to take home. I heard of incidents amounting to over $100,000 a week lost by unlucky dealers. More victims always followed. Certain local rip-off gangs had honed this trade to a fine art. They'd drive up with a truck full of kilos and then, when the buyer pulled out his money, he got a shotgun in the face and the robbers left with both dope and cash. Sometimes these robberies went wrong, resulting in a victim's death, by either accidental weapon discharge or just some cold-blooded whim unexpectedly rising to the surface. A fine art.

I knew that rip-off season had started after reading of an incident in the local paper. A couple of broke losers were passing through town and knew that they only had to say the right lines to some college kids spending their summer vacation trying to get rich in Tucson. Three kids were talked into driving out to the desert with these thieves, ostensibly to buy $9,000 worth of bricks. The cons sat in the front seat, the victims in back. After relieving the kids of their money, with the car doing seventy miles an hour down the freeway, the thieves just turned around and started firing at the kids. Amazingly, it was the one in the middle who wasn't killed, and he jumped out wounded despite the car's speed. A driver behind them picked him up, and the two killers were soon apprehended. They fried, and for a lousy $4,500 each. The news of my young Mexican contact, found dead by the park, soon followed.

The eighty-five-dollar gram I'd purchased from Yaqui Jim wasn't the profitable item that I'd hoped for. I stayed *really* high for three days but still ended up paying thirty dollars for my dope. There just didn't seem to be enough aside from what I used to sell more than about five and a half dimes.

"It seemed like you were making those papers awfully big," commented Nazi Paul when I complained about my costs. "I mean, didn't you notice how glad people were to get them? I bet they were all back for more the next day!"

I grinned sheepishly. "Yeah, I guess they were, at that. It's too bad. When I went back to Jim's to get another one, they were out. Just had the same old tiny papers with that stupid white cut in them."

"Oh well, those'll do in a pinch. Can't complain about that." Paul shook his head. "Things seem to be getting a bit tighter everywhere. Here, thanks for letting me borrow this." He held out the brass bar taken from my window. I had a brief flash of Paul climbing into some darkened abode, ruefully considering all the property he had to leave before making off with part of some unfortunate's belongings.

I had just turned twenty-five and treated myself to a birthday shot. My funds continued a slow shrinkage despite my doing thousands in business that month.

Traffic in and around my upstairs room had increased. I missed the quiet of the basement room but somehow felt more at ease away from it. Still, I was now in the midst of a whole little community of fiends who occupied the third floor. Any time of the day or night I might hear some frantic running down the hall, accompanied by a panicked call of "Anybody got some salt? Does *anybody* have any *salt*? It's an emergency! Salt or milk!"

Shooting salt was the well-known antidote for an overdose, milk seeming to run a close second, though I doubt the latter did much more than dilute a heroin-rich bloodstream. It seemed like overdoses were becoming more frequent. The interruption of normal supply routes forced purchases of unknown quality from strangers, increasing the chance of an OD. Of course, if salt didn't work there was always the option of taking a swing by some emergency room doors and throwing out the body, then perhaps phoning in to inform them of a possible corpse on their doorstep. (I recall tales of people shooting up salt solution when they were out of junk; they claimed that it could feel like a real shot. It's called the saline reaction.)

Some users just seemed more prone to the overdose experience, misjudging proper amounts or shooting too many times in one day. Most junkies are greedy about the day's first shot; they want the maximum rush on a clear head. Following shots just aren't the same. So they try to get as much into the first shot as they think is possible, often erring toward the greater end. This can have devastating consequences, for other people in the room as well. They're the ones who get stuck having to care for the overdose victim, keeping him alive, shooting him with salt, slapping him awake, throwing him into the shower, twisting his ears, breathing for him, walking him around. For somebody trying to enjoy his afternoon shot, this can be quite an irritating interruption. Who needs a corpse suddenly appearing in the room?

Believe it or not, some rare shooters actually made a habit of overdosing and were greeted with trepidation whenever they showed their faces.

"Ollie just ODs for attention," sneered a little junkie chick before he appeared. Ollie was a mustached, chubby, curly-haired slob, his cheeks flushed with youth or embarrassment. He was notorious for his routine of bringing down roomfuls of heads by hitting up and losing consciousness. And indeed, as Ollie got ready to do up, I impulsively joined the rest of the room in a rush for the door. Everyone was wise to his tricks.

"Oh, come on" came Ollie's distant whine. "I don't want to get high by myself!" With an act like his, I don't imagine that he did.

I had the luxury of fleeing to my room, just a few doors down. The people stuck out in the hall were muttering. "I'm not going back in if *he's* doing up in there. No way. I'm tired of his shit. It never fails with that guy. . . ."

As I closed the door to this pathetic scene, I heard Ollie start negotiating. "I promise I won't OD! Come on! Don't be ridiculous!"

Determined to ignore the outcome of this little farce, I rolled a joint and stared out the window. There was a knock on my door. "Who's there?" I growled in exasperation.

"Andy," answered a voice I was relieved to hear. I let in my old high school friend. As usual, he was bedecked in high-quality Indian jewelry, in which he had dealt since we were students. He'd amassed quite a collection. The bright turquoise and coral rings, bracelets, and necklaces seemed to accent his shortness. He pulled an expression of mock horror on his face as he entered.

"Jesus, Scott! Does this go on all the time around here?" He'd caught the end of the Ollie show.

"Oh, that shit." I shook my head in disgust. "The usual story. I've learned to just ignore it."

Andy spied the decrepit armchair near the window, making another mock face at the cloud of dust that exploded around him when he sat down. His legs were too short to reach the floor.

"Scott," he began. "Things have been incredible lately! I've been meeting all kinds of women! I'm telling you—it's never been like this for me. I don't even know where some of them come from. The other day I woke up in bed with some woman, and I had no idea how I got there or even who she was! That's one of the strangest experiences . . . she was in the same condition!" As he continued he got more earnest, leaning forward, grabbing the ends of the chair's arms. I enjoyed Andy's jovial character. "This other one is absolutely beautiful, Scott. And she loves me—she wants me to marry her!"

Andy often regaled me with tales of feminine conquest. A dark, Russian complexion and thick, curly, black hair, combined with his height, made him both appealing and unthreatening to many women. He also had a Russian's capacity for intoxicants, could probably drink a six foot five, 300-pound man under the table, and was one of those rare people who was able to combine heroin and alcohol with no ill effects. I say no ill effects, but he got wildly inebriated at times, and I'd often seen him passed out on a couch, thoroughly bedecked in striking, expensive Indian jewelry—as pretty a picture of decadence as a girl could want. And many did.

"I'm telling you, Scott," he implored me. "I have been meeting them everywhere! Even in supermarkets! The other day I was just pushing my cart down the aisle, and I looked at this woman and went like this—" He made some lewd spasm with his tongue, slathering it around his lips. "And she just kept looking at me and gave me the weirdest expression. But she was interested—she didn't look away! It was incredible!"

Andy was also a chronic liar. Constantly compensating for a short man's inferiority complex, he manufactured outrageous boasts and marvelously ornamented stories. "I started screaming at the guy, and he just backed away in fear! I *wish* you could've seen his face, Scott. He just couldn't believe I was as tough as I was!"

Of course, when telling so many lies, he often ended up contradicting himself. When he realized that he might've done just that, he'd covertly watch me through slits in his eyes, hardly turning his head, trying to evaluate if I'd accepted his last statement. There were too many lies for him to keep track of or for me to bother pointing out contradictions, so I generally kept a straight face and let him ramble on. This aspect of his character hinted at a darker side, a hostile, vicious, defensive streak lurking under the joviality. It surfaced when anyone disagreed with him.

A sudden commotion developed out in the hall. Someone ran by, frantically knocking on my door and others as they passed.

"Does anybody have any salt? *It's an emergency!*"

So Ollie had done it again. I felt no concern for his situation and even snorted a sardonic laugh as I imagined the poor sucker who had been talked into getting high with Ollie. Andy, however, let his mouth drop open, gawking at me in disbelief. "My God, Scott! I can't believe you have to listen to this stuff! Come on, let's get out of here. I didn't want to hang out here, anyway. I wanted to take you up to this friend of mine's house."

"Well, I don't mind that. Someplace different would do me good. But I wanted to do something up first."

"Oh, don't worry about that. You can do it up there. Please, Scott, I'm sure you'll like visiting this place. Can you sell me one of those papers? Here, I'll pay for yours, too." He pulled out a twenty. "Just hold off until you get up there. I'm sure you'll be glad you did."

"Okay, I guess. I don't see what the difference is, though."

Andy gave me a piercing look. "There is a difference, believe me." Then, seeing that he'd gotten his way, he became jovial again. On the other hand, who wants to listen to cries for salt on death's doorstep?

Many people like to espouse this little gem about "all junkies have a death wish," but this is just nonsense. In this crazy world people who go to war do it because they want to feel good about themselves and people who want to feel good by using opium have a death wish? Still, one cannot ignore a case like Ollie's. Now that guy had a death wish. Or a supermanipulative personality. I could see how Andy wouldn't want to sit around partaking in the Ollie experience, because Andy himself was one of those junkies who seemed to suffer a greater incidence of overdose. Listening to those absurd cries for salt caused Andy some unpleasant associations.

"I don't really like to listen to that stuff, Scott," he explained as I got ready to go. "Did I ever tell you about that time I OD'd in New Mexico, up in Bernalillo? Now Bernalillo, there's a little junk town. About 5,000 people live there, all Indians and Mexicans. I was one of about a dozen white people. But because of my dark complexion and my black hair, they thought I was Mexican, too."

I nodded. "I've passed through Bernalillo. I had the strong feeling that there was junk there."

"Shit, are you kidding? That place is crowded with junkies, man. And they have strong dope, too! I used to go down along the main street where they all hung out. Man, it was so obvious. I got to be friends with this guy, Chicatín. Chicatín and I bought these really good dimes one night. The stuff there was always cheap and good. He warned me about it, saying it was extra good, but I thought, hell, I'd been doing stuff around there for a while already."

I was changing my shirt, brushing my hair as I listened to his tale. I rolled up a joint for the road.

"I don't remember anything after I shot the stuff in. The next thing I knew, I woke up and I was trying to figure out where I was, what the hell was going on. I knew I was moving, but, man, I was fucked up. And it was really dark, you know? After about five minutes I realized where I was. I was lying on the floor of a car, behind the front seat. It took me all that time to figure it out! Then I was trying to think, What the hell's going on? Is someone taking me out to the desert to kill me, or what? Finally I stuck my head up and asked, 'What's going on?'

Man, Chicatín was driving, and he practically wrecked the car when he heard me. I scared the shit out of him. You should've seen his face—he was Mexican but he turned white! 'Andy,' he was saying. 'Man, am I *glad* you're alive. I was just taking you out to the desert to dump your body!' " Andy gave an open-mouthed, can-you-believe-it? look.

We hopped into his parents' car. It was hot outside, but Andy switched on the air.

"I'm taking you up to my friend Alice's house, Scott. She used to be the editor of a famous women's magazine in New York. But she lives out here now because she's dying of emphysema. She loves me, man. I'm telling you! Alice's daughter is an ingrate. I'm trying to get her to put me in her will. I think she's almost ready to leave her stuff to me instead." He peered at me through slits in his eyes without turning his head. I kept watching the road.

We drove up to lush northern Tucson, at the foot of the Catalina Mountains. There was still a lot of undeveloped desert there, and roadrunners whipped across the asphalt in front of us. The writer Joseph Wood Krutch had lived near our destination, and his eyecatching mailbox of dead cholla branches remained at the start of the road we turned off on. The Rillito River stretched out for miles behind us, now just a wide, dry gulch, but its banks were covered with greenery in that part of town; Prohibition photographs show it as a full, flowing river. The road became a dirt path barely wide enough for the car, and mesquite and paloverde trees slapped our windows as Andy whipped up the drive. Clouds of dust billowed behind us. I couldn't see much beyond the trees because they were so thick and old.

After a couple of twists and turns in the road, we coasted into the circular driveway of a hidden, large, old dwelling. A well-monied, secluded residence. Getting out of the car, I just stood and listened to the wind blow through a grove of hundred-foot-tall eucalyptus trees. An amazing roar of rustling leaves. A covey of quail zipped through sand and brush, turning left and right as one manic formation. Though hardly out of the city limits, it was markedly cooler and quieter there. The thought that I hadn't yet done my shot interrupted my reveries. Andy resolutely walked up and knocked on the door, obviously familiar with the place. A faint call came from inside.

"It's Andy, Alice. I brought a friend with me," he answered cheerily, letting us in. We entered a cool, dusky, spacious room. Off to the right was a sunken living room with a fireplace, and the whole dwelling looked homey and well lived in, if just a bit messy. Subdued daylight eased in southern glass doors, turquoise necklaces hung on the walls, feathered kachina dolls sat in a row above the fireplace. To my left I noticed a small, green oxygen tank on wheels, a little, clear plastic nose- and mouthpiece dangling on the side. Then a woman slowly, deliberately entered the room. She had the startling bluish gray pallor that I'd seen in other emphysema victims. Tucson is the last stopping place for many of these sufferers.

"Alice, how nice to see you!" crooned Andy as he delicately touched her shoulder. She didn't look like she could stand much more than that. Her reply was faint, and she smiled a strained smile. Alice was very weak; she couldn't walk without wheezing, but she seemed happy to see Andy.

"Alice, this is my friend, Scott. I've known him a long time. He's also in the Indian jewelry business." A small lie, though I knew enough to hold my own in conversation with most people.

"I'm so pleased to meet you, Scott," offered Alice in a labored, hoarse whisper. I touched her outstretched gray hand.

We made small talk about bracelets and necklaces. Carrying on the simplest conversation was obviously taxing on Alice.

Awards and framed magazine covers were a good indication that the woman in front of me was used to an energetic, independent life. Now she could barely speak and finally had to sit down.

"Andy," she rasped. "I hate to ask you this, but could you move that over here for me?"

"Yes, of course, Alice." Andy wheeled over the little green tank. "Don't feel bad about asking me to get you something. Is there anything else you need?"

As Alice applied the oxygen mask, I figured that enough time had passed for me to take leave for the bathroom. As I rounded the corner, I dug into my pocket for my sock, which held my works. The bathroom, a large, blue-tiled affair, had enough daylight entering a line of small windows near the ceiling that I didn't have to turn on the light. Eucalyptus trees brushed the windows when the wind blew, and there was a soothing atmosphere. I wasn't worried at all about Alice becoming suspicious.

Efficiently I poured the paper's contents into my spoon, added a few drops of water with the syringe, and lit a book of matches to cook it up. I pinched a few of the cotton balls sitting next to the sink, pocketing some for future use. The solution felt nice and warm as I drew it into the fit, and I deftly tied myself off and shot it into my vein. After pulling water into the syringe straight from the faucet stream, I sprayed a vivid, red line of blood along the blue sink.

Seconds after, a luscious wave swept my entire body. I blended into the bathroom's gentle, blue light. Sitting back on the closed toilet seat, I let my body meet the perfect temperature and felt my mind become one with the silence. It was a lovely bathroom. The borders of my flesh seemed on the verge of vaporizing. I could've sat there for hours.

"I'm misting."

Staying as long as I dared, I regretfully stood up, flushed the evidence down the toilet, then turned on the fan to dispel suspicious odors. I rinsed out the sink. It had been a shot worth waiting for.

Back in the living room Andy and Alice stood facing each other. I joined them, dutifully ready to jump into conversation. The conversation, however, jumped at me. Andy's mouth hung open.

"Andy! My God! Do you realize what's happening to me?" Alice was frantic. "Don't you understand what's going on? *Andy, what am I going to do?*"

Andy could barely think of a word to fit in. Standing next to both of them, I was overcome by the contrast between what I'd just left in the bathroom and what I now saw. A strong emotion was welling up inside me, and Alice rasped hysterically, grabbing Andy by the shoulders and shaking him.

"Andy! Do you see what's happening? I'm dying! *I'm going to die! My God!* What am I going to *do?*" Her voice cracked as she fought to raise the volume of her panic, but the deadly damage in her lungs allowed only a rumbling, hoarse rattle. Pressing my lips firmly together, I suddenly realized that I was ready to throw up. Sweat popped onto my brow and above my lip. I felt color leave my face as I strained to keep the stuff down. I didn't want Alice to think that *she* was the reason I needed to vomit. Finally I could wait no longer and, uttering a hasty, garbled "Excuse me," I fled from them, my hand rising involuntarily to my mouth.

I made it just in time. Good thing I knew where the bathroom was.

Lingering a couple extra minutes in there, I rinsed my face with cool water. I had tried to vomit as quietly as I could, but I think they heard me anyway. Afterward I felt better. When I walked out again, Alice had left the room. Andy gave me his openmouthed, can-you-believe-it? look.

"Jesus, Scott. I've never seen her act like that." Then he gave an impotent shrug.

"It's quite understandable, really, considering her situation," I replied. "I just had to barf. I tried to hold it down as long as I could. Shit, I hope she doesn't think *she* was the reason I had to. Fuck, there was nothing I could do." I stood there shaking my head.

Andy nodded knowingly. "I had a feeling that was going on," he answered reflectively. Then, nodding quickly at me, he declared, "Well, it couldn't be helped. I don't think that's what she thought."

"I'm afraid that's exactly what she thought." I shook my head again. A loud hiccup spontaneously erupted from me. "Oh, shit, now I gotta put up with these."

Alice reentered the room, much more composed. "Andy," she immediately began. "Please forgive me. I don't know what got into me."

Andy was quickly conciliatory. Alice's expression showed puzzlement when she turned to me. A strong, silent hiccup made my head and body jerk. Even if I'd been able to think of something to say, I was afraid to talk for fear of emitting some damned raucous chirp. After a while my side started to hurt from them.

I wandered from Alice's line of sight, feigning interest in her books and paintings. Then I popped back into the bathroom to grab a few hits on a joint. When I returned I heard Alice's mild, gravelly protest. "But she's my daughter, Andy. She's entitled to *something*. Anyway, I love her."

Mercifully, the visit came to a rapid close after that. We all said farewell as genially as if we'd just had tea and crumpets.

It saddened me to leave that desert for the town again. Resignedly, I watched the gnarled, twisted trees pass as we drove away. Andy was unusually silent until we got back onto the paved road and into traffic. Then he shrugged lightheartedly. "Welp, so much for that inheritance."

Dropping me off at the Geronimo, he handed me another twenty. "Look, why don't you buy us another couple papers?"

"Andy, I don't know if I can find anything. Things are pretty tight lately."

"Oh, don't worry about that. Just see what you can do."

"Well, okay, like I say, I can't guarantee anything. You know I'll try, though, especially if I'm getting a free dime out of it. Want me to call you?"

"No, no, Scott. Really, don't worry about it. I'll be by again in another couple days. If you get it, then you get it. If you don't, then you don't. I'll be by again."

Getting those papers was, in fact, quite difficult. None of my regular contacts had anything. I felt lucky that I wasn't caught short even though I was down to my old cottons. After a couple days of fruitless searching, I went onto automatic pilot. Instinctively, I made my way down to Fourth Ave and Sixth Street, then a well-known hangout for drug dealing in Tucson. There I quickly zeroed in on a solitary, somewhat furtive figure lurking in a corner doorway. I must've looked pretty beat, because he approached me.

"Twenty dollars, man. And it's really good. I mean *really* good."

His desperation to sell made me wary. Most drug salesmen insist that everything they sell is "really good." Not wanting to get burnt too badly by this stranger, I counteroffered seventeen.

"Oh, what the hell." He accepted. "I really need the money. Don't try to do it all at one time. Just do a quarter. I'm not kidding about it. It's really strong. You'll see."

His so readily taking my lower offer told me that the stuff

was probably overpriced. When I opened the paper, there was only a tiny bit of some dark brown, almost black uncrushed heroin chunks. The meager amount dismayed me.

Andy showed up at my door toward evening, just minutes after I'd walked home from making the purchase. "Impeccable timing, Andy. I just got back. It wasn't easy finding anything. I had to buy this twenty minutes ago on a street corner from someone I've never even seen before."

"Really? That's okay, that's okay. I'm glad you were able to get anything at all."

"Well, we'll see about that soon enough." I pulled out the three dollars change from the purchase. "Here, you should take this. I'm sorry that there's so little in the paper. He kept saying how good it was, but he knocked the price down right away."

Andy scrutinized the minute granules lying in the paper. "Geez, there's hardly anything here. Fuck, is this all you could find?"

"I'm afraid so."

"Ahh." He resignedly shook his head. "I know things have been tough lately. I appreciate you trying. Anyway," he added more brightly. "The proof is in the pudding. Maybe doing up half of it won't be that bad." He frowned into the paper again. "Shit, there's not very much here. You mind if I do it all?"

"Andy, I don't even know about doing half of it. He did insist that it was really strong. He said to just do a quarter."

"A quarter? We won't even feel that! No, I need to do more." He paused to view my expression. "Well, okay, since you say the guy was so insistent. Maybe I'll do just a third of it. Hopefully that'll be okay."

He carefully scraped about a third of the hard, black bits into a spoon, pulled out his own needle, and prepped his shot. The resulting fluid was rather dark for the little amount he'd cooked up. Then he briskly pumped his veins up. He was one of the few people I've seen who could raise his veins and administer the shot without tying himself off.

"I hope I'm not wasting my time with this." He grimaced, centering the needle point into a scarred, bulging vessel. When it registered red he shoved the stuff in. Leaning back in the chair, he got a studious look on his face. "Boy," he muttered. "This stuff seems really strong." Then he fell back into the chair, a detached picture of repose.

I thought it was a joke and gave a little laugh. The stuff wasn't good, and he was pulling that old junkie joke and pretending it had just killed him. Then I figured he should work on his timing and delivery. Suddenly I tensed as I saw his lips and eyelids turning blue.

"Fuck," I breathed. "Andy? *Andy!*" I shook his shoulder. This made him slide onto the floor. His legs bent hideously back under his body. Just looking at them was painful. Shit! I thought. I don't believe this! A glance at the phone. No, I wanted no ambulances, no medical personnel and cops traipsing through the room. That would end the whole affair for me. Grabbing Andy under the shoulders, I pulled him up onto the chair again. Then I placed my head near his mouth and nose—he might've actually stopped breathing for a bit there, but my tugging him up caused him to start again. Despite this he continued turning deeper shades of blue. Brief flashes filled my mind: driving to an emergency room and dropping off the body by the doors.

Resolutely, I took hold of my senses, determining not to call for help until he stopped breathing. Panic constantly prodded my logic. A few firm slaps in his face produced no results. He just slipped over on his side. I straightened him up again and again.

"Andy! Andy, wake up! Wake up, dammit!"

This went on for a half hour, slapping him, then throwing water on him. A soft, low moan escaped his lips. I jumped on this as encouragement and kept calling him, moving and slapping him. To my incredulous relief, he finally groaned and opened his eyes halfway. Pulling him to his feet, I thanked Fate that he was only five two and easy to lift.

"Walk, Andy! Stay up! Keep standing up. Walk! Keep walking . . . that's right." I walked him in circles around the little room. Anytime I started to let go he began to fall, so I kept up the routine for a while.

"Man," he whispered. "I have never been so fucking high."

At this I had to laugh. I kept him moving for a while longer. Finally, he groggily announced, "It's okay now. It's all right. I'm okay now." When I let him go he remained standing. "I'm okay. Just show me to the bathroom."

I led him a few steps over to the doorway of the dark bathroom. He peered bleary-eyed into the blackness.

"Oh, Pamela," he crooned. "You look so beautiful tonight."

I rolled my eyes. At least he was alive. At least my little boat hadn't been tipped over. I was still shuddering at visions of ambulance attendants and police with walkie-talkies combing through my room, shaking their heads in disgust at our stupidity. Then I found myself annoyed at having to wait so long to get off myself. Andy emerged from the bathroom.

"I cannot believe how high I am," he muttered in wonderment.

"I guess that guy was telling the truth." I snickered. Then I realized that he had no idea of the scare he'd just given me. "Fuck, I didn't know what I was going to do with you. You were completely out. Christ, you were turning blue!"

"Well, I'm okay now. I'm gonna drive home."

"What? You think you can drive? Maybe you better stay here awhile."

"No, no. I'm okay now. Thanks. I'm going home." The capacity of a Russian. "Boy, I have never been so high. This is really good stuff."

After he left I remembered that I'd been putting off my own shot for a long time. I needed to calm down. Hopefully some junk would contribute to that end. Taking a few breaths of relief, I opened the little paper and measured out my dose. Andy had used about a third. I lifted out less, glad that there were a couple good shots still left in the paper.

As soon as I did it up I knew that I'd done too much. Darkness suddenly prodded the edges of my vision. I fought panic. Blood rushed noisily in my ears. My head felt like it had just been placed into a tall, tight-fitting tube. I struggled to remain conscious, and even as I did was telling myself just how stupid I was to have put myself into the same spot. Then I told myself how stupid I was for wasting so much good dope on one shot. And all the time I fought the panic of knowing that I was absolutely *alone* in my room. There was no one to help *me!*

My breathing became labored as I struggled to maintain consciousness. I knew that I'd be okay as long as I stayed awake. It wasn't like fighting off overwhelming fatigue at all. More like battling an almost irresistible force that kept dividing my attention, distracting me from the simple task of keeping my eyes open. Involuntary moans purred from me as I forced myself to breathe deeply. I pressed my sweaty palm firmly on the desktop like it was a connection with some vital current. And all the time I kept berating myself on just how *stupid* I had been for doing the same thing Andy did! This didn't make it any easier.

After thirty or forty minutes of this (it could've been more, I don't know), I felt awake enough to let myself relax a bit. The crisis had finally, barely passed. I let go. One thing was sure: I had never been higher than this either!

And I felt great! My mood was elation, partially at having so narrowly escaped death. It was so easy to feel good! I could hardly walk straight, and I didn't care. Looking forward to hours of solid, strong, ethereal euphoria, I wandered down the hotel stairs in an expansive mood.

As soon as I hit the street, I gregariously waved down some acquaintances who happened to be driving by. The couple stopped, and I climbed into their car without even asking permission or where they were going. One or two blocks of car travel was all it took for me to have to vomit, silently, onto the back floor. When I stuck my head up again, I perceived that they hadn't heard a thing. After a couple more blocks I asked them to let me out, waving cheerily as they drove away.

11 As if awaiting the cue provided by that evening, my behavior became more unpredictable. It was just a day or two later that I found myself foisting the most ludicrous laudatory praises upon a policeman walking his Geronimo beat.

"You guys are doing a great job!"

I brashly spewed this into his face. I don't know what I was thinking—perhaps of walking off arm in arm, basking in some stilted light of manly brotherhood. As it was, the cop snapped his scathingly dour expression at me as if I'd just offered a disgusting proposition. There was no humor in his eyes. My praise was totally inappropriate, to be sure. Seeing that my compliment had fallen flat, I tried to redeem the situation with a firm nod of my head and a stout "Keep up the good work!" I could feel the cop's eyes boring into my back as I walked away. Then I realized I'd been absentmindedly rolling and unrolling my sleeves the whole time.

Perhaps the summer's heat was contributing to my wayward actions. School had recently ended, and the streets were oppressive with inactivity. Strength-sapping waves of heat shimmered up from the asphalt, their eerie, clear illusions convincing me that sobriety was pointless. My dreams and realities were starting to mix. Was so-and-so really back in town, or did I just *dream* that I said such-and-such to my neighbor? To this day I dread the onset of desert summer and readily attribute to it almost anything bad taking place during those months—discomfort, bad living conditions, fatigue. Much has been written about the desert's awesome summer power, rich descriptions of the white-hot, baking sun, dangers of exposure and dehydration, bleached cow skulls and the constant buzzing of cicadas. These last are totally hypnotizing, and all daily business in the desert is conducted to their vibrating drone. It's been written that it fades in and out of consciousness, making one feel like an overmedicated patient struggling to wake up.

There was one more brief flurry of Geronimo economic activity just as the students made ready to leave town. A lot of junkies enjoyed these end-of-semester times, when thousands of kids piled their belongings outside their dorm rooms, waiting to load them into taxis and parents' cars. Enterprising fiends could take leisurely walks through student dorms, helping themselves to radios, tape players, and other small items, drawing no more than the slightest suspicion. Then, with the students gone and the already tight junk supply, a situation arose more severe than any I had yet experienced. It seemed that everyone was scampering around as old sources dried up and new lines sought to connect in the junk network.

Clean syringes were now a rarity for me. I had long since

given up my initial practice of using a brand-new needle for every shot, or even for every day or two, often employing the same fit for so long that the point became dull. Then I'd throw it or give it away. People would clean these plastic syringes with alcohol, but it often left a stinging residue inside. Some sharpened the points on the striking surfaces of matchbooks. I avoided that, though, because of little burrs that could develop on the point, causing it to catch painfully under the skin.

Even matches were becoming a source of irritation. I found it hard to supply myself with the many books needed to cook up dope and light all those joints and cigarettes. The most convenient place for them was a little grocery store situated right under the hotel. An old mom-and-pop affair, it had sagging, dusty wooden floors and poorly maintained shelves. Pop, quite stern despite his bald spot and spectacles, had become suspicious of the rate at which matches were disappearing from beside the cash register, and, in the true cracker spirit, he put up resistance at that point rather than deal with the problem logically. Pop didn't know why everybody wanted matches, but he didn't like the smell of it. They were doled out pack by pack to qualified recipients who'd bought tobacco. Indeed, having to supply free matches to the entire population of Junkies, Inc., could drive a business into receivership rather quickly, but the process of approving each customer's application for matches could send one's sanity to the same place.

Nazi Paul chose to make subtle rounds of the shelves while I engaged the store owner with my profitable plan of letting me pay two cents a pack while removing our mutual source of irritation. To this Pop was doggedly resistant. As I walked away he smoothed his white apron and continued to chat with one of the Geronimo's pensioners.

"Now me, I'm nothing in the mornings until I have my coffee and Danish!" His proud, stupid voice filled the store.

Paul sneered under his breath. "Yeah, and what is he after he's had his coffee and Danish?"

Paul seemed to supply himself exclusively from this little store when he bothered with nutrition at all. Resenting having to waste money on food, he got progressively and more alarmingly emaciated. His money situation was always pathetic as well. As supply lines dried up, he got more morose and introspective. There were numerous interruptions in his daily supply, some days he was sick, and I saw him getting tired and discouraged with this regime. He took to shooting a variety of pills, Ritalin, Valiums, codeines, anything he could get his hands on. Sometimes he'd inject simple saltwater solutions, claiming to get a decent pseudoeffect. One meager day, after I'd gone through my old cottons for the umpteenth time, I walked into his lodge as he proceeded to inject himself with a healthy amount of some clear liquid.

"What's that?" I asked with hungry curiosity.

Paul showed a childish smile. "Water." He grinned, sheepishly. "It makes me feel better to at least be doing something."

My own financial situation was hardly better. There were days that I found myself with no money and no dope. Then I sometimes hitchhiked or took a bus to my parents' old house, picking up various little collectibles or salables of my own that were lying around there. Since I always made it a point to arrive when my father was gone, I usually raided his supply of Valiums and Dexamyls for resale. Valium, a muscle relaxant, helped ease withdrawal pains.

I remember one particularly difficult trip during which I hid behind a wall at a bus stop to grab my sides, tight and painful from lack of junk. When I finally arrived at the house, I found that my father had gone out of town, installing his young, icy secretary to watch the place. She absolutely refused me entrance, citing my father's orders. This stumped me, since I was broke and had an old antique brass box of change in the house. I explained that I'd have to walk back miles for the lack of bus money, but she refused to budge and threatened to call the police. The gall of this intractable woman denying me my property and barring me from the house in which I'd grown up filled me with fury. I kicked in the front door, shredding the wood around the lock, then grabbed my things as she cowered in the bedroom. I kept an eye out for cops as I walked briskly back to the bus stop but saw none.

When I did manage to put money together, through either pot fronts or orders for papers, I found that my most reliable contacts were no longer dependable. Once, I showed up at Yaqui Jim's and Bill's and watched them turn away a host of business, claiming that they had nothing to sell. When we were alone they produced one tiny paper for me, in light of my being one of their best customers. I was very happy to get that minuscule dime with its absurd white powder cut. Perhaps it had helped that I'd quietly and fatalistically received their initial refusal. But I knew that it does little good to whine and complain, especially among hardened addicts. Kicking is just a risk of the game, one that everybody's been through, and it doesn't do to snivel about it in front of others. Anyway, Marty, the pregnant redhead who gave cheap hand jobs, dominated the conversation.

"But what am I going to do?" she intoned, sitting scrunched up on that moth-eaten couch. As I rounded the end of it, I saw her more clearly. Her pregnancy had grown obvious. And her right hand and arm had swelled up to three or four times normal size. It lay grotesquely on the cushion beside her. I'm sure she saw the alarm on my face.

"Look at my arm!" she frantically called to me, like it would make a difference. It was the last thing I wished to see. Would it have been impolite to turn away in horror? I was speechless.

"You'd better see a doctor, bitch," advised Jim. "That arm looks pretty bad."

"A doctor? How the hell can I do that? *I* don't have any money!"

"Well, go to some clinic or somewhere. You better do something." Jim was short and curt about it. Warmth wasn't one of his attributes. He was simply stating the obvious, and it was clear that he didn't like looking at that painfully distorted limb.

Marty gazed out the window in shock. "Look at my arm," she whined flatly to the glass. "What am I going to do?" She was suffering from phlebitis, not an uncommon affliction among pregnant women. A blood clot gets lodged in the arm or leg, causing the limb to expand to alarming size. Blood-thinning medications and absolute rest are usually prescribed, lest the clot loosen and end up someplace worse. Marty clearly would've been glad to detach the offensive appendage and just walk away from the gross affair. No more hand jobs from her for a while.

Yaqui Jim stood out of her view, shaking his head and rolling his eyes. Days later he told me that she'd ended up going to an emergency room, where they dealt with her problem, then took her to jail for drug use. Pregnant addicts are especially frowned upon. When relating it Jim looked like he was glad to be rid of her.

As is the case during most shortages, new people got hooked into the supply net and assumed the position of dealer. Someone will always be there to take that place. Even if the penalty is death, there will always be someone to buy dope from. This time the role was filled by a couple of brothers living down the hall. Ron and Terry became known to me through Nazi Paul, who had rented the room before them.

Actually, they'd only seen me hanging out with Paul, but

when I knocked on their door, Terry readily made me for junk and invited me in. It was a rather large room with a few beds lined against the walls. Paul was already lounging on one, reading some old World War II picture books on the SS, left from when the room was his. He had no shirt on; his stringy, blond hair fell on his Germanic bronze shoulders. Afternoon sunlight was stealing across the wooden floor from western windows. It was a bit warm, and the others were also bare chested and in khaki pants. A pathetic sight, like a collection of mistreated British POWs. Terry sat back down after letting me in. "Come on in and wait like everyone else. My brother's out copping something right now." He hoisted his blond hair onto his ear, a freckled, innocent country boy, and continued with his tale.

"So I got the money up for an office visit and had the doctor examine me. 'Yep, it's hepatitis, all right,' he told me after a bit. I asked him for a letter, and he wrote one out saying I couldn't work for six months. Now I just take it down to the welfare office every month and they hand me some money. They *have* to!"

The other people sitting on the beds seemed impressed with this exploit, showing exceptional initiative for this group. "It's not a lot of money, but it covers the rent, anyway," he emphasized. Dee-Dee, a junkie chick I'd seen around, sat aloof, curled up in a corner. She was leafing through magazines. In her early twenties, she still had some baby fat on her, but it was rapidly turning into that peculiar, unhealthy paunch that some addicts develop instead of emaciation. Her dark hair, hennaed to haphazard reddish hues, needed attention. It matched reddish freckles on her face, probably imported from Brooklyn. A loose-fitting, rust T-shirt completed the color scheme, all topping a very short skirt, with which she displayed some moles on her thighs. The slick, high-fashion women's magazine she browsed provided perplexing contrast.

While Dee-Dee attended to her reading, the guys could check out her almost nonexistent hemline. They were, however, preoccupied, displaying subtle edginess, picking their fingers, smoking cigarettes, and rubbing the backs of their red necks. One fellow looked like an ex-athlete whose former body development only meant that much more junk-sick weight for him to lug around. We were all anxious for some dope to show. Only Paul, as usual, seemed to glide through these times without displaying concern, an ability honed by having survived six years in prison. He was quite content leafing through his World War II paperback, a soldier's face similar to his on the cover, sporting a cap with a death's-head medallion on it.

It's incredible how much time is passed every day by customers waiting for contacts to show. It's not normal time, sliding by without meaning, providing only a puzzle piece between one shot and another. A suspension during which I caught myself holding my breath from tight stomach muscles; my body tried to hibernate until release arrived. I could've written a book in the amount of time I've spent waiting for dope. Lack of supplies, however, makes meaningful activity impossible. Those endless hours I recall as but a few quick snapshots. When we heard Ron turn the key in the door, it was like air was suddenly released into a vacuum chamber. Everyone spoke at once.

"Did you cop?"

"Is it any good?"

"You have my money *or* my dope?"

Ron, the older brother, let a flicker of disgust cross his face before playfully announcing, "The guy didn't have anything. . . ." Before anyone could groan, he just laughed at his own lousy joke. He had copped after all, but, as I would soon learn, he'd say he hadn't to make people more appreciative of his notoriously short counts. Ron didn't look at all like Terry, who was boyish and robust. He had stringy brown hair, more freckles, and sinewy, thin arms; his cold, hard eyes were set in a face carved by deception. These two worked some bad brother/con brother routine, refined through the years.

"Ohhh," Terry would whine. "Did my brother rip you off, too? I'm *really* sorry. It's not the first time, you know. He's even done it to meee!"

With a pair like that, I appreciated getting anything at all. Ron and Terry huddled together a moment, squaring away their own supply. Then, with the homing instincts of the truly desperate, customers began knocking on the door to plead their cases.

"But, please, I'm getting some money this evening. Come on, I don't feel very good."

Ron cast his stern eye at the supplicant. "Are you sick? Well, *are you?*" And he glared. The beggar backed down, too embarrassed to fake illness. "See?" Ron explained, as if to a troop of ensigns. "People'll tell you if they're really sick. Hey! If someone's *really* sick I'll give them something." He switched on the radio, then brightened. "I really like this song." It was called "How Long Has This Been Going On?"

Ollie came in to buy a dime. After he paid Ron made to put it into his meaty hand, then pulled back. "You do this up someplace else. You're not getting off here, you understand?"

"Okay, don't worry, don't worry." Ollie sulked, took his paper, and left.

"Ollie just ODs to get other people's attention," called out Dee-Dee in her scratchy voice. It was one of those cloying, little-girl voices that some people find sexy. "He knows what he's doing each time. Man, what a waste of good dope." She squirmed larvally on the bed, tugging at her miniskirt. I expected her to break out into a Betty Boop routine.

Ron finally serviced the rest of us, me last. My brow rose as I viewed the meager amount in the paper, but I was in no position to complain. Clearly, it was a seller's market. Ron looked me square in the face, daring me to say something.

Terry prepped his shot. He was efficient and deft, startling me with the speed of his actions.

"Jesus Christ, that was fast!" I exclaimed.

"Lemme use that fit, will ya?" called the big ex-jock as Terry set his works down.

"I wouldn't advise that," he answered. "I've got hepatitis."

The big guy shrugged. "I don't give a shit," he murmured bitterly. The rest of us shook our heads. I was glad when the jerk left.

"See that chick Barbara down the hall?" Ron asked his brother. He turned to us. "She said she'd fuck me for a paper."

"I'll fuck you for a dime, Ron," announced Dee-Dee, putting a little extra squeak in her voice. "Just don't tell John. I have to live with him, you know."

The room fell silent as we all watched Ron narrow his eyes and consider the proposition. I expected the order to clear out, but he suddenly turned away from her. "Never mind. I don't like the conditions," he answered firmly.

When the nightstand had cleared of shooters, I sat down and prepared my own stuff. I could feel the others evaluating my performance, so I was glad to hit the vein effortlessly. Apparently I passed muster, for I detected no disdain. Picking a hardback chair in the middle of the room, I sighed as the shot's languid warmth undid tense muscles. My stomach loosened, like I'd just removed a tight belt; an attitude spontaneously struck me of having completed a hard day's work and getting on now with my real life. The whole group was more at ease, I noticed. Speech was superfluous. For a few minutes we all knew that words would only provide bumps on this beautifully smooth road.

Cigarettes were lit. Silently, I pulled out a joint, lit it, and passed it. The sunlight slowly spread across varnished wooden floorboards. The small radio quietly played the "Limbo Rock." An earnest Chubby Checker piped from the tiny box, his compressed, nasal voice sounding like some genie trying to get a crowd of autistic patients to rub his lamp.

"Boy, this stuff's good," someone finally said. "Too bad it's so expensive."

"Too bad it's illegal," agreed Terry.

"Too bad it's addictive," murmured Ron.

Nazi Paul looked up from his book. "Now Himmler, there's a guy that had the right idea!"

Terry rolled his eyes. The others smirked and snickered. Paul must've been used to this reception, for it didn't deter him in the least. "Oh, sure," he continued. "He was a little off about a few things, but the world would've been a lot better place if he'd been allowed to carry through most of his ideas."

"Like the Jews?" asked Terry, sarcasm dripping from his voice.

"He was right on about the Jews!" Paul proclaimed enthusiastically. "They had a lot of advanced ideas. Those Nazis used to take people and immerse them in freezing water to the point of death. They'd see how far they could take them and still bring 'em back. They found that other human bodies were the best thing for that. Guys that thought they were dead would come to between a couple beautiful women. Nothing like a couple warm fräuleins to rejuvenate you!" Paul's eyes were wide and positively leering sparks at his vision of ultimate relief. The lusty fräuleins! The heady marching tunes! Those were the days! The fact that Paul hadn't lived those times did nothing to lessen his sense of poignant loss.

"I don't think," I interjected, "that Himmler would've been very happy about this little scene here." The others grunted assent, like some misplaced parliament.

"Oh, I don't know about that," countered Paul. "Göring had a taste for morphine and that stuff. He was a doper from way back." The grin on his face matched the death's-head worn by the grim SS trooper on the book. "Shit, he was just a little different, that's all. Lotsa famous people wear makeup, man!"

I smiled and closed my eyes. Swirling dots on my lids grew more complex as I watched. A snowy landscape filled my vision; an aerial view of endless barracks and Auschwitz stretches before me. The baby Himmler wanders into the living room with no clothes on. "Really!" his father blusters. "The child must learn a sense of shame!"

Jerking awake, I almost fell out of my chair. The others were chuckling at my nodding out. I stood up to go. "I'm starting to fade. I think I'll go out to enjoy this stuff before I fall asleep."

Wandering between the lodges and among the trees, I felt glad to be alone again. Those groups forced me to suppress so much of my personality. The instinct for self-preservation demanded not attracting curiosity, which would mark me as a target—for rip-offs, burglaries, informers. Being different would inevitably be taken as a challenge or conceit. The whole pack would simply consume me. Weakness as well as strength drew this treatment. In all animal packs difference invites attack. Weaker members are always targets. Then again, some people just get "special treatment" in life. Those who hand it out steadfastly deny it, since acknowledgment would end their little game. And those who receive it must avoid mentioning it, as that only draws more "special treatment." This was the term used by the Nazis to mean extermination.

I leaned back against an old stucco wall in the warm shade of a lodge. As plaster crumbled under my back, I breathed the antique dust that I liked so much. I loved the way it smelled like an oncoming rainstorm. But the sky was a glary, cloudless blue slate. My secret essence for smelling oncoming rain only caused a longing for relief from the heat. A distasteful, hot, bright red-orange smoldered beneath my eyelids; I opened them again. Too bright for any dreamy pictures to form. Insect buzzing filled the air, emanating from lush trees; it was so loud that the trees were practically shaking. I was sweltering out there, and it seemed almost as if the specters and visions of the old, great Geronimo had fled the bright daylight. Burning stabs, piercing glares had driven the tender, ghostly romances to cower in secret corners.

Having fulfilled my physical requirements for the day, I felt weighted by boredom. There was no longer the edge of anticipating questionable supplies. And the rush of the shot had passed all too quickly. Those shots just didn't seem to be lasting as long or doing as much. The answer, of course, was to up my dose, but that didn't salve my immediate, cloying ennui. Almost robotically, driven by a ceaseless press of heat, I found myself turning around, mouth hanging open, sweat running into my eyes. The old tower came into view. Mandate of Stegman the Guardian. Like an automaton, I moved forward and up the steps.

I wiped moisture from my eyes and face. Two steps in and I found the relief of his cooler air. Thank goodness he was there. I gave the desert greeting: give a sigh, bow the head, bend the knees. Thanking desert deities for letting me stay conscious.

"Stegman! How're the angles doing?"

He seemed taciturn, tinged, perhaps, with melancholy. "Ahh, the days of the old Greeks are gone," he muttered, giving a little wave. "I am a man born thousands of years too late."

"Yeah, well, the heat's getting to me, too," I replied. "Had any luck retrisecting that angle?"

He shrugged. "I did it once. That's all I have to do to prove it can be done. It's just like I thought it'd be. Most people don't understand what it means, and those that do don't believe I did it."

"I was never too good at geometry. I like writing instead."

"The first writers were mathematicians, son."

It was dusky and almost cool in there, but the outside glare was so strong that it hurt. My eyes were sensitive from the shot and the smoke. "Stegman, people are always resistant to those who step off the beaten track."

He shook his head woodenly. "Science is just another religion . . . it's just a young pretender." Stegman would not be mollified. His downcast mood was contagious. And it made me sleepy. As usual, he soon took up the slack in the conversation, gazing over the courtyard, homilizing distant, wistful mutterings, almost like he was nodding out. "Days of the Greeks . . . produced a magnificent testament . . . rise of the universe . . . born too late . . . down by Ionia . . . a man like me . . . to the Pillars of Hercules. . . ."

At the far edge of the courtyard stood a gateway and stairs, bordered by two ancient columns. They beckoned like an undetected doorway to another age, reminding me of those romantic old paintings with ornate, chipped stone steps leading down to the sea. The lay of the lawn, the crumbling walls all led the eye to that gateway. This is what Stegman's gaze drifted to in moments of repose. I could see why I once dreamt that I was standing in that room viewing a 3,000-year-old Egyptian harbor. Naturally, a man with Stegman's outlook would find himself pining for millennia past if he spent much time above that vista. My mind was drifting from the simple etiquette of conversation. The cards strewn over the desk, the blue-gray light—that tower was such a meditative spot. How I wish I could've spent hours, days, *years* sitting, watching, dreaming there.

"Boy." I sighed. "I am so constipated—" I came to suddenly, red spreading over my face. I could not believe what I'd just said.

"It's those erections!" snapped Stegman, not missing a beat. "One good erection'll constipate me for days. 'Course," he lowered his voice, "I don't have to worry about that too much these days."

"Well—uh—" I stammered. "I don't think that's the problem."

"Well, if that's not it, then what is?" He peered at me, suspicion spreading across his face. Inadvertently, I had planted the seeds of drug hysteria. I hastened to dig them up. "Nope, nope! You're right! Must be those erections!"

"Yep, those erections'll do it every time!"

Back up in my room it was business as usual. People wandered in and out, bought a little weed, needed a place to get off, or were just roaming around making one more stop to ease boredom. The usual tough talk flourished.

"Stuck a knife in his face and told him to split!"

"Fucker ripped me off. Fucker better hope I don't see 'im."

"Had to kick his ass."

This bluster is part and parcel of the junk scene. Transparently false braggadocio must be received with a straight face at the risk of challenging touchy egos. Somewhere the meanest, bad-ass, pockmarked junkie traverses a fawning crowd of addicts. Supplicants reach to touch his garment, stroke his tracks for luck. Sometimes I heard a more pleasant reminiscence of a time when money and junk were plentiful. It was often related in a tone of mean, hollow conceit.

Later in the afternoon an old high school acquaintance wandered in with some other people I knew. He didn't realize that it was my room he was entering. I actually knew Don C.'s sister better than I knew him.

"She's studying to be an international stewardess," he told me. "She says it's an incredible amount of bullshit but that she'll be able to smuggle really easily after she graduates." As it turned out, the bullshit got to her and she dropped out. But I was surprised to see Don there. I hadn't known that he did junk.

"Me? I haven't done a thing for the last couple months. I just bought some stuff from those guys down the hall. That shot's gonna feel *so good* tonight. Boy, I love to do something up after I haven't had it for a while. The dreams are incredible with that first shot! Man, I'm gonna dream in Technicolor tonight!"

My own dreaming I had to forestall until well after sunset. I just couldn't relax with my body constantly covered with sweat. There was a moment of relief around 9:30 P.M., when the temperature dropped enough for the cooler to actually do something. Then they turned it off. I heard some swearing down the hall when it happened, but I didn't even have the energy to swear. It wasn't until practically midnight that I felt the invigorating cool spark. Getting up, stretching, letting out a groan of release, I grabbed a couple hand-rolled cigarettes and moved out to the upstairs porch.

"Now," I said to myself, pulling up the old wooden chair with the peeling gray paint. "Now, at last."

I lived for "Now." My whole frame of mind had become compartmentalized into two areas: one was "Soon," waiting to feel better; the other was "Now," feeling good. And when "Now" arrived I made the most of it, driving as many anxieties away as I could. Of course, like a wrapper that refuses to stay unfolded, my worries and fears soon engulfed me again, but I staved them off as long as possible. Lighting a cigarette, I regarded the empty street below.

I heard no footsteps; only occasional passing cars invaded

the scene, rudely throwing the tenuous light of reality onto my dreamscape. The glare of my match annoyed me, and I quickly tossed it. I drew comforting fantasies of being a rich man gazing over postmidnight Victorian London. In my silk smoking jacket, I'm free to get my opium from the chemist whenever I desire. Laudanum. Hashish from the Arab quarter. Heroin cough syrup. Cocaine is the rage of high society. Nose douches. Hookahs. Cocaine-wine infusions. *Cannabis indica* extracts. Black gum opium. Paregoric. Cocaine lozenges. Heroin reefers. I am a man born a hundred years too late.

I shuddered at Old Stegman's fate: facing his last years knowing that he was born *3,000 years* too late. Images of robed philosophers who had called entire systems of maths and sciences into being through mere thought, swimming round his head. Smooth new Greek pillars, the first Roman arches clean and sharp; one would barely be able to imagine them crumbling into ruin. Hermits crawling out of caves to announce basic discoveries to virtually no one. Learned discourses that deftly combined fire, water, earth, air. And the ether. Their world hung precariously, mysteriously in some undefinable ether. An elemental vapor that drifted with obscure but inevitable purpose around our Earth. Knowledge coddles us with the illusion that we're the center of the universe and that all things revolve harmoniously around us. There are sweet musical tones to be heard by those who would but listen. The music of the spheres, playing a serene lullaby to a bunch of smug philosopher-scientists. I took a deep drag on my cigarette, and it filled my limbs with delicious tingling. Old shades danced round my head, pulling a dark curtain over my eyes.

I knew I'd fallen in between. A lush half-sleep, whence I could see dreams forming to the sound of gentle winds in the old Geronimo's trees. In this sublime state I watched: the desert grew and spread before me, a nighttime desert of which I could nonetheless see all detail. Armies of the night roam its floor, my surveillance undetected as they advance on their objectives. Wealth pours from the sky; bricks, duffel bags, bales of weed land with heavy thuds on some secret, sandy spot. Huddled couriers helplessly tense as they pray they aren't crushed. A kilo of counterfeit bills breaks up on the way down, raining thrilled groups below with floating C-notes. And there! Between the hills, a line of knapsacked smugglers winds along a dry, murky gulch as luscious breezes kiss moist brows. Up ahead, unseen figures await in dark ambush.

I'm approaching an intersection, a kaleidoscope of red and green traffic lights. Its clarity is astounding, and I advance with alarming speed. The passing houses are but marked targets, previously staked out by a troop of wiry, silent housebreakers. Yet I can still hear the sounds around me on the porch. Cars pass. The tinkle of breaking window glass. Many sleepers hear it besides me; no one will do a thing about it. I picture the shade of Nazi Paul stealthily easing into a residence. I pick and choose my images; aware of them all, I float above, secure in the ether. Blackness at the edges.

Only minutes of life left. The sun's gone out. How shall I spend them? Frenzies of rape, desperation, of blind, pleading fear fill every hotel room, every street, every town. I have no one to express eternal love to. The last light will take eight and a half minutes to arrive. Behind it, the invisible, dead sun; a dark ring grows from dead center. Huge airborne bales of weed land with a dull thud. A frigid reception committee, preserved in the act of rushing for them, will forever fear being crushed by falling duffel bags. The line of smugglers freezes in midstride, all leaning away from the deadly, grinning, endless leer of a frozen Mexican Federale. C-notes float serenely through the endless night, silently wafting onto the frozen desert floor, gently cracking into pieces. In the distance a plane engine fades until it flies into the Catalina Mountains.

Paul's shy smile. He grins with embarrassment at me as he prepares to inject a hypo of pure water. His smile peels back into a rabid, gaping, icy crystal skull for all time. The old glass hypo cracks as water in it freezes and assumes its shape.

I stare out from my dreams to the dirty floodlights around the night lawn. They shatter and explode as their heat meets the finality of absolute zero. An eternal circle of frozen junkies await future excavation. Clouds form above me from decaying steam of dead cities. They dissipate, and a star-filled firmament, clear as the dawn of time, glimmers cold, white light. Reflections twinkle on graceful columns, on a heritage of ancient porticoes glistening with frost. In eternal blackness, my greedy eyes harden beholding a Parthenon of shimmering temples, of the mysterious, ever silent arches of . . . the Geronimo.

That night I had one of my more common dreams: Among a group of musicians, I'm holding a guitar, but despite all the music I hear, no one lets me play. It was quite colorful and quite obnoxious.

I feel so light! Turning, I'm amazed to view myself lying on my bed, quite dead to the world. Faint white light surrounds my corpse. To my delight, I find that I can pass through walls into other rooms. A brief tour among the tenants of the third floor. Alkies alternate with junkies from room to room. All look dead. I move on. Just passing through.

My eyes are half open. It's morning. Startled, then helpless, I find I cannot move. I'm stuck in another Heat Dream. Footsteps tread cautiously behind me, just out of sight. Steaming, vicious hissing fills my ears. I must swallow the fear. *I must swallow it!* Straining, sweating, struggling, I can do nothing but gaze through half-opened eyes at my bedspread and windows. They are horribly bright with sweltering, threatening daylight. Yet I would do anything to wake completely up to that life-sapping heat. A vibration starts to fill my head. My ears are hissing. I push, strain and—finally!—break awake.

Hissing in my ears fades to insect buzzing as cicadas announce another killer summer day.

Later that same day, I hear that Don C. has OD'd. He is dead. It's not the first time I've known someone this has happened to, but I'm still struck with fascination at having been witness to some of his last hours. I'm glad I didn't sell him the stuff that killed him.

The sudden, unnecessary end of a boy who only wanted to dream.

coming to

a parallel ballpark

12 Everyone knew someone who had died from an overdose. It's practically the first thing a novice learns. In Tucson, people who had no idea what heroin looked like still knew of an OD. The newspapers spread the alarm, publishing notice after notice of heroin death. During that summer, and many others around here, the rate of overdose surpassed that of traffic fatalities. Emergency room doctors were complaining that some people were ODing purposely to get the antidote. At that time it was intravenous cocaine. A number of victims told me that when they came to it was the best they'd ever felt. But I can't think of a more obtuse evaluation of the problem than that offered by those doctors. Most incidents arose from lack of steady supply; victims underestimated the potency of unfamiliar dope. Occasionally someone got stuck with a poisonous cut and died from that.

Many of my days were spent trudging through the summer heat, going from one contact to the next, usually receiving a negative response to requests for dope. Hardly anyone could get it; certainly no one had a steady supply. Manny, who I used to count on for decent papers, no longer even answered my knock. The only indication of his existence was a childishly scrawled sign on the door. "You'll never take me alive!" it proclaimed to all comers, each polka-dot balloon letter a different, bright color.

I hit up my family dentist for a Percodan script. A soft touch, he suffered at the mere mention of pain. "How many would you like?" he asked. He did look a little bemused at my request for fifty. The trick was getting by his secretaries, who weren't fooled in the least by my entreaties. I'd raise my voice enough for the doctor to hear, vehemently insisting that it was up to him, not them. Once he got on the scene, they just threw up their hands, knowing that he could never turn anyone down. He eventually lost his license.

Upon returning to my room that evening, I realized that I'd gone all day without dope. I wondered if I could get through the night without it. Since I was tired enough to sleep I lay down, pulling the purple spread up to my waist. It was too hot to cover up all the way.

A minor itching began to make itself known on my ankles. Soon it had spread up and down both legs. The more I determined to ignore it, the more it asserted itself. A sensation of crawling insects grew more insistent beneath the spread. Intellectually I readily denied the existence of even one bug on my legs, but *physically* the feeling was so present, so constant, and finally so convincing that I suddenly, madly tore off the cover. My mouth fell open. There was, of course, nothing there.

"Why suffer?" I asked myself, the answer ready. I grabbed a couple Percodans and swallowed them, then lay back down. Without knowing it, I fell asleep for thirty or forty minutes. When I awoke, it was to the most exquisite, all-encompassing pleasure. This, I languidly mused, is what it must've been like to drink potions from the Old Man of the Mountain. Fall asleep and awaken in his Garden of Delights. His hashshashins would murder on command at the prospect of return to this delicious state. A song played and replayed in my mind, some droning Arabic ditty:

> *There is no treason*
> *   No oath from us transcends.*
> *There are no brothers*
> *   Nor relationships in sin.*
> *We all live together*
> *   And are all assassins.*

The Percodans carried me through the week, even after I sold some for food money. However, I avoided shooting them and was soon hungering for the full-fledged rush of a shot. I talked Mark and Luke into fronting me $300 to get them more stuff. But it was nowhere to be found. I was frustrated at having to scramble for money and then being unable to find the dope. For the habit won't let you forget, and the money's just a mocking reminder of what could be.

For two days running I asked everyone I knew in the vain hope that $300 buying power would miraculously raise something on the dried-up market. Finally one afternoon, a woman I'd seen around the night lawn approached me. She claimed that she could get stuff easily but that I'd have to front her money. This was a bottom-line no for me. I, who heard of thousands of dollars in rip-offs every week, would not be played for a sucker. And the surest way to avoid that was to refuse to front money. Eventually she acquiesced to take me over to the apartment. Some guy, her friend, drove us there. When she arrived she started with the same front-the-money bit, patiently explaining that she was simply walking up to a door, which she pointed out, and that the people refused to meet anyone, but not to worry because I'd see where she was going. I gave her the money, and she entered the complex. As she started picking up speed at the other end, I knew that I'd been taken and ran after her, only to see her leave the grounds. Sprinting over, I was just in time to eat the dust from her friend's car, which had swung around to pick her up.

Infuriated, with myself most of all, I soon felt dread at having to inform Mark and Luke that I'd lost their money—and in such a stupid way, at that. It wouldn't dent their wealth much. But there was always the lingering suspicion that I was lying and had simply kept the money.

I had no cash to pay them back. In fact, I can't remember where what little money I had came from. I recall having little to eat but not feeling much hunger. I didn't steal or burglarize, but I always seemed to have at least one shot a day. I suppose I just kept up the petty deals, procuring papers, selling bits of weed. I no longer got the calls for packing, which cut into my income. People tipped me to hit up in my room or use it to parcel stuff up for sale. Those I'd helped out of past jams, like Nazi Paul, came through and returned the favors. This hand-to-mouth existence carried me along for a while.

A variety of brief scenes come to mind:

I'm visiting Terry at his new apartment, a cubbyhole in Manny's ramshackle complex. I hand Terry two twenties for dope, for which he must step out a couple minutes. I strongly suspect that he's buying from Manny, but I can never get Manny to answer his door, so what can I do? Terry dislikes leaving me alone in his place for even a short time.

"I'll just be gone a bit," he mutters. "And you better not touch a fucking thing!" To emphasize his point, he produces a pistol with an ugly, homemade silencer and aims it right at my gut. His scowl contrasts with the silly laugh I give.

"Hey! That's pretty neat!" I am grinning like an idiot despite feeling my stomach evaporate. He holds the gun and silencer on me until the split second my smile fades. Then he goes and cops.

Paul shakes his head. "Man, this having no money is getting really old. Someone wanted to buy my gun yesterday. Told 'em to buzz off! But, God, I actually considered it for a second."

My mouth falls open. "You have a gun to sell? Shit, if I had something like that I'd sell it right now!"

Paul looks incredulous. "Sell my gun? No way! Man, I'll never sell that! Shit, why that'd be like selling my means of . . ." His voice trails off.

I run into Terry.

"They got that fool, Manny," he relates. "Went in there in the morning while he was asleep. Didn't give 'em any resistance at all."

A parolee named Steve is hanging around the Geronimo. Crude, abrasive, a lout obviously on his way back to Florence Prison. He shoots into the back of his hands, figuring his parole officer won't see the marks as easily. Steve doesn't seem to have any permanent place to live; he appears without warning at various tenants' rooms to get off, giving them a few dollars of dope. Then he barfs and doesn't flush the toilet.

Steve starts hanging out at Paul's lodge, much to Paul's chagrin. But they are both longtime prison inmates, and they relate with each other on a whole different level of understanding than they do with someone like me. Steve simply bullies Paul, addressing him as Stupid.

"Hey, whataya think of that, eh, Stupid?"

He outweighs Paul by about fifty pounds. Even an Arizona prison diet makes someone look positively healthy next to Paul.

"What'd I tell you about that, Stupid?" he growls threateningly. Paul cowers resentfully in a corner of his own room. A most distasteful exhibition, which I and the rest of the visitors do our best to ignore. Later on I hear that Steve kicks Paul's ass around the lodge.

People around the hotel no longer call him Nazi Paul, instead assigning him the permanent name Stupid.

I spend an entire day on the scent of some Demerol pills. Blocks of hours laboriously pass as I try to kill enough time to justify going back to my contact again, then again, then once more. Finally, as I dismiss the whole wretched affair, he shows up outside the hotel grocery store and hands me one white hundred-milligram pill for two or three bucks.

I thank my good fortune! Excitedly popping back into my room, I notice that I feel no more discomforts or symptoms. Why not see just how long this sudden, surprising state will last, an effect of the knowledge that I now have something to shoot? Within ten minutes I'm feeling the aches and tensions I've been fighting all afternoon. Now it's evening. The entire day has been spent in the quest for one pill. I decide to crush it, soak it in a small amount of water, draw it up through a cotton, and shoot it. It has the foul, piercing, hospital odor of all Demerol.

The shot provides a full, unpleasant bodily rush. I've done too much, but not so much that I'm going to pass out. Within minutes the drug provokes a deep depression—a complete let-

down after all my trouble to get it. And I'm fighting to stay
awake. Despondent, I call up Earl. "Earl, all this stuff I've been
doing is fucking killing me. I've got to stop. I feel like I've got
to put my head down and sleep a bit. . . ."

Alarmed, Earl yells into the phone. "Scott? Scott! Don't go
to sleep! Scott?"

I hang up and lay my head on the desk. In what seems like a
mere five seconds, there's a hammering at my door. To my
surprise and delight, Earl is standing right there, even though
he was thirty minutes away!

"Earl! How did you get here so fast? You were just on the
phone!" A vague, distant memory of a pounding door comes to
mind. "Have you been knocking long?"

"Jesus, *yes*, I've been knocking. I was just about to break
down the door if you hadn't opened it!"

Paul sits and just shakes his head. "There comes a time when
everyone must stop living beyond their means."

I'm confused. What is he talking about?

"I'm getting sick of this shit. Man, I think I'm gonna have to
quit for a while."

"Wow . . . you sound as if you really mean it."

"Well, nothing like getting back to zero level again. I know I
can't keep up with what I need now!"

To return to zero he sequesters himself in his lodge over
four days. I stop in once to see how he's doing.

"It'd be simple if my goddamned legs didn't hurt so much."
He groans. "I'm telling you, that's what gets me every time.
My legs. They just hurt so bad. Man, it'd be a snap otherwise."

I can barely see in the dark gray of his room, basically locat-
ing Paul by spotting his white boxer shorts. "I have a bit of
Valium. You want to try that?"

"Shit, I'll try anything. It certainly couldn't do any worse."

* * *

Throughout this vague, choppy period at the Geronimo, the weather provided the only stability in anyone's life. Every day was over a hundred degrees. The sky was almost always glazed hot, blue, and clear. A dry, feverish wind added to the misery. There was abundant insect buzzing. Nights were short, desperately needed periods of recuperation. When I had the energy, I'd join the circle of fiends gathered on the night lawn, beneath Stegman's tower. Some nights there were two dozen junkies there. If I wanted solitude, I'd hang out on the porch or hoist my feet on the windowsill and lean back in a chair. I borrowed a guitar and remember coming to, my feet up on the sill, my hand still holding a fading chord.

Then clouds began to gather over the five mountain ranges that surround our town. Humidity was trapped inside them, which made them take on odd pink, yellow, and blue pastels. Like a set of moist, punched-out veins, they shied from us for weeks. Summer heat maintained steady mercury levels, but the added humidity gave new meaning to the word *oppression*. Life, of course, writhed on as it will. But now it squirmed and slid in a salty, generous sweat, which caused those who had to go outside to cringe, wince, swallow in despair, and, finally, roll over and stew in their own stinging, stinking juices.

At this point we'd gone over fifty days in a row without rain, virtually every day above a hundred degrees. The fireman in the room next to mine went into a drunken rage, ordered his friends to stop calling him Captain, and kicked them out. I heard it all. I imagine he could hear things that went on in my room also. I knew that the heat wave could last another fifty days, and miserly, humid clouds lingering on all horizons made it more irritating. It was in this poor, sopping condition that my talks with Richard took on a new turn.

He had rented one of the lodges; I'd finally been offered the opportunity, but I didn't have the money by then. He resided in Number 1, on a corner of the property, peeking out into the street from behind some bushes by the courtyard wall. As usual, entreaties and probes into drugstore robbery resulted in stalemate, he insisting on seeing the money beforehand, I insisting that this point was nonnegotiable. These discussions always ended with me shaking my head and closing with some "too bad this opportunity's slipping by" statement.

"Ahh, it's a shame," I muttered. "Too bad I can't just buy it on the other side of the border and get someone to bring it up."

"Shee-it!" Richard sparked up. "I can always get it down in Nogales. I just don't have the bread. Getting *chiva* is never a problem down there. Not for me, anyway."

Our eyes met. A tender, searching recognition flickered in Richard's shifty brown orbs, like he'd just realized I was human. Then mutual psychic probing began, as I explored this sudden new supply option.

"I won't, I absolutely won't take the stuff over myself," I stated firmly. "I don't deal with borders, personally."

"I know someone that'll do that. That's no problem. We'll just have to give him a little. I'm more worried about how we'll get down there."

"My car's a real clunker. I wouldn't trust it to get us back. Can't we just take the bus? Hardly costs a thing."

"Well, we could, but we'd stand out more. Those Border Patrol are always boarding the buses a few miles this side of the line, looking for wetbacks, they say. But I don't think they'd behave if they saw us. No, bus isn't a good idea. We need a car." He gazed down into his crotch, as he did whenever he got reflective.

"A car, huh?" I pondered. "Mmm, maybe I could borrow something. I don't know if I could count on that, though. I doubt the people that'll front me the money will want to risk their car on such a small operation."

Richard's head popped back up. "There's no risk! Not to the car, anyway." He laughed. "We park on this side and walk over. That's a lot safer than trying to drive the shit over." Nodding his head curtly, he came to a decision. "Don't worry about the car. I'll take care of that. You just come up with the money. We could probably do something for $300. That's the least I could ask my people about."

I didn't relish Mark's reaction at being asked for another $300. That $300 loss I'd engineered was still recent memory. It seemed almost improper to ask, quite nervy, really. "I don't know," I hedged. "I can ask the guy. I can't front you the money, you know." My habit quickly manufactured sublime yet pertinent reasons why it couldn't possibly hurt to ask Mark for money. In no time the boundaries of my gall had cleared the field.

Richard was enthusiastic. "Three hundred dollars is the least I can work with. They won't even talk to me for less, but that'll do it. Don't worry about the car or taking the stuff over. Just come up with the money. We can go down there tonight if you get the bread this afternoon."

I was also excited by this new idea but maintained a cool demeanor. "I'll see what I can do. I don't know, but I'll try my best."

As I suspected, Mark was not enthusiastic about the proposal. It wasn't the borderline that scared him—he regularly funded projects involving dope crossing the border just before he received it. With weed, he generally placed an order with the Mexicans, having no responsibility for any payment until the load actually cleared the border and reached Tucson. Sometimes little chunks of heroin were included gratis. On the other hand, funding a junk run, which he'd sometimes done on a smaller scale, did involve a direct risk of his money. To my knowledge, he had yet to lose out on any of these propositions, though, which was in my favor.

The TV was on with the sound off, showing an old *Mr. Ed* rerun. "Heroin," by The Velvet Underground, played softly on the stereo. Clothed in blue gym shorts and a V-neck T-shirt, an unshaven Mark was staring vacantly at his wall. But, as I'd feared, his recent memory of my $300 loss made him actively cantankerous toward my request. It took weaseling and repetition on my part. Christ, he gave Marie $300 to buy Chinese food for the day, something that arrived only if he was lucky. I found his reluctance a bit much by the end of the conversation. But I subjected myself to it anyway.

Mark groaned and twisted on his floor mattress. "Allll-right! I will do it just this one more time. And I don't really know why I'm bothering to do that. You better not have any problems with this, or it'll be the last time that you ever get any money from me!" He counted out $300 into my hands. "Remember, I don't want to hear anything about how you lost this money."

"Oh, don't worry, don't worry, there won't be any problems this time," I brashly and obsequiously assured him. Though I was glad to have the money, its weight in my pocket felt like I was starting a climb up a steep hill. I was unsure if the risks I planned would be worth the returns.

I did know of other successful border crossings. Once, an old girlfriend of mine stuffed four ounces of heroin up her vagina and waddled across with no problems. And I recalled when Andy had gotten a cash front from Mark and hired Earl, of all people, to bring the stuff over, again a walk-through at Nogales. Earl had agreed to do it for six dimes, a pitiful price for what he went through. It involved him swallowing a double prophylactic full of heroin and walking through customs. The only thing he had to fear was an X ray, a minuscule possibility.

That, and the chance that the rubber would burst inside him, which would kill him. As it went, neither thing occurred, and they arrived back up at Andy's, where Andy refused to let Earl leave the house until he relinquished the junk. Earl spent a couple hours attempting to vomit the stuff up, but it wouldn't come. The whites of his eyes were solid red from the pressure of trying.

"Just relax, Earl," counseled Andy. "It'll come out when you go to the bathroom. Don't worry, I've been through this many times." Earl made to go to the store for cigarettes. "No, Earl, you're not going anywhere until you produce that dope. And don't you open it up, either, after it comes out. You just bring it in here to me, and I'll give you what's coming to you."

It finally appeared when Earl moved his bowels hours later. They'd taped the toilet handle so Earl couldn't reflexively flush the toilet, which had happened to others. Andy hung around the bathroom, and then they dug it out together. It was close to an ounce of stuff, almost 28 grams. Andy and Mark paid Earl about a half a gram for his troubles. Despite his pleas, they steadfastly refused to give him another grain.

These memories and other tidbits were bouncing around my brain as Richard, his friend, and I took off for Nogales, Mexico. They'd borrowed a large, old, white car. Strip searches, Mexicans who sell and talk, rip-offs, lousy stuff. All these things were registered and filed beneath my calm exterior in the backseat.

It was night when we left Tucson for the one-hour drive down I-19. Just a few miles south of town it cooled off appreciably. Weeknight traffic was sparse, and we passed through a number of brief, pleasant rainsqualls on the shiny, empty highway. The cool, wet breeze was a positive panacea for my weary mind and body.

"My God!" I implored myself. "Why am I rotting in Tucson when I can live out here?"

There was no moonlight. Rare oncoming cars illuminated sparkling raindrops that shot by headlights like diamond chips. Sometimes we passed an exit or crossed a bridge, bright islands of bluish-white light along the dark interstate. The lights were swarming with armies of moths and grasshoppers, panicked as the cool, wet gems shot through their squadrons. Yet out in the bushes and cacti stretching for miles unseen along both sides of the road, I sensed a friendly, gentle peace; memories of my desert, which I achingly longed for. There was an alluring, clean, live smell in that vast space.

"Boy, Scott, this was a good idea," Richard spoke up. He was more relaxed than usual. "I don't know why we didn't think of going to Nogie before."

Reluctantly, I returned to business. "Yeah, well, I hope it works out. How's he gonna take it over, anyway?"

I don't remember the name of our courier. I don't think I bothered to learn it; who needs to know the name of someone who might shortly be swept off to jail for the next ten years? Both of them, however, were reticent concerning details of their part of the operation. "Well?" I pressed them. "Are you swallowing it? Sticking it down your pants? Shoving it up your butt? Or what?"

They remained quiet until Richard answered. "There's no need for you to know. Really, the less you know, the better."

"I doubt it'll be very difficult," chimed in the other guy, briefly turning paunchy, freckled features toward me. He casually brushed reddish blond hair from his eyes. It was a forced ease.

"Oh, it'll be really simple!" Richard agreed. They were psyching themselves up. "As long as they don't strip-search you, you're okay."

The body-for-hire nodded hesitantly in agreement. A slow, fatalistic rigidity stiffened him as the mileposts inexorably flashed their countdown. Richard caught his worried pause.

"Ahh, don't even think about it. I've seen this stuff go down dozens of times. It'll be over before you know it! See?" His brow furrowed at me in the rearview mirror. "Now you're gettin' 'im spooked." He turned to the courier. "Forget about it. It'll be over really quickly."

That last sentence produced a dread so palpable that I thought I must be imagining it. We continued down the road, chatting about nothing in particular, keeping our minds off the big game. When we got to Nogales, Arizona, we parked the car along a quiet city street, a mere block from the border. On the other side of the crossing lay Nogales, Mexico. Though it was a bit cooler here than in Tucson, the refreshing light rains remained hovering on the sixty-mile stretch we'd just driven. A glistening, sweaty humidity covered the twin Nogaleses, the same slippery muck that we'd left up north.

The game really began when our trio passed through the international crossing, a large concrete and glass affair arching high over the road running from the United States into Mexico. Many lanes existed for traffic going back and forth, as the place was often quite busy. But now it was starkly silent, garishly lit with tall, ultrabright lights swimming with crowds of bugs—who seemed to be observing border regulations. Picketing casually below were green-uniformed members of the U.S. Customs Service. Our adversaries. I tried to avoid showing my face as we walked into Mexico, but that was impossible. We maintained a relaxed but pleased air as we crossed their line of vision.

Then we were in Mexico. Glum, brown-uniformed Federales mutely regarded us with a distinctly different posture, leaning on the outsides of their red, wooden guard boxes. *Their* hands weren't tied by protocol and silly regulations like those of their brothers but a few yards to the north. To fall into their clutches would be a painful and unpleasant affair, yet they weren't our main worry. Visas aren't required for tourist visits to the border towns, so Federales spend most of their time harassing Mexican nationals trying to sneak in electronics or too many American cigarettes. Nogales is a normal Mexican border town, overflowing with overpriced, mass-produced tourist crap, with a hepatitic water supply and a scent of criminal activity lingering a few yards off any main drag. Every Arizona kid grows up to tales of vicious bar fights along Canal Street, and, as I kept pace with my companions, legends surfaced of bullshit cigarettes, Spanish fly, women copulating with donkeys in mysterious side street taverns. This is the fare that boys are fed as they enter adolescence around here, and I can recall many young cowpokes recounting how their fathers handed them eleven dollars and sent them down to Canal Street for sex education. A striking, ominous silence lurked between our echoing steps as these raucous memories bobbed into mind.

Richard soon led us to a residential section in the hilly eastern side of town, then down some dirt alleyways that crisscrossed these hills. Houses behind us were slightly higher than the ones below and in front. A few dim streetlamps hung from twisted, weathered telephone poles. Garbage cans, cats, and dogs seemed the main purpose for this eerie, tenuous alleyway.

"You're gonna have to wait here," Richard suddenly announced to me. "I can't bring anybody over to these people's house. And I'm gonna have to take that money now." He held out his hand.

So, I was back at this point again. He knew that I didn't like to front out money, so he'd waited until I was at this distinct disadvantage. When he saw me balking, his impatience rose. "I know, I know, you didn't think you'd have to front the bread. You think I'd bother taking you all the way down here if I wanted to rip you off? Shit, I coulda done that without leaving town." Then his manner eased up. "Don't worry. Nothing's gonna happen. We're just going into one of those houses there. You're gonna get your stuff. But there's no way you're going in there with us. Come on, let's get this over with."

Reluctantly, I counted out $300. My situation was becoming more alarming every minute.

"Wait here." Richard motioned as if walls rose on each side of the spot where I stood. "You'll be okay here. No one's gonna bother you. We won't be that long." They climbed up some piles of dirt and disappeared between some houses.

The homes appeared upper middle class. Multibedroom, single-family affairs, probably a pretty good part of town. A man opened a gate and tossed some bags into his garbage cans, doing a double take as he turned and noticed me standing there. Regarding me with brief curiosity, he shrugged and went back in. I found myself imagining what would happen if some upper-middle-class U.S. citizens saw him standing in *their* alley. He'd probably get some attention quickly.

As it was, I spent a long, indeterminate period there, and no one bothered me. Cats jumped out of their skins when they perceived me, and at one point a pack of dogs surrounded me and sniffed heartily at my pants, then rambled on. However, I sweated there long enough to begin to wonder if I'd really just been taken for my $300. I was relieved when I saw Richard and his friend come back up the alley.

"You still here?" He laughed. "Shee-it, I thought you'd have given up by now!"

"Did you have to take so long?" I was deliriously glad to be getting out of there. "Are we ready to go? Everything in order?"

Richard made a sharp motion to cut off my jabbering. "Don't worry. It's fine. Good *chiva*, too." He looked like he'd taken a strong shot while I was festering out in that stupid alley.

We returned along basically the same route. The Federales paid absolutely no attention to us.

"You want to go through separately?" I asked Richard.

"No, that'll just raise questions. They saw three of us go in. We'll all walk through together. Okay? Let's do it!"

I put myself into a practiced, relaxed mode, one I could readily assume during operations or whenever under scrutiny. Some people have a natural ability to stay calm under these pressures. This inbred acting streak is one thing that makes the difference between a long-term dealer and one who crumbles under pressure. The instinct not to avoid eye contact, to refrain from being talkative or otherwise displaying nervousness, an awareness that you're not flaring your nostrils or raising your brows, enforced languidness regardless of what you might be feeling inside. I placed myself into this familiar chameleon-like disguise. The other two guys seemed relaxed as we approached under the amused gaze of a green-uniformed border guard. He shook his head slightly, as if we were wayward lads who might try to lie about having chewing gum in our mouths.

"Just here for the evening, boys?"

"Yep, just visiting."

"Have anything to declare?" He was a tall, round, blond fellow, regarding us from under a balding, furrowed brow.

"Nope," answered Richard. "Nothing to declare."

"Why don't you guys come over here for a minute?" The guard motioned for us to enter the green and glass maze within the arches of the large customs building. I noticed that he kept the ornate handle of his pistol away from us as he held the door open. Leading us to some stairs, he had us proceed first. There was a door at the top.

"It's open," he called from behind. Richard opened up, and we all filed into a small, trapezoidal room with a large, bare desk and a few hard-back chairs. One side of the room had windows that looked right down to the street where we'd just been.

Tantalizingly close, yet impossible to get to. All three of us appeared unconcerned but tight-lipped. I wondered, Is this leading to a strip search? I'd never been strip-searched.

"Just have a seat, guys. I want to talk to you a little while." Everyone sat down, the guard on the other side of the desk from us.

It's just a bluff, I told myself, knowing that a mere wink from him could get us body searches. That would bring the whole scam crashing down.

The guard brushed back strands of blond hair over his bald spot and assumed the posture of a friendly, decent, good ol' guy. "So, just down here visiting, huh, guys? Come down here very often? No? I didn't think so. I don't recognize any of you . . . I'm glad to say. Mind if I take a look at that arm there?" He motioned to Richard's inner elbow. Observing a healthy smattering of needle marks, he gave a friendly, knowing nod. "Mmmm, well, well, how 'bout the rest of you? . . . mm-hmm, so you all do it, eh? That's okay, boys, that's okay! We don't mind *what* you do, as long as you do it over there." He jabbed a thumb behind him, toward Mexico. "Really! I'm not kidding you. We have people that go over every day for a shot. We *know* that they do. And they know we know. And they know that they better not try to bring anything over, otherwise the whole thing changes. But we don't care. You guys want to go over every day and get high, that's your business! But just remember—this is *our* ballpark, and we play by *our* rules here."

From where I was sitting the place did somewhat resemble a ballpark, with us up in the press box. The guard leaned back and smoothed his green shirt over his stomach with both hands, smiling a warm, just-a-night-at-the-game smile. He made light small talk with us, really, with just the other two. I kept my mouth shut, making sure to laugh at appropriate times. It was nerve-racking. Anytime I expected the whole show to change pace, and I avoided making eye contact with our courier. Occasionally another guard would pop his head in the door, but our buddy assured him that "everything's under control."

I must say, the other two guys held up remarkably well, looking as they were into a yawning chasm of jail time. Both of them had records, something I lacked, and that made my own situation a bit more bearable. I was hopeful of fading out of the visible light spectrum at any time. Our guard looked at me. "Well, how 'bout you? How come you're so quiet?"

"Because you haven't said anything to me yet!" I brashly fired back.

"Oh, he does talk." The guard smiled. "Just wanted to see if you could. We never know around here. Sometimes people like to keep stuff hidden in their mouths. Well, I guess we don't have that problem with you, do we?"

All three of us chose a smart-alecky, flippant attitude to enhance our images of innocence. The customs man seemed at ease with our posturing. Now that he'd broken the ice with me, I ventured to make a little small talk myself. "So, do *you* ever go over there?" I asked.

"Me?" He cocked his head, then frowned. "I haven't ever been over there. And I hope I never go. Worked here twelve years, and I'd be happy if I never set foot in the place. There's no way I ever *want* to go."

So much for the Hands Across the Border routine here.

"Now those guys over there," he continued. "They do things a little differently. When *they* arrest you, you'll be in a shitload of trouble. They're not like us. Well." He stood up. "You boys can go now. Don't forget some of the things I told you. Have a nice evening."

We trudged back down the stairs. Anytime I expected a "Wait a minute!" or a "Hold on there!" to sound behind us, but, to my utter amazement, they were actually letting us go! All of us kept silent as we walked back to our car, still in sight of the border station. Instinctively, none of us displayed any emotion or relief that might get us called back. We climbed into the car quietly, subdued.

"Could you believe that shit?" Richard broke the silence.

"Oh, God! That was incredible!" I chimed in as the feeling of elation started to glow.

Our courier just smiled and rolled his eyes.

Richard was more talkative. "Those fuckin' guys. After a while you get to know how to handle them. They're all the same, in a way. Now we just have to get our asses back up to Tucson."

"Ah, shit." I dismissed him. "Nobody's going to bother us now. They'll know that they already checked us out." I hoped, in my light-headedness, that I was right. We had sixty miles to drive, and, especially within twelve miles of the border, we were still at risk. Most people don't realize that the twelve-mile border limit actually works in both directions, and that search and seizure laws are virtually suspended within that range.

"Well, don't take the stuff out yet," Richard advised our man after a few minutes on the road. "We don't need you stuffing it back in if we get stopped."

"I doubt anything'll happen," I repeated. Seconds later Richard glanced into the rearview mirror. "Oh, shit," he uttered. "Don't look back!"

I knew better than to peek over my shoulder. Red and orange flashing lights of the Highway Patrol car filled the interior of the car. After what we'd gone through at customs, I found it incomprehensible that we should get caught now. "Ah, it's nothing," I announced, confidently. "As soon as he calls on the radio he'll figure out that they checked us out thoroughly back there. Just relax," I told the guy with the dope.

"Shit, I wasn't even speeding," Richard muttered.

The cop strolled to the driver's side of the car and shined his flashlight in. He checked out Richard's license; all paperwork seemed to be in order. "Ever been arrested?" he asked Richard.

"No," he lied back.

"How 'bout the rest of you?"

We both shook our heads.

"Hmm, that's pretty good." The cop nodded, somewhat disbelievingly, I thought. He looked briefly down the long, black, empty highway, then back to our trio. I got the impression that he felt a little funny standing alone out in that desolate spot with the likes of us. He strolled back to his car and chattered a bit on the radio.

"He's going to let us go in a minute," I assured the other two. "He's checking down with the border now."

The cop returned and handed Richard his license. "All right, thanks. You guys drive carefully." He walked away.

Released again! But this time I had been so self-assured about it that my reaction was more matter-of-fact than one of relief. Or, perhaps I simply had no more energy to expend on utter gratefulness. The last forty-five minutes of the drive are a blank. I know I didn't doze; though almost overcome with exhaustion, I didn't trust the other two enough to sleep. I was so drained from the evening's pressures and emotions, plus the fact that I'd volunteered for it, plus the fact that the rewards seemed *so slim for what I'd just put myself through*, that I was spent with emotional fatigue.

My next memory is being back in lodge Number 1, Richard's place, his small front room packed with six glistening, sweaty junkies. All were electrified to be in the presence of people who had just run heroin over the border. Except Dee-Dee, the tough talker, who acted as if she saw this kind of stuff every day. The courier seemed to be struck mute from shock. He could've been Richard's ventriloquist dummy. The other guys, some of whom I'd never seen before, were more animated. Richard became wiry and enthusiastic.

"I'll just be a minute," he breathlessly remarked, then bounded into the back room with the courier.

I didn't know what arrangement they'd made, but I didn't like the dope disappearing back there, nor did I enjoy the fact that I'd gone through all this and still had yet to see anything. "Goddamnit! Bring that stuff in here! I said, bring it in here now!"

In a couple of seconds Richard popped back into the room as if late in delivering his lines. "Here you go! Geez, whataya getting so worked up about? See? There's your stuff, just like I said."

I glowered at his weasely attitude, taking the small, clear plastic bag he offered over to a softly lit side table. The weight in my palm pleased me, but when I got a better look at the stuff I saw some strange coffee-colored crystals in which lay a smattering of tiny, black granules.

"Oh, fuck!" I let loose. "What is this shit? There's hardly anything in here. What is this brown stuff they've thrown in here?"

"Whataya mean?" Richard came over by the light. "That's heroin!" He pulled out a few little black specks. "That's good dope! I don't know what the fuck that other stuff is they put in. The Mexicans are always doing shit like that. I don't know what it is. You pick that black stuff out of there, and you'll see that you have something."

I removed a black speck for a sample shot, taking care to keep it small. I remembered my last encounter with these little black specks, the stuff I'd done with Andy. This stuff felt okay, but somehow the shot just didn't ease my evening's burdens or the nakedness of being the object of a dozen hungry, leering junkies' eyes. After a few minutes a feeling enveloped me of being coated in lead. The thought of how little, if anything, would be left over after delivering the insatiable Mark his share effectively took the rest of the wind from my sails. Sitting down, I felt a small, defeated smile steal over my lips, and I resignedly shook my head. The lighting in the room assumed a burnt quality, like I'd been watching TV for hours and had suddenly looked up. Edges of objects seemed fuzzy and frayed. They appeared almost flat, as if ink had been running out when they got printed. Dim lighting barely reached the windows, which stood like silent, open gateways to a deep, black space. That room felt like it was flying through endless reaches of freezing, lifeless emptiness. Vague shadows and afterimages lagged behind anything that moved in there. When I lifted my arm, a shadow arm tardily chased it. When someone crossed the room, a dull, gray aura trailed lazily behind.

My world was rapidly shrinking to this softly lit cube, the lamps and tables, a half dozen junkies, the only things happening as a Ptolemaic universe spun around us, its center. I was in my cave, biding my time to announce that, dependent on my observation of shadows, the sun, the stars, the music of the spheres all spun around this little cube. I felt tired. Objects were too fatigued to move in one piece, always trailing that gray afterimage behind them. My mind detached gradually, knowing that the room, the Geronimo, the world is but a play of shadows on a background of the Void.

"Come on, honey, don't you *wanna* have a good time?"

Dee-Dee was curled up at my knee. A set of thick brown eyebrows implored me with unction, a pathetic enticement to hiring her services in exchange for some of my dope. She pawed at me. "I can show you a real good time." Graveling her voice, she cloyed. "I know what you like. Why don't you and I get away from here and go up to your room?"

Embarrassed, I sat silent during her groveling. A tingling

blush crept over my stupid grin. The room was quiet but taut with the same tension I'd noticed when she'd offered to screw Ron for a dime.

Finally Richard rescued me. "Whataya doing, idiot? Can't you see that he's not interested? Would you leave him alone?" I was relieved when she moved away. The other guys breathed again, now that their source wasn't being kidnapped.

"Ahh, it doesn't hurt to try," she whined.

"You want to sell some of that?" one of the guys ventured.

"Oh, shit, this is fucked up," I muttered. "Here." I turned to him. "Just take a little. Somebody might as well get something out of it. I'm not going to." I handed him a couple granules.

"Geez! Thanks a lot!" The guy was incredulous as he backed away. In a hungry surge, the rest protested their zeal for my evening's efforts. Passively, I handed them gifts of little black grains also.

"What the fuck are you doing?" Richard exclaimed. "That's good dope! You'll make money from that. Jesus, if you're giving it away, I might as well get in on it too." He tried to suppress a sly, embarrassed grin.

Soon there were almost no black grains left in the coffee-colored cut. I did a little shot of the cut to see if it had any effect. It did nothing.

Richard frowned. "You keep shooting that stuff up, and you *will* get sick. You're not supposed to shoot up stuff like that. I don't know what the fuck it is."

Something in me sagged. I knew that when I dug out the last granules from my bag I'd be out looking for more. My situation had changed for the worse. Realizing that Mark could no longer be counted on as an economic boost, I assumed that I'd just finished the last in what seemed a browbeating series of blown, improperly managed, or unfairly handled deals.

I was floating in a bittersweet cloud, facing some unblazed

trail with that irony felt when you've finally tapped out your last nickel. Absolutely nothing to lose, the whole world at your feet. I was broke, at frayed loose ends. With the accoutrements of freedom but not free. My little world, this cube rushing haphazardly through a black void. Everything outside those windows seemed a parallel universe away. Totally unreachable and irrelevant. For all practical purposes it was as if the sun had burnt out, all life outside the room had stopped, and my unimportant but explosive, tenuous but irresistible situation wasn't affected an iota. The world had shrunk to a tiny singularity, the point that's the end of old time, the beginning of new time, of all time. I was lost in fresh everything. Free and ready to explode into the vacuum to create new reality. A parallel ballpark. All materials will be forged afresh, all structures will be vibrant, all cardinal directions will be determined by *me*. An empty, new universe to escape to, and the startling, awesome recognition that time has stopped. Let me begin it anew. I'd brought only one thing with me through the strange portals of parallel existence.

My habit.

13 A summer's day in the Geronimo:

I lean back on the head of the bed, facing east. The sun is far past my windows, the one saving grace of my room. It dispenses its longest rays, from noon all the way past 8:00 P.M., into the rooms on the other side of the hall. Sometimes it's warm in here, but a step outside makes me appreciate the steady humming of the old engines that pass for coolers. It's so quiet that the air being pushed around is usually the loudest noise. Occasionally, a soft, round mushroom sensation grows in my brain, pads into consciousness, and becomes the discrete, gentle sound of footsteps moving somewhere down the hall. Sometimes vague voices drift through dusky passages, like echoes through a long tube, gliding along varnished floorboards, apologetically slinking into empty halls that demand silence. A muffled laugh, a whispered deal, mere suggestions, the bulk of the plans held back until the conspirators are behind one more old door.

Rarely, a raucous chortle or a vehement complaint would be salvoed off the long walls. The pagans exit quickly, and then I'd practically hear seismic decay: grains of brown, ancient dust sifting off old lighting fixtures. Things got so sepulchral that I could tell when I was about to get a phone call from the faint click that occurred when Mrs. Nutting plugged into my line to complete the switchboard circuit before actually ringing the phone. I used this knowledge to perform the parlor trick of announcing that my phone was about to ring to unsuspecting visitors.

Outside a daily chorale was meticulously composed, a dirge really, of the continuous rapid staccato of insect buzzers against a counterpoint of long, haunting calls from mourning doves. A rhythmic bottom filled in every half hour—deep chimes from the old campus bell tower. This completed the dirge: the mirror that ensnared the local ghosts.

I'd almost jump out of my skin when a dust devil swept through the grounds, slapping sand and dead leaves against my windows. Running to the window, I'd spy a crooked, tan spout of desert floor spinning furiously 500 feet into the air. It sucked baked trash and grit through a funnel a yard wide. In the wobbly dust cloud on top, crisp, yellowed newspapers floated fulfilled until carried out of sight. All these sounds and sights were made lethal by the heat's never-ending oppression, a steady, billowy pounding of hot puffs, which, given enough time, caused flesh, hair, and psyche to bake, dry, and crumble just like the powdery, tortured stucco of the Geronimo.

I had little appetite under such conditions, which was just as well, as my money situation was pathetic. This fueled calculations on why it was better to save up for dope. When I bothered with food, it was usually from the understocked grocery store below the hotel. This meant bananas, canned soups, which I fixed on a hot plate, chocolate milk, candies. Sometimes I was lucky enough to get packs of matches from beside their cash register, but I still didn't buy tobacco.

Though at times a meager portion, I managed to find something to shoot every day. Some days I could afford only a few dollars' worth or got stuck doing up my cottons. When supplies got that low, I'd wait until the afternoon or even almost evening to take my shot. I'd lie down to ease pains, avoid heat and exertion to minimize sweats, stay alone to lessen sources of tension, take aspirins to fight off headaches. When I finally couldn't stand it any longer, I'd do up whatever I had. If it wasn't adequate, I'd find myself mulling the weird irony of feeling mentally intoxicated but still suffering the physical discomforts accumulated all day. High but sick. This incomplete, unpleasant effect left me lethargic, too lazy to get more and too tight and sore to be happy about it. The other side of the coin was even more common: enough for a decent shot, but within minutes after the initial rush I felt the inescapable sense of having had a thick coating of lead poured over my limbs, torso, and head. Far from being physically euphoric, it was as if my body weight had increased two- or threefold—just the thing when it's baking outside. After a shot, a joint, and a walk in the 110-degree heat, the Beat Generation had nothing on me.

This heavy feeling became such a common reaction that I sometimes didn't want the shot. And, if I held off long enough, my mind began to awaken and I no longer felt that physical weight. In other words, I had energy that I wouldn't have minded putting to good use. But, as the hours progressed, withdrawal pains magnified and I was soon faced with no choice but to end them with another shot. This, of course, covered me in lead, effectively ending any ideas for activity. So it was mandatory that I get high, a morbid experience.

I hated going out into the heat anyway; there was no way I'd subject myself to it under these conditions. Consequently, I unwillingly forestalled activities until nightfall. Almost invariably I could be found in my room during the day, but not that many people looked me up. My dealings lessened as my economic base weakened. Because I had so little money, anyone who saw me soon figured out they'd have to pay my way everywhere. Barring that, the only option was sitting around with me in my room, watching me smoke joints and nod out. Not that I didn't have takers for this gala event, but they were getting fewer and further between. When on a rare visit, I'd nod out in people's living rooms; looking up I'd catch them pointing at me. Even Nazi Paul didn't seem to be showing up much. It had been a while since I'd seen him when he tapped on my door one afternoon.

He took his usual seat, the dusty, gray-upholstered chair by the window, but there was a different air about him. Though he was just as emaciated, I saw a more active, livelier, *more frantic* look in his eyes. Lifting his knee up onto the chair, grasping it against his chest, why, he looked ready to vibrate right out of the room. He could hardly contain himself.

"Man, I have to thank you," he chattered. "That Valium you brought was just the thing. I don't think I would've been able to make it without that. Man, my legs were hurting me so bad, Christ, I was ready to go out and maybe do myself harm!" His eyes glimmered madly, and his mouth stretched as he spoke, revealing a glinting, skeletal set of teeth. The point where his lower jaw met his head seemed like a hinge that was threatening to come undone any second.

I assured him. "That was no problem. Hell, my father gets that stuff all the time. So." I peered sideways. "Were you successful?"

"Hell, yeah, I was! I've definitely cut back. Back to zero, man! Shit, I'm gonna lay off for a bit until I can get up some bread. Matter of economics, you know? Why spend thirty dollars on what I can get now for ten? Shit, I remember when I used to get—ahh, but that was a long time ago. . . . It's always just a matter of getting over that big hump. The day you came into my room was the worst. But that Valium was just the thing. Took the pain out of my legs and let me sleep for a while. Just what I needed. It wasn't all roses after that, but that was the big hump."

I recalled the time when I'd kicked in the downstairs room and Luke had given me that sleeping pill. In the nick of time it had pulled me through my worst day. Paul was right; there definitely was a big hump to get over in the kicking process. And that little bit of help I had made all the difference in the world. Wistfully, I viewed the pitch things had reached since then.

"Listen," Paul spoke up again. "I really hate to ask you this." His eyes narrowed to blue-gray slits, cold marbles that held more light than I'd ever seen in them before. "Could you lend me two dollars? I am so famished that my body feels like it's going to consume itself!" He widened his eyes on *self.*

"Oh, yeah, sure, no problem." I pulled a couple bills from my pocket.

"Man, thanks a lot! I knew I could count on you!"

He returned with packages of little cakes and pieces of fresh fruit. These he proceeded to wolf down like he'd just been freed from cruel captivity. "Shit, I got the chucks," he warbled, bits of apple falling from his mouth. After he finished, and it was very quick, he thanked me. "Man, I was so hungry I was to the point of insanity! I'll get you back that two bucks real soon, don't worry. I know you're short of money, too."

Everyone was short, not only with money but with supplies. Somehow I'd survived this far. An ambivalent sense of relief struck me as I recalled the victims of ill fortune who'd accumulated over the last month or so. Don C., the fair-haired, freckle-faced boy, unaware that he was spending his last hours in my room. That Mexican kid, in his clean, white T-shirt, his sneering white teeth, stained with blood from three bullet holes in his head. Marty, her hand-job career come to such a sudden end, viewing with horror an arm so inflated that it looked ready to detach and float away. I pictured some well-tracked, grotesque arm, bent at the elbow, lighter than air, bouncing around Yaqui Jim's ceiling.

Later that week I heard that Yaqui Jim's finally got busted. Well, they'd been doing a land-office business for months—what did they expect? A couple days later I was unable to score anything with anyone else when it suddenly occurred to me that it might be worthwhile to give them a try over there.

"No way," chimed Jim and Little Bill. "We don't have nothin'." They repeated this to a line of old customers; then, when we were alone, they produced a couple papers for me.

"Shit," moaned Jim. "I gotta come up with legal fees somehow. Now I only sell to people I *really* trust! What do the cops expect? Yeah, I've been doing it up myself, too. Now I see why all you guys like it so much." I might've raised an eyebrow, but he acted like I'd expressed true shock. "Yeah, that's right! Even *I'm* doing it now! Fuck, I gotta have *something* to help with the pressure. It's intense!"

One week later the cops raided their place again. It didn't take much to figure out they were still at it. And, again finding myself at loose ends, I of course showed up a few days later.

"No way," Jim and Bill repeated to me. "And this time we're not kidding!"

Their house, never overdecorated, looked more bare and decrepit than before. Nothing had been removed, but there was something about the white walls and the hard tile floors that echoed voices and reflected daylight differently. Almost as if the house itself was no longer intoxicated and was facing the boredom and flatness of life as best it could.

Jim rattled complaints to me like a businessman listing beefs, his mouth hanging open and his arms flailing and shrugging. Black, straight, shiny hair moved up and down his thick shoulders like a market graph gone wild. "Now I'm facing *two* counts of possession of heroin for sale. Busted twice in one fuckin' week! Whataya think that feels like?" His broad body faced me wherever I moved. "I'd rather just go to jail and get it started, get it over with as soon as I can. But now I suppose they're gonna fuck me around with that, too." He looked like he'd lost twenty pounds.

The whole scene was shaking and shivering like a poor junkie with a bad case of cotton fever. Nothing was dependable anymore. Anyone who knew what was happening from one day to the next kept it under his hat, jealously guarding a contact who might disappear in three days anyway. Almost no business took place during the day and not only because of horrendous heat. Not everyone had transportation to pursue wild goose chases that often extended past twelve at night. People were working or not at home or dealers simply wouldn't sell anything earlier because they believed that business didn't start until after dark. Then, after sunset, our tatterdemalion army swarmed over the town. Often running around past 2:00 A.M., I never felt safe after midnight. It was like trying to follow a script far too complex for a B movie, some long, dull adventure story that led to an anticlimax. If I hadn't been addicted, it would've been utterly pointless. The fact that I and everyone else was provided a stupid drive to the whole fiasco.

After I learned that it was useless to try to score before sunset, I spent summer-lengthened days reading and attempting to nap, the latter almost always a failure. Lying down produced a thin layer of sweat wherever my skin touched the bed. I'd turn over, savoring a coolness that lasted about two seconds when the moisture met air, then I'd lie there and feel sweat form on my other side. An interesting book was as good as gold during these dull days, and I remember spending many pleasurable hours, which I tried to stretch by reading slowly, with a copy of *The Job*, by the old junkie William S. Burroughs. A nonfiction interview collection on mainly scientific subjects, it contained esoteric facts rarely discussed elsewhere. He pursued investigations into the nature of junk addiction, citing successful cures forbidden in the United States. From what I could gather, heroin addiction (and many addictions) is the result of metabolic alterations in the body's chemistry. Ionic imbalances cause basic shifts in the body's clock, producing cravings and physical symptoms of withdrawal. For example, drug use blocks up calcium-related channels, so the brain creates others. When the drug is stopped, all the channels start firing. So taking calcium can reduce cravings, especially psychological ones. Substances also exist that can correct the body's metabolism. Apomorphine, a morphine derivative, is one. Naturally, it's illegal in the United States. None of this "once a junkie, always a junkie" routine but a logical, chemically based, sound reasoning that makes me wonder why our policy makers choose to extend the so-called drug problem when simple solutions for it exist. Of course, when one considers the money in the twin industries of law enforcement and drug dealing, this question answers itself. Once a junkie, always a junkie becomes a highly profitable political morality.

Burroughs's books are filled with tales from another time, stories of old-time junkies and alternative lifestyles of the Beat Era. He recalls junk corners like New York's 103rd and Broadway or Third Avenue and Fourteenth Street, and old characters with names like Joe the Mex, Old Ike, Pantapon Rose. These old-timers spent years sitting around coffee shops in their trench coats, dipping pound cake in coffee, waiting with eternal patience for their Man to show. Indeed, a check of some of the corners mentioned reveals that they are still frequented by gray, discreet customers, huddled in trench coats, still dunking cake in coffee. A row at the counter, still trying to stop time while waiting for their Man. Only now they all have names like Jason, Jeremiah, Justin, Joseph, Jeremy, and Joshua.

Richard started selling it. I went down to his lodge in the late mornings to purchase supplies for a day or two at a time. It was a convenience, this simply taking a walk across the courtyard lawn within the Geronimo proper, instead of a rambling, exhausting race around town. "This is what the place was made for," I thought.

"I think you're just buying back your own stuff," mentioned Paul. "I hear you went a little crazy down there the other night." He was referring to my giveaway session, but even that didn't bother me. Easy scores from Richard were well worth it. They brought a little stability into my life just when things were getting really chaotic and energy sapping.

One morning I awoke feeling more rested and relaxed than usual. I decided to lounge around my room, eat some breakfast, take it easy for a while instead of rushing right over to Richard's. At about 2:00 P.M. I mentioned to Paul that I was going down there.

"Oh, I don't think you want to do that," he observed. "I guess you haven't heard what happened."

I stopped in my tracks. "What do you mean?"

"They busted him this morning. He's l-o-n-g gone."

As my mouth fell open, I realized just how close I'd come to getting it myself. "Jesus, how much longer is my luck going to hold out? Yaqui Jim's got busted twice in one week, and it was only luck that I wasn't over there when it happened. Man!" I hit myself in the head. "I usually go down in the mornings to cop from Richard. It's just blind luck that I decided to wait until this afternoon!"

"Yeah, well, blind luck. That about sums it up. I don't think they were very happy with him. They tore that place apart, came down on him pretty hard." Paul winced as he recalled it.

"Why, what'd he do, rob a drugstore?"

"I don't know. Judging by the way they took his place apart, I could believe it. I told you I didn't like that pharmacy business. It sounds great, but they really come down on you hard for it."

I shook my head absently. "Mmm. I guess we won't be seeing him for a while."

So, it was back to the old grind. After hours of chasing down leads, I ended up one night in a strange house down by Punks' Park, on Fourth Ave. I bought papers and did a shot with people whom I'd never seen before, whom I'd never see again. They were tense with me until they saw that syringe go into my arm. In fact, they didn't want to let me leave until they had. I reluctantly used the filthy fit they offered. One of the guys was on parole and hit himself in the back of his hand. It was covered with freckles, which made for pretty good camouflage, but he was displeased with the mark he'd left.

"Shit! Look at that. All I need is for my parole officer to see it."

I meandered the five or six dark blocks back to the Geronimo. Silent, spectacular sheets of heat lightning flashed on the eastern horizon. No thunder, no rain; more unfulfilled promises. I hung out in the nighttime lobby for a while, went upstairs, rolled cigarettes, smoked out on the porch, fought off anxiety attacks.

"My God! What's going to happen to me?"

The next afternoon I found myself up at Park and Speedway, a busy university intersection, loitering around the Jack in the Box, trying to figure out my next move. I was hungry but didn't bother wasting money on food. It only caused nausea in the heat. The traffic went shooting by, giving me an unpleasant feeling of insignificance. Summer session students passed me, lolling through the baking sun. Rigid, combative college girls regarded me with distaste. They wore cutoffs and reminded me of girls in elementary school who drew horse pictures. Some would snort around the grounds acting like horses. Now some were starting to look like them. It was depressing to watch so many future government workers, young men and women who were soon going to learn just how worthless a degree really is. Hopefuls who didn't know that their minds were taking a busy walk to the end of a long gangplank before they dove into the workpool. All the subjects they'd studied so avidly would be nothing less than despised. Just drones, really. Drays and drones.

A warm wind brushed me incessantly. My blue jeans felt like two rolls of burning canvas around my legs. I was soaked, and I stunk. Crisp, yellowed newspapers rippled and crinkled around my feet. Out of boredom I picked one up.

An article at the top of the page caught my eye, something about a local chemist. He'd just sold a brand-new, six-hour heroin cure to a California medical firm. Something about drinking a solution of three salts—sodium, calcium, and potassium—then repeating the process six hours later. That's all it took? The guy's name was David Blackman.

That took me aback. I'd known a David Blackman a few years earlier, a big, sloppy, Jewish-looking guy with whom I'd attended antiwar rallies. We'd taken our draft physicals together. Seemed like a real goofball, but upon further reflection I realized that he was just the type to study chemistry then invent something this earthshaking. Well, it was earthshaking to me, anyway. As it turned out, the whole treatment was just buried, and I never heard another word about it. Today, people to whom I mention this simple cure express complete disbelief. They cannot comprehend that the so-called drug problem might have such a simple solution. That would make it a totally fabricated affair, and *that* makes them feel very uncomfortable, like someone's shaking a rug out from under them.

A couple nights later I was roaming around that area and actually encountered David Blackman. He looked almost exactly as I remembered: baggy pants, shirt hanging out, black, bushy hair, Semitic appearance, a real space case. He was quite suspicious when I approached him. Now, I figured that this guy Blackman owed me one for a favor I'd done him at our draft physical.

Determined to get a deferment, he had appeared there in an old army jacket covered with a plethora of antiwar buttons. This was already a sure hit at the Phoenix induction center, but he juiced up the outfit by pinning a dead bird to one pocket and a bag of shit to the other. Clearly, he wished to demonstrate his unsuitability for the armed forces. We got to talking up there.

Not everybody wanted "out" at that physical; in fact, many were hopeful of passing and looked forward to their military stints. Unlike the regular personnel, these young recruits had few constraints on them and soon made Blackman an object of their attentions. To escape he visited my room. Four pursuers found him lying on my floor and began dragging him out by his feet, sliding him on his ass. He was absolutely terrified. I yelled at them to stop, which, to my surprise, they did. For that, Blackman was grateful. The next day, despite all his valiant efforts, he got classified 1-A.

After reading that fascinating article, then running into him, I wasn't going to take no for an answer when I queried him

about his formula. I had already learned about ionic imbalances through Burroughs, but my unusual knowledge only
made him more suspicious at first. I finally calmed him down,
recalled our draft physical, and got him to open up. I'm sure
that my appearance, which by that point was pretty beaten, had
something to do with his hesitancy.

"You mean all someone has to do," I asked, "is mix spoonfuls of calcium, potassium, and sodium salts in a glass of water,
drink it, and do it again six hours later?"

His brow rose into a shock of curly, black hair. "That's just
about it. Not exactly, but you could almost describe it like
that."

I thought a bit. "Of course! Since it's an ionic imbalance of
the metabolic system, and since salts are a great source of ions,
why, that explains a lot!"

"Hmm." He frowned. "You *do* know a lot about this, don't
you? Where did you find out about this stuff?" I could see the
words "industrial espionage" dancing around his brain.

"Don't worry," I assured him. "My interest is purely personal. But, yes, I do read a lot about it." I refrained from telling
him just how personal my interest was.

"Those salts are three of the four body salts," he added.
"The treatment helps with kicking nicotine, too."

We sat at a bus bench and, as the evening got cooler, carried
on one of the most captivating conversations I've ever had.
The cars continued to whisk by, but I didn't find them nearly
as depressing.

After midnight, in the cool hours, I roamed through the
graceful arches and dark passages of the Geronimo. How I
wished I could've lingered in those shadows forever. I soon arrived down in the main lobby. Finding it empty, I felt at my
ease, surveying aged furniture and the huge portraits of prim

old women in frilly collars. They gazed down from large frames, some glowering severely, others regarding me with kind serenity. In the corner stood an old phone booth made entirely of polished oak and glass. It had a seat so smooth from use that you almost slid off when making a call. On the east wall remained the frame of a large fireplace. It was sealed off, and a black-and-white TV sat in it, resting on a cheap, brass-colored frame with wheels. I leaned back into a cushion of the hotel's humming calm, replete in the plush security of a once classy chair.

With obstinate homing instincts, my mind continually returned to my situation, to my conversation with the chemist, to my readings about addiction. Obviously, I was dwelling more and more on the possibilities and intricacies of—did I dare say it?—kicking.

"Why pay thirty dollars on what I can get now for ten?" I remembered Nazi Paul's logic.

Mark, who had been nursing his own habit for a while now, commented, "It's easy to think about quitting when I'm on the stuff, but when I'm not and it's time to start trying, it's next to impossible." As it turned out, Mark's wealth supported his habit for years. He eventually experienced "reverse tolerance." This is the last stage of addiction, when the body rarely feels high, instead demanding dosage just to feel normal. The user doesn't have to reach this stage if he avoids constant overindulgence, choosing moderation instead, even if it includes regularity. Addiction doesn't have to be a spiral of need. Intravenous use, however, changes this, and tolerance readily increases with the needle. Be a food hog, get fat. Drink like a fish, become an alcoholic. Be a junk-hog, develop reverse tolerance.

I thought of old alcoholics I knew, sloshing down copious amounts of booze, always seeking the pleasant lightness of their first drinks but never really feeling it again. They were obsessed with chasing an illusion in a body embroiled in metabolic war. Alcohol is the worst taskmaster, for it leaves the system quickly then demands to be replaced, allowing no time for food or sleep. And the only alternative alkies ever hear is that, since they're sick, they must stop, never drink again and see a shrink. This just didn't ring true to me. It ignores the physical disease that addiction is. The "once a junkie, always a junkie" crowd, the either/or simpletons spouting off about "cold turkey—that's the only way!" I just didn't buy it. Even without my investigations I instinctively knew that their philosophy was incorrect. Imagine someone who doesn't even have the discipline to cut 1,500 calories from his or her weekly diet heartily urging "cold turkey" on someone else.

I asked myself, would my problem even exist today if I had money and an adequate supply? A resounding "No!" practically echoed off dusty venetian blinds and rattled around the Reader's Digest Books huddled in old shelves. Then I remembered how unrewarding my shots had been of late, the leaden feeling that poured over me a few minutes after the initial rush. I was obsessed with an illusion. I was hooked on that needle's "Inside Touch." Like an old lush hankering after his initiate's body of bygone days, my mind dwelt wistfully on the pleasures of having my own rich supply of dope. How I could sell it! Pictures of smug repose poured into my brain, the sheer enjoyment of never having to run around this burning, lousy town for dope again!

With a warrior's stubborn resourcefulness, I nursed an image hatching in my mind's eye. It started with the Ptolemaic cube that I remembered as Richard's lodge, and with practiced, calculating efficiency, I peeled away the burned, flat lighting, the dark gateways to empty space, and erased the half dozen leering junkies malodorously glistening in there. The room, I realized, was now empty. Legends came to mind of fiends sneaking into busted rooms and houses after the cops had left, ripping open mattresses and finding *ounces* of heroin. Why, anything that the police had missed was lying there, *right now*, waiting for the first taker! This simple possibility all but floored me. I sat unmoving in the lobby chair, dreaming and scheming. Dawn drifted in around me. That gentle, blue, cottony light just before the sun appears. It's when time takes a breather. I quivered in this diluvian dawn, balanced between "Don't bother, it's useless and you might get caught" and "It's there to be had by the first taker."

By the time I rousted myself, the sun was up. It was a weekend morning; very quiet, everyone sleeping in. The course was clear: *I had to take a look.*

It was only about 5:30 A.M., but outside the temperature was feverish. An unpleasant warmth festered in the courtyard. It was already close to 90 degrees, and the buzzing cicadas were fitfully starting and stopping, influencing the dreams of sleepers and announcing another scorcher. The sun hadn't yet risen above the roofs, and I snuck between the shade of flame trees and thick bushes. I didn't want to be seen at all, not even by another junkie. As I skulked through the shadows, along the edge of the lawn, along the wall, I surveyed an eerily desolate court. It was like sunrise at an ancient ruin. Doves cooed long and mournfully. I slipped into the bushes next to lodge Number 1.

The door facing the street had been torn from its hinges and stood open invitingly. After peeking into a window to determine it was empty, I made a sudden spring into the lodge. It was totally unlike I remembered. Sunlight streamed incongruously through windows that had been black eternities. The long wooden floorboards dazzled me with glare. No furniture remained; not a nightstand or a chair. Only a beaten, half-collapsed, stripped bed. The mattress was already knifed wide open. Halfheartedly, I lifted it up and looked under it, then dug around in the cut, finding nothing. The destruction laid down by the police raiding party was overwhelming. Every door in the place was torn off the hinges. Holes, big holes had been punched into the walls, the floors, the closets. Any barrier, any conceivable hiding place for dope had been enthusiastically bashed apart. No regard had been shown for the property owners. The violence of that morning echoed stark and real in the silence. Amidst those shambles it was painful to imagine what they'd done to Richard. Soon it was clear that my treasure-hunting brainstorm had no merit. I gave up.

I had remained vigilant, tucking myself into a wrecked closet whenever I heard a passing car. From this vantage point I could peek out without being seen. None had been cops. Then my head and body froze to involuntary alertness. The sound of tires from a slow-moving car pierced my reverie. I made the quick jump into the closet.

A softly purring vehicle halted. Shit! I backed into the shadows and didn't move, praying that I hadn't been seen. Ten or fifteen seconds passed. The car gunned its engine and moved again, but not far. Stealthily, I moved my head, letting the frame of the open front door come into view. Suddenly I saw part of a white car hood and jerked my head back. Tucson Police cars are white. The car wasn't moving. Very stiffly I edged my head some millimeters until the doorframe again came into view. Then the white tip of the car. Then a blue number painted on the side, by the headlight. Cursing softly in the shadows, I pulled back and held my breath.

The cop must've seen something. He was just sitting there, his motor purring. This went on for tense minutes. Finally he moved his car a few feet forward again to change his vantage point. And he just sat there. I couldn't budge. He was obviously quite vigilant and not very busy. Shit! Somebody call this guy on his radio! I was stiff from squeezing myself into that little demolished nook. He could've stepped out and walked the few yards into the lodge.

Eventually, to my relief, I heard the car move away. Even then I waited another minute. Then I got on my hands and knees and crawled to the door, first peeking out the window to make sure the coast was clear. I burst from the doorway and rapidly blended into the trees and bushes, quickly putting distance between me and lodge Number 1.

The sun was now over the rooftops, and I felt sweat on my brow. Buzzing in the yard had reached full pitch. Different birds were chattering above the cooes of the doves. As I scampered past the lodges toward the hotel and safety, I noticed an alleycat, a gray, roughhousing tom. It was perched on its haunches, holding a loud, buzzing cicada in its mouth without crushing it. The insect was vibrating madly and must've been shaking the cat's head into a stony state. Natural high. The cat, out of habit, glanced furtively to the left and right, but I could tell that it really wasn't very vigilant.

Paul had been keeping himself scarce. He hadn't been buying dimes from me or anyone else. No one knew where he'd been hiding, so I was surprised when he knocked on my door.

"Here's that two dollars back. Thanks a lot. I don't know what I would've done without it." He sat down in a hard-back chair instead of his usual seat. I was looking at a meaner, healthier Paul, with more meat on his bones, more color in his skin, and a wide-awake, vicious glint in his eyes. Clearly, he was not intoxicated. Showing a disdain for my reconnaissance of Richard's lodge, he let on that he'd fruitlessly scavenged it before me. After some introductory patter, he began more serious conversation.

"You know," he offered, "those Nazis weren't all bad. They actually had some good ideas about improving society, economics, stuff like that."

"Well, some people like that stuff," I mouthed. "That's their business. I don't care what people do as long as they leave me alone." I resigned myself to more tired old Nazi horseshit.

He continued his piercing regard of me. "For instance, we should've let them carry out some of their programs on the Jews. The world would've been a lot better off, you know. If they had just had a couple more years they could've gotten them all. Those Jews have been making things bad for people like you and me for a long time. Yep." He nodded. "In prison we're pretty hip to this stuff. A lot of people have the right idea up in those jails. They're pretty right on. That's where I realized they know what they're talking about."

I was not really in the mood for this recruitment speech. "Now, how do the Jews affect people like you and me? They don't even give a shit about us."

"Bull*shit!* Why do you think that people like you and me are stuck down here on the bottom of the economic ladder? The Jews are the ones that control the world's money markets. They're behind the big business moves and all that." He shook his head, turning his palm up lightly. "Check it out sometime, man. If you look close enough, you'll see that it's the Jews that control the world monetary scene."

"Oh, just because somebody's Jewish doesn't mean that they're greedy. Shit, there's probably Jews that would do something nice for you."

"Oh, you're missing the point. There's probably a few nice ones." Then he shook his head, making a downward cutting motion with his hand. "No, never mind! I take it back. There's not. If somebody's Jewish it means that they have it out for someone like me!"

"Well, now, I don't know about that. You might've had somebody do something nice for you and not even known that they were Jewish."

"That I seriously doubt."

I leaned back, looking him full in the eye. "You know that I've done you more than one favor, and I'm Jewish."

His eyes sparked, and his head jerked back like I'd slapped him. Then his mouth fell open. Collecting himself, he shook his head gravely. "Man, I really wish you hadn't of told me that. Now, why did you have to go and say something like that, huh?"

For some reason I felt embarrassed. A red flush burned my face as I groped for words. "Well, really, I hardly think—I mean, I've been pretty generous to you sometimes. That proves not all Jews are bad."

Nazi Paul rose sternly from his chair. "Man, I don't believe you! Shit! I'm gonna leave before I do something I'm sorry for later!" He exited, slamming the door behind him.

He looked like he wanted to break my jaw.

14 Paul disappeared after that. Big deal—I'd liked him better strung out.

Days later my eye was caught by a blurb in the local paper. Describing a Southern Arizona Bank robbery, it said that the armed robber, impatient at the tellers' speed, had jumped marble-covered counters, then run the row of windows, shoveling money into the bag himself. Jumping back over, he slipped on the slick floor, sending money flying.

At those last words a shockingly clear picture popped into mind: the robber slipping and sliding on the bank's shiny floor with an embarrassed, tense grin, waving his gun around, recovering as much cash as possible before complete panic grabbed him. I imagined the nightmarish cartoon horror felt by the bumbling fool, tottering in a crowd of shocked, gawking, *nor-*

mal citizens. An involuntary whisper blew from the canyons of intuition.

"That was Stupid."

So Nazi Paul had resumed his old profession. He'd been destitute for so long that I was surprised it hadn't happened before. I'd suspected he'd been thinking about it. ("Sell my gun? No way!") Well, I thought, I hope he gets to spend the money this time.

Being almost completely out of funds myself, I hardly ate. I remember borrowing quarters from people to buy bean burros. Revulsion still boils up when I recall their self-righteous moralizing at my needing and requesting this large sum. It probably would've been easier to beg change, but the idea has never appealed to me.

I barely managed to feed my habit from occasional visitors requesting papers. Apparently word had spread, and acquaintances I hadn't seen for years looked me up. One, a high school friend named John, had been in jail numerous times but just couldn't stay off the needle. He'd even burglarized my house once, but desperate as I was for junk and money, I discarded qualms about getting stuff for him. The son of a successful Tucson lawyer, he must've been a total embarrassment to his dad with the police record he was building. I sometimes see him these days, a chronic junkie, lids drooping, a name tag on his wrist from a recent con of some hospital emergency room. He seems unable to leave the path that's leading to a lifetime prison sentence. At that time he was sleeping on a friend's couch and mentioned that he was staying about a half block away.

This hand-to-mouth existence was quite uncompelling. I was completely at the mercy of waiting for someone, anyone to show up at my door asking for dope. I avoided the mirror, for large, round, black shadows under my eyes accented an already consumptive appearance. Because I was rarely getting the amount of dope I wanted, my habit had probably been reduced, but, because I had shot up every day of the previous five or six months, it would still brook no long interruption. About this time I sold my car—for fifty dollars. It was a relief to get rid of the irascible vehicle, and the cash was like manna from heaven. It was soon gone. With no money and the difficulty of finding dope, I finally concluded that when I ran out of stuff again I'd just curl up on my mattress and, for better or worse, kick.

As always, it was easier to plan and imagine this course of action after I'd taken a shot. But a greater irony was that after I had chosen this course, when I had virtually not a cent, people came by daily who had heard that I was in a bad way and returned favors or showed appreciation for past business. For a week I received enough to stave off withdrawal symptoms and sometimes get high. Every day I was mentally prepared to start suffering, and every day someone would surprise me.

Then I'd grab my spot on the third-floor porch, puff on cigarettes, try to dream and fight off anxiety attacks until dawn. At those hours no business took place, no one was awake, no opportunities materialized. Nothing happened. Cool, postmidnight air seemed the only advantage of my time out there.

On nights that I wasn't adequately sedated, a restlessness drove me to wander up and down nearby blocks. Most were residential, but around the main gates of the university a block and a half away sat a couple silent rows of gloomily lit closed stores waiting to capture what little summer business might show when the sun rose. These were filled with such knick-knacks as records, sweatshirts with school logos, equipment for hamburgers and tacos and ice cream. All made me feel alienated, for I had no use for any of these things. Women's boutiques displayed obnoxious, expensive patterns. Bookstores offered selections so costly that I couldn't imagine paying for one when I knew I could better utilize the money for a couple decent shots and a snack. I strolled by a jewelry store, its windows mostly cleaned out for the night. Those few items, fancy watches and cheap rings, glimmering behind the glass, were so irrelevant to my existence that it depressed me to see them. Fighting despondency, I wandered over to where John was staying. I smoked a joint with my high school friend, keeping up a front to disguise the insignificance and despair that I felt. His friend Mac, whose house it was, stayed inside and ignored us. He didn't smoke much or use dope, but he'd seen so much shit that our activities just rolled off his back. The evening was cooling off, but the pot, sensitizer that it is, only intensified my depression. I knew it useless to moan to John, so, keeping a stiff upper lip, I returned to my dull little room.

There I fell prey to the plague of any who carry the burden of imagination—boredom. The steady hum of coolers, with their unchanging, almost subliminal vibrations, taunted my lack of options and brought bursts of exasperation gusting from my lips. Wind rustling through the trees caught my attention, then angered me by failing to provide a punch line. A beetle with its leg caught in the screen buzzed oafishly. I stewed up my usual imagery of blown deals and uncollected money, the blockade that kept a world of enticing possibilities from me. If-onlys beckoned maddeningly through the mirage. Pictures of a long gone pile of twenty-dollar bills greened in my mind's eye. I saw a repetitive scene: my hand holding money, then collecting stacks of papers again and again. Like a broken record, and the only way of escaping it was by imagining a languid dreaming in cool, dark mornings of seasons past. This produced a hungry longing for just a taste of the river of shots that had carried me relentlessly to this point.

My arms and hands tingled, not from lack of dope but from

stubborn, seething energies: I was completely bored, and I needed something to do. But in order to do something I needed money. But I had to figure out something to do to get money. But I had nothing to do. This little whirlwind of circular logic soon spun a colorful picture in my idle brain. A shimmering, static scene, accompanied by a sudden, absolute conviction of ability. Charging me with the knowledge that it was there, a still life appeared of the early-morning fluorescent window in the jewelry store.

No traffic passed on the dark street outside. The silence pounding in my ears as I sat on the bed was, I knew, the same silence that I'd hear when I stood in front of that window. My mind focused on a brief fantasy. I walk half a block down the empty street, a rock in my hand, break the display window, coolly reach in to help myself to whatever is there, ignore the clanging alarm bell. In this scenario the bell was ringing but it had no sound. And I was filled with the conviction that *I could do it!* It was there to be taken! All I had to do was get off my ass and do it!

I phased with a parallel universe of possibilities. A nod and a smile autonomously moved my head. That action caused a reaction: I stood up. I put on a jacket. It was warm out, but I knew I'd need the pockets.

In a light and buoyant body, I stealthily left the room, easing the door shut behind me, then slipping down the back stairs of the Geronimo. There was something utterly thrilling about finally taking my fate into my hands. The release of energy was soothing. Again I ran the scenario through my mind. Survey the street. Walk to the display window. Firmly, assertively smash a rock through it, and confidently reach in and help myself to whatever I could grab. Ignore the alarm bell. Keep my fingerprints off of glass and anything else. I could run over to where John was staying, a mere half block from both the store and the hotel. John would know where to sell the stuff. I knew that there wasn't much there, but they left a few things out every night. Not much for them could be a lot for me. Reaching the sidewalk, I quickly scanned the street. Empty and silent. I picked up a good, heavy rock, about twice the size of a softball. It was from a riverbed, and its warm smoothness, radiating the day's heat, was soothing. Placing it in my jacket pocket, I continued toward the store without breaking stride. The street was abandoned. Approaching the shop, I took deep, slow breaths. I was so glad finally to have something to do! No use lingering around the place, no leery passing back and forth. I simply stopped in front of the display window and looked both ways. No cars, no sound of traffic on side streets. The window had a set of wrought-iron bars in front, which I hadn't considered, but with careful aiming the rock would fit through. I held my breath and aimed.

A startling sound of crashing glass was immediately covered by garish ringing of the alarm bell. The quaint little display of overpriced watches, all the same model with different-colored bands, had a huge piece of glass land right on top of them. When I reached in to move it, I cut my finger. A nice, clear, bloody fingerprint glared back at me. Hastily sticking the piece of glass into my pocket, I filled the other pockets with about six or eight watches and a couple of cheap rings. Then I took off down the street, the alarm growing more faint the farther I ran. As I turned the corner, I slowed to a brisk walk, passing through an empty lot over to John's house. His friend Mac answered the door immediately.

"Is John here?" I asked, forcing my panting back, making my voice quiver. I could feel sweat glistening on my face. That absurd piece of glass was still in my pocket. My friend came to the door and let me in. I had made it!

"Hey, John, how's it going? Can I use your bathroom?

Come on in there. I want to talk to you." My diaphragm felt almost uncontrollable with vibration.

Since John was a junkie thief from way back, he didn't see anything odd about my request. When he closed the bathroom door, I produced the watches, the piece of glass, my bloody finger. I had bled all over the inside of my jacket pocket. The glass had a long strip of that silver tape used for burglar alarms. The watches had blood on them.

John gave a little wry snort. "So you're the one that set off that alarm, eh? I had a feeling you might do something by the way you were talking tonight. Shit, that looks like a pretty bad cut. We oughta let Mac look at that. He used to be a medic in Vietnam—he'll take care of it. Why don't you put those watches away? Shit, you brought the glass with you, too?"

The medic came in, looked a long second at the glass with silver tape, shrugged, and went about washing and bandaging my finger. The deep cut stung horribly under the water; in fact it brought tears to my eyes. In my adrenalined state I laughed it off. A small, ugly gash, but I wasn't going anywhere to get stitches. The last place I wanted to be was in an emergency room. John seemed a bit embarrassed by the glass shard. After all, he was sleeping there on the good graces of the other guy.

"Here, why don't we just get rid of this little thing?" He picked it up and disposed of it, then returned. "Shit, you shoulda just dropped it somewhere. I wish that Mac hadn't of seen that. Well, don't worry, I don't think he'll say anything."

"You want to buy these watches?" I asked.

"Shit, I don't have any money. But don't worry, I think I know someone we can talk to. We can go there tonight if you have a car."

"Well, I sold my car. Maybe we can go there tomorrow."

"Naw," drawled John. He was completely at ease with the situation. Me, my heart was still pounding, and I was having trouble catching my breath. Having to talk in whispers made it worse.

"Maybe," John volunteered, "I can get Mac to lend me his car. We need to get this stuff out of here." He disappeared for a minute, then came back with the keys. "Okay, let's go. Listen, don't say you were here."

We climbed into an old, white car, drove down the alley and out onto the street. When we hit a red light on University Blvd., I looked furtively to my left. A private security car was in front of the store, along with a city cop car. The goddamn bell was still yammering away.

"Hmm," mumbled John. "Wonder what happened there?"

I was glad when the light changed. He drove to a nearby neighborhood, close to Manny's old place, and we entered some little hovel. There we were met by a pretentious Mexican junk dealer. In his bright red beret and slick purple shirt, he looked like a foreign fashion plate. Huge water marks on the walls made the room look like recent ocean salvage.

I threw the watches on the table. "What'll you give me for these?"

"Ah, shit." He sneered. "I don't want this fuckin' stuff. Get that shit outta here." The guy was totally disgusted. I felt my buoyancy deflating. The adrenaline was wearing off.

John stepped in and bargained for me. "Hey, don't worry, Eddie," he cajoled. "This is good stuff. I can sell one of these for you tomorrow. I'll get you twenty for one of these watches for sure." John smiled and fingered the goods. "Shit, I wouldn't mind havin' one of these for myself. Yeah, this is nice stuff. I can sell it easy. Why don't you take all of these and let us have a couple dimes tonight? I can definitely sell one of those for you tomorrow."

The Mexican waffled around a bit, then consented to the deal. "Don't say you were here, man," he warned me. John handed me one of the papers. I had just smashed a jewelry store window and stolen the paltry contents for one thin dime. It was nice to get that hot stuff off my bloody hands.

Back in the car John seemed pleased with himself. "See? That's how you deal with people like that."

I longed for the sanctuary of my little room.

"Let me know if you happen to come up with any more of that kind of stuff," John cheerily suggested when he dropped me off at the lobby of the Geronimo.

"I doubt I'll be coming up with any more." I frowned.

Quietly I unlocked my door, hoping that no one had seen me come or go. As I finally caught my breath, I saw that I'd have to change the dressing on my wound. It hadn't stopped bleeding, soaking through the bandage. I fashioned a clumsy setup with layers of toilet paper and Scotch tape. The white paper stuck out like a beacon, and I automatically began to devise some cock-and-bull story to explain it. The coolers weren't running, and I could almost hear the exchanges as I rehearsed them in my mind.

"Yeah, locked myself out of my room and tried to get the lock open with a knife. Practically sliced off my finger, heh, heh."

"Where'd you get the knife?"

". . . tried to get the lock open with a knife *I borrowed* . . ."

As far as I could figure it, my makeshift bandage was the only indication that I was connected with the store incident. I'd seen nobody on the street from before I smashed the window until I knocked on John's door. Of course, I couldn't be sure that I'd gone completely unnoticed. Perhaps someone had seen me after all. But I was sure that no one had seen where I'd run to. I also knew that there were no fingerprints. Most of what I had touched was just the felt material that's often found in jewelry store displays. The shard of glass with my bloody fingerprint on it was disposed of.

A clear image of that bloody glass, first on top of the watches, then sitting on John's bathroom sink made me lower my head into my hand. I squeezed the bridge of my nose between my thumb and forefinger, shaking my head. "Jesus!" I laughed softly, filled with embarrassment. My nose crinkled involuntarily.

Fingerprints weren't a problem anyway, since I'd never been arrested. As far as I could see, the only weak points in the whole affair were the people whom I'd gotten involved. I knew John wouldn't talk. I prayed that his roommate wouldn't. The guy who took the watches wouldn't be able to place me; we'd never seen each other before. After a lot of rationalization and self-assurance, I convinced myself that it was safe to go to sleep without doing up the paper; the cops probably wouldn't show up at my door before I shot up in the morning. In a dead exhaustion I fell rapidly to sleep.

I awoke feeling well-rested and relaxed. This pleasant feeling lasted about two seconds, until the ludicrous tape and toilet paper affair on my finger came into view. Another poorly paying project had been completed. I understood that I'd have to take a step I'd been avoiding. There seemed no way out of it: I would have to contact my father and take advantage of his professional contacts to get methadone assistance and kick.

Months before I never would've entertained such a notion. Since then I'd skidded through so many humiliating scenes, had poured so much energy into fallacious deals, had presented so many self-deprecating con stories to get money or dope that I thought I had become immured to self-abasement. Calling him felt like just another con I had to pull to get relief.

My father, as usual, was not thrilled to hear from me.

"How long has this been going on?" he muttered in a low, professorial voice.

"About six months." I wasn't sure, but that would do.

"And how much do you do a day?"

"Six dimes," I lied. I wanted to make sure of getting enough medication wherever I might end up.

"Jesus, you really are strung out, aren't you?"

"Mmm-hmmm. . . ."

"Well, I'll have to get back to you after I make a couple phone calls."

As I expected, I felt utter repulsion at talking to an authority, a professional in the social services and my father to boot. After being so secretive, it went against my grain. All of my disgust for the social services came back in a rush, buried reactions developed over decades of listening to endless double talk, a feature of all psychologists' households. The countless accusations of being passive-aggressive; seeing my mother whither under charges of practicing transference; hearing Möbius intonations from my father that began "I see a pattern here . . ." and mysteriously turned into "I resent. . . ." Had I detected a hidden degree of satisfaction in my father's tone? Was there pleasure in finally bringing the rebellious son under the influence of the profession? All of these things I thought, then rapidly pushed them into the vault where I hid other revolting memories I'd collected: Nazi Paul's skull; Manny's mottled stomach; my crimson, oozing tracks; Andy's lips turning blue; Dee-Dee's Brooklyn face.

The phone rang again. My father. "Okay, I got you on a waiting list for a program run by a psychiatrist I know down at County Hospital. The list is about six weeks long."

"Six weeks? Can't you get him to do you a favor and move me up on it?"

"I've done that. But you'll still have to wait three days. They're only allowed ten beds in this ward, and they're already over the state limit. Can you wait three days?"

"Well, it doesn't sound like I have much choice." I shuddered with nervous despair. How would I be able to supply myself for the next three days?

"You'll have to wait. You're the one that got yourself into this mess. I made an appointment for you to start the process tomorrow. They have to interview you first, to make sure you qualify."

"Qualify?" Disgust at having to qualify for the clutches of psychiatrists and social workers combined seismically with annoyance at actually hoping I would, plus the realization that I'd just tipped my whole rotten hand and still didn't have what I wanted. The appointment was for late the next morning.

Impulsively, I stepped outside. It was almost noon. I didn't want any more paternal phone conversation. Drawn irresistibly toward the scene of my crime, I spied the owner of the jewelry store, a tall, thin, balding man in a gray suit, out in front of his shop. He was sweeping up piles of broken glass. The iron bars were still in place, even though the store was open for business. Coolly, I stuck my bandaged finger into my pants pocket as I walked by. The owner glared into my eyes. Pure anger radiated from his every pore as he regarded me. Rather than avoid his look, I put on a questioning expression of surprise at the mess on the ground. The owner was giving all the passersby the same treatment. I saw that he had no particular suspicions of me. My bloody finger felt like an unlawful object hidden snugly in my pocket. Once safely past the scene, I let elation and cruel humor envelop me.

The next morning, after a small shot, I took a series of bus rides down to South Tucson and the County Hospital. South Tucson, a one-square-mile township, has steadfastly refused to be incorporated into Tucson proper and has ended up being completely surrounded by it. It's mostly nonwhite and antiwhite. When I transferred onto one of their 1940s buses and into that foreign, crumbling part of town, I felt like I was entering a time warp, a disconcertingly familiar feeling. Used tire and body shops, run-down bars, and good Mexican restaurants gave the streets the atmosphere of a border town. These and dope were the backbones of their economy.

The County Hospital was a deteriorating edifice, which has since been torn down. A waiting room offered rows of horribly colored plastic chairs, all facing front. Emergency cases found them quite uncomfortable, some choosing to lie on the filthy concrete floor instead. I gave my name to a cheerful Mexican woman behind a glass window, who found it on a list and called me in a few minutes later. She directed me to the small office of an older, white, blond nurse, who took the particulars. She was the one who would "qualify" me. A look at my arms seemed adequate for her.

"How much do you do a day?" she asked. Her voice was calm and friendly.

"Six dimes."

"You've worked up to that much in six months?" She sat back, surprised. Putting her pencil down, she looked me in the eyes as she continued. "Now, Mr. Frank, a lot of people want to exaggerate their daily dose because they're afraid they won't get enough methadone once they're in here. But you don't have to worry about that. The first couple days they'll give it to you whenever you ask, until you're comfortable. So don't worry about not getting enough. Have you actually been doing six dimes a day?"

I admitted that I'd been doing only two dimes. Actually, I'd gotten by with even less. Some days only five dollars' worth, but that left me uncomfortable and sick enough to make me afraid of kicking without assistance. The nurse seemed to accept the lower figure. The lines around her eyes and mouth loosened a bit. These were crevices formed by a life of self-denial. She seemed to be laboring under a ceaseless, leaden fatigue. Long, blond hairs covered with face powder ran from her cheeks to the backs of her jaw.

"The body detoxes itself after eighteen hours," she explained. "The methadone covers up the pains and discomforts of kicking without actually fixing you. All of the symptoms are there, you just don't feel them while you're on it. But you can only take methadone until you're over the withdrawals; otherwise you'll end up being addicted to it instead."

Having known people who were methadone addicts, I knew that its kick was twice as bad as heroin's. "I dreamt I was a flying gorilla," claimed Earl, describing it. "I flew up, up, up into the sky and exploded and woke up and it was finally over. Make no mistake, it was hell."

I felt that I knew more about the general topic than the nurse did. She was surprised as I explained concepts of ionic imbalance and metabolic disease, but she was open to the ideas.

"How did you cut your finger?" Casually she motioned to the ridiculous paper and Scotch tape bandage.

I unleashed my well-rehearsed spiel—the locked door, the borrowed knife, making sure to stress idiocy. "That's what made me realize I'd better get help," I embroidered.

She remained doubtful. "When methadone candidates arrive here with injuries such as yours," she explained in her genial manner, "we find that they're often connected to some incident. Are you sure that's how you cut your finger?"

"Oh, definitely. I've never done burglary or any of that stuff. I know a lot of people who have, but I've always avoided it."

"We've found," she warmly and obstinately continued, "that when we check the police logs for incidents that have occurred near the residences of the people applying here, they're often involved. We cannot allow people into this program when they've committed these crimes. Did you get that breaking into someplace?"

Of course, I felt like admitting to it so I could end up kicking in a *jail cell.* For the first time I thought that this "qualifying round" was starting to get difficult. Keeping up a lighthearted portrayal, I presented my idiot self as having been illuminated to seek help by an accidentally cut finger. I didn't see how I would be helped by undergoing felony prosecution. I was relieved when she finally let the subject drop. Bandages were provided to replace my improvisations.

Toward the end of the interview, she reminded me that I wouldn't get into the ward for a couple more days, then handed me a little packet of pills for help with cramps. "These will make your mouth really dry, but avoid drinking water. Take them at the first sign of symptoms. Don't wait. And don't worry, I think you'll find them pretty helpful."

"Ah, yes, it probably gets a lot of water out of your cells. Moisture gets stuck inside the cell walls and can't escape because your ions are depleted. That's one thing that causes cramps." I was chattering like an imbecile. Talking about an ionic imbalance and suffering from one are two different things.

"Yes, well. . . ." She'd had enough of my lessons for the day.

"If this stuff doesn't work," I added nervously, "I'm going to have to take a shot." Announcing to authorities that I was planning to shoot up heroin struck me as odd, totally disconcerting.

"I know, I know, just try to keep from doing it. The longer you go without a shot before coming in here, the more chance you'll have of succeeding with the cure. Call us if you have a problem."

Yeah, sure. Three days. Why don't I just kick before coming in? Should I call you before or after I do my heroin?

The nurse stood up, ending the interview. "We'll see you in two more days."

I had qualified.

15   I had two days to kill before entering the hospital. It meant fighting off apprehensions, raised in part by having lived for so long on the edge of withdrawal. The first morning I did my last cottons. Only for a little while did this stave off discomforts. Existing on the borders of my habit had honed my mind to a keen awareness, but my physical energies remained low. In my lethargy, sounds, impressions, the passing of time were uncomfortably distinct.

I held little faith in the tiny pills the nurse had given me for cramps, but when they started developing in the afternoon a pill actually brought slight relief. It was only physical relief, though; my mind remained fraught and strained. The pill made me quite thirsty. As I had been instructed, I avoided drinking water, which I knew could increase cramps. Bits of Valium helped take the edge off my nervousness and muscle tension.

It was now July, the very depths of summer, and a heat wave had vigorously instituted itself, ringing in at 107 degrees, a temperature that made many people actually glad to go to work to take advantage of a cooling system. It stifled my urges to leave the room, so I lay around, reading, watching the lighting change, with a couple breaks to fix cans of soup on the hot plate. I avoided weed because of its tendency to magnify my symptoms. The day streets were silent, the heat having driven most everyone inside. It was the same at night, staying in the nineties till past midnight. As much as I desired sleep, I lingered in a sticky, half-conscious state for hours.

The next day was just as hot and slow. Cramps developed in my lower back by afternoon; the pill did nothing for them. This didn't surprise me, but still I battled a worried panic. I knew that I was in no state to go out breaking store windows and running away, bleakly picturing spasmodic collapse in the middle of the street. Some of the junkies had heard of the jewelry store grab and viewed my finger with knowing suspicions.

"Sure you didn't have nothing to do with that?" asked Terry, one of the brothers, on a sales visit to the hotel. "It's too bad when that shit starts to happen, 'cause the cops come down on all of us, you know?"

"Welp, it wasn't me. I don't do that shit, you know that."

"Yeah, I remember." He nodded, still regarding my bandaged finger. "You want to cop anything before you go into the hospital? Maybe something for when you get out, you know, if things don't go well in there?"

"I wouldn't mind, but I don't have a cent. All I have is a few Valiums and the bus fare down there."

Terry nodded slowly. "Things seem to be changing for everybody. You seen Stupid, you know, Nazi Paul?"

"No, haven't seen him for a while now." I didn't relay my theory of him as the character who'd fallen during the bank stickup described in the paper.

But Terry had already put it together. "I think he's gone back to robbing banks."

"Yeah, well, I wouldn't be too surprised by that. It seemed like he was thinking about it sometimes."

"Shit, I know he was! I'd hate it when he pulled out that gun of his and started talking about shit. He wanted me to go in on it with him, but I told him to leave me out of it. Hey, I'll sell you my cottons if you can't afford anything else."

I remained reluctant. Terry sensed it and continued on his rounds. He worried me, since he could probably pick up a few months' expenses by turning in Paul for bank robbery and me for the break-in. But at least he'd taken my mind off my physical state for a bit. I tried to dispel concerns over him. A thin coating of nervous sweat soon covered me, exacerbated by ceaseless heat and no dope. Soon afterward I heard a knock and was actually relieved to see that crumb Steve in the doorway.

"Mind if I use your room to get off in?" he asked, walking past me as he spoke. I realized that he'd quite likely lay some dope on me after his shot. I had to turn off my mind to patiently watch him prepare it. After he poked around for a while, a gruesome, cursing affair, he finally found the vein. As his shot started coming on, he pulled out a wad of money, at which he squinted, and drunkenly leafed through it, counting. There was $300 or $400 there. I surmised that between the marks he'd just made on his hand and the probable source of that money he was well on his way back to prison.

"Aren't you even curious where I got this bread?" he baitingly asked.

"Not really," I replied. "It's not my business. I figure if you want to tell me, you'll tell, but I don't really care." He'd obviously just robbed someone, so why did I need to know the details?

Consternation crossed his face. "Boy, you're a strange guy. Most people would wanna know where this came from. You sure you don't wanna know? Well, here's a little something for letting me use your room." He peeled off a measly three bucks, then handed me a few grains of junk, for which I was more grateful. "Man." He patted his belly between caresses of his money. "I just had me the greatest dinner. Shit, they sure don't feed you like that in the can."

Then he stood up, walked over to the bathroom, and threw the whole thing up. Didn't flush the toilet. I never saw him again after he left.

Now that I was again undistracted, my physical discomforts asserted themselves. It was only a matter of waiting overnight to get to the hospital, but the symptoms were getting so strong that I had to take the small shot. Briefly, I worried about the combination of the pill and the heroin, but I discarded those concerns. As it turned out, nothing bad happened, and the shot went a long way toward easing my suffering. I didn't get too high, but it did relax me enough to enjoy a joint. Trying to milk the shot for nodding dreams, I perched my legs up on the windowsill and smoked the last of my tobaccos, but there wasn't quite enough medicine in me. It was nighttime already, and the shot helped me to get to sleep quickly. The only thing that kept me awake was an ambivalent pondering on the hospital. It included a tentative sense of relief that my nightmares might be ending. I fell asleep to images of nurses delivering me doses of methadone. White-clothed angels of mercy smilingly wheeling in trays at my request. My tax dollars at work.

I had no problem getting up for my morning appointment. I straightened up the room and made the bed, rare actions for me. Not knowing what my state of mind or body would be upon my return, I didn't want reminders of the depressing existence I'd be coming back to. It was a small, pathetic attempt at buffering my homecoming.

The lengthy bus trip into South Tucson was easier since I knew the way. I didn't have bus fare home. A Mexican driver was making an imbecile of himself for the benefit of two adolescent Mexican girls. They briefly stopped laughing to gawk at the Anglo's torn blue jeans, with impolite leers at my long hair. My eyes held deep shadows, and I felt a scowl on my face. They unleashed a stupid giggling whenever the bus driver said, *"Abre la puerta!"* (Open the door) while actually closing it, and then their demonic eyeteeth flashed. I swear that they knew just how irritating their sharp, thin, forced laughter was for me and the other passengers. My scowl deepened as I got up at the hospital bus stop.

"Abre la puerta!"

The idiot driver closed the door on me while I was still on the steps. In a rage I spun around, ready to rip open the doors and tear off his face, but he pulled away. The girls' shrieks blended into exhaust and fading engines. Within seconds my anger was beaten into passivity by heat and vicious glare off unfamiliar sidewalks. I turned and saw a collection of dull, dark faces eyeing me carefully. Quickly I entered the hospital waiting room and announced myself to the secretary. After a few minutes she motioned me back to see the nurse I'd spoken with before.

The nurse seemed pleased when I related that I hadn't done any dope since the last time I'd seen her. "Good. That means your body has already detoxed itself. It takes only eighteen hours for the body to detox itself. You shouldn't find it too hard in there."

This didn't sit well with me; my greatest apprehension was

to be committed to the ward yet not receive enough medicines. So I told the truth, that it had been only the previous evening since I'd had something. It made no difference. Then she started in about my injured finger again, but I so readily assumed my previous casual, cheery attitude that she almost immediately gave up. Some people so enthusiastically get into the confession mode that they talk themselves into a felony rap, but I wasn't going to be one of them.

The nurse pulled out some paperwork outlining an odd set of conditions, which I had to sign in order to enter the ward. These included that I couldn't say I'd ever been in a psycho ward, even though that's where I'd be for the next five days ("Don't say you were here"); that I couldn't claim having been on a methadone treatment program, despite the fact that I would be for five days; that I'd never have to admit that I was ever treated for heroin withdrawal anywhere except on the stand in federal court. Odd, but nothing I found objectionable. I suppose that they were worried lest I use my brief internment to get monetary benefits.

I didn't have that much experience with methadone, having taken it orally only one time. I had felt no real rush and had suffered nausea. It was devised by the Nazis to counter wartime morphine shortages and was originally named in honor of Adolf Hitler. I had once shared a hospital room with a youth who had made the mistake of shooting noninjectable methadone. His arm was black, and he didn't know if he'd still have it when he awoke from his operation.

After I signed the papers, they led me down a long hall to a pair of locked doors. When they let me in, they watched my face as the doors were relocked behind me. I found myself unperturbed at being placed in the psycho ward, though I felt the location inappropriate to my treatment. In a way, I looked forward to it with great interest. How many people get to live in a psycho ward on the condition that they can't say they were ever in one? I was given some hospital garb to change into and shown a bed. The ward normally held only ten beds, but extras had been set up despite lack of state approval. I had bed number 13.

Actually, there were adjoining wards to separate the sexes. A nurses' station stood in the fulcrum between the two. Just slipping behind an opening in the counter gave one access to rows upon rows of pills, all brightly lit with labels facing out. Because of this temptation, the patients were periodically gathered and warned not to attempt to get at them or they would, whatever their condition or circumstances, be arrested and carted off to jail. The second day I was there a little, wiry Mexican girl, who was kicking a barbiturate habit, was caught red-handed trying to grab some Seconals. Sure enough, within minutes she was handed over to a sheriff's deputy. Barbiturates is one of the hardest kicks there is. It can be fatal. Placing them before an addict is like waving water in front of someone dying of thirst. She tried a little begging for mercy, but they wouldn't budge. Then a look of real fear evolved onto her face. Carting her off to jail seemed the height of medical negligence.

White-clad nurses loitered behind the counter, sporting various odd caps denoting where they'd trained. The nurses' station was fraught with the tension that often passes for operating efficiency among groups of professional women. There were a couple of male aides, in street clothes, who associated on a more down-to-earth level with the patients during the daytime. One casually mentioned that I might be interested in going into "Group" but that it wasn't mandatory. I indicated that I wasn't attracted to group therapy, and he didn't press it, saying only that I might change my mind.

I was given a dose of methadone within minutes of my changing and getting into bed. I asked for and received one an hour later and soon had a fairly good buzz on. The nurses kept a leery eye for any sign of me nodding out, which they'd interpret as meaning that I was taking too much. The rush was nonexistent, and there really wasn't much sense of euphoria, just a pleasant, relaxed intoxication. This was augmented by Valiums three times a day. They also gave me acetaminophen, which is surprisingly effective for minor withdrawal symptoms. At night we all got a Dalmane sleeping pill, rather mild, and it didn't work if you tried to stay awake too long. The food was plentiful and good, served in our beds, and snack trays were rolled in between times. All I had to do was lie there, take my medicine, and eat. After the duress and starvation of the previous few months, I found this quite a welcome relief.

During the first day my father stopped in, bringing a beat-up guitar he owned and a couple packs of cigarettes I'd requested. I initially appreciated his visit. "Well, what do you think?" he asked with a frown, indicating my dubious surroundings.

"It's great!" I enthusiastically replied. "It's like a vacation!"

He scowled, seeming to take my reply personally. I think he felt that family members he committed should be properly despondent. But I couldn't help the relief that I felt; it *was* like a vacation, and a badly needed one at that.

"You should think about getting into Group." He glowered and stalked away.

Lest the reader be disappointed, understand that I'm not going to unfold some vertiginous snake pit panorama. While the male side of the ward was overcrowded, the dozen guys there were generally pretty quiet and well medicated, and they provided diversion in the variety of their symptoms. One tall, muscular black had been committed by the court after shooting up his lawn with a .45 pistol. He seemed as sane as anyone I'd met on the outside. Another black, a youth, had taken too much LSD, which seemed to have whittled his attention span. He was always drifting off in midsentence.

An unobtrusive old Yaqui Indian spent long periods kneeling and praying to a colorful picture of Jesus. The small, gray man wept when I accompanied this with soft guitar music, and his tightly braided hair shivered gently on his back. In the bed next to mine lay a rather high-strung Mexican guy about my age. He was as normal as the day is long. But evening was another matter. Then he would indicate to a nurse that it was "that time," and she'd strap him into bed with strong leather belts. Through the dark hours he'd jerk and struggle, foaming and shuddering in sheer terror at some collection of invisible demons who accosted him at night. His face was a study in horror as he regarded the foot of his bed. Sometimes I'd hold a cigarette in his mouth for him.

The first day a tall, thin man was wheeled unconscious into the ward and strapped into a bed. A failed suicide, he'd had some sort of horrid mercury compound pumped from his stomach. He seemed pretty disappointed when he came to. Parents and siblings came in for a tearful visit, and we all tensed when some asshole of a doctor started scolding the patient, telling him that suicide was against the law. The doctor was personally insulted that this felony had occurred. It was nauseating, especially when he acted like he was doing everyone a favor by not prosecuting. Talk about living in a fantasy world.

Then there was this kid transplanted from the East Coast who, from what I could see, served as a warning on the dangers of overindulgent parents. Harry was about nineteen, and he proudly announced to them that he was pregnant.

"I talked to Father about it, Mom," he explained. "It's okay with the Church."

"Now, Harry, we've been through all that before." Mom sighed resignedly. These were the people who make desert natives scream, "Go back to New York!"

I was the only one there for methadone treatment. Some of

the patients found their own personal demons easier to understand than the idea that I'd cultivated a heroin habit.

"Shee-it, now whud you wanna go an do thashit fuh?" asked
the tall black. "Doan you know thashit's the *worst* of all?"

I smiled and shrugged. "It just happened." This guy's shooting up the neighborhood with a .45 and he's still copping the
old "There's nothing worse than a junkie" rap. At least my
shots couldn't hit anyone else.

The first couple days passed pleasantly. The aides enjoyed
getting paid to play games of chess with me, and I was free to
eat and nap as I wished. No one pressured me in the least. By
the second afternoon I was a bit surprised at how little effect
the methadone pills were having. I had expected to be nodding
out for hours, but evidently my tolerance was higher than I
thought. The treatment plan allowed as much methadone as I
desired the first day, then four the second day, three the next,
two the next, and one the last, before checking out the day
after. The last one I could take anytime I chose on the day
before I was to check out.

By the second day I was kicking back and thoroughly enjoying my good fortune. No one minded if I made a complete pig
of myself, and, after having lived on starvation rations for so
long, I took full advantage of the policy. Valiums helped
smooth over the boredom, and I didn't fight the sleeping pills,
preferring a good night's rest. I do recall that I didn't dream
any night there, always falling into a deep, sound sleep.

It was in the midst of deep sleep, during my second night,
that my eyes suddenly opened as if I'd just been tapped on the
shoulder. The ward was gray and silent. I was instantly awake
and looked around for a second or two. Then I felt two long,
bony hands grab my guts, squeezing my intestines as hard as
they could. I rolled on my side and doubled up as cramps
stabbed at me, trying to catch a breath with my knees pressed

on my chest. I didn't have enough wind left even to yell. I knew it wouldn't do me any good, anyway. I waited for the strength of the spasm to pass, then, clutching my abdomen, I struggled up to the nurses' station. A single nurse held down the fort at night.

"Ahhh—I need another methadone. I have terrible cramps!"

The nurse calmly looked up from her magazine. "Are you sure that you don't just have gas? Why don't I give you a Donnatal for gas? That's what it turns out to be in a lot of cases like yours."

"I don't think this is gas."

"But what if you take methadone and you don't really need it?"

"It's not gas, damnit! I know what it is. I need methadone—they said I could have it whenever I needed it." I was reaching a point of impotent fury, yet so severe was the pain that I could speak only with teeth clamped. "I need methadone *now!*"

She gave a little laugh. "Okay, no problem, Mr. Frank. Here you go." She handed me a little mustard cup with a pill in it. It had been sitting there ready to go. I looked at it and hesitated. "It's okay, that's really methadone, just like you wanted. Go ahead, take it."

I slobbered it down with a little water, then continued to stand, leaning against the counter. With dismay I realized it would be another thirty to forty minutes before the pill took effect. But I felt better standing there stretching out my stomach muscles, so I spent the next hour talking with the nurse. She was calmer than any of the day crew and, once past the methadone problem, was pleasant to converse with.

"The withdrawal pains are always really there," she explained. "The methadone covers them up until it wears off. Actually, you've just been getting placebos since this afternoon. They like to check and see if you're really addicted or just faking it."

After about an hour the pain subsided enough for me to return to sleep.

Soon after awakening the next morning, I got to meet the architect of this quaint little deception. The head psychiatrist swept in with an entourage of interns and students in tow. They were a splendid collection of the robotic types found in this line of work. Most had learned to exude the mandatory aura of tolerance. This is nothing more than a skin-deep sham in the social services. A good look made it clear why the psychology profession has practically the highest suicide rate among job categories; they were rigid and clearly under a lot of pressure. The head psychiatrist, on the other hand, had long ago dispensed with any allusions to sympathetic, empathic postures. Displaying an abrasive, cover-my-ass manner, he was clearly used to having orders summarily followed by charges and patients alike. It was he who had designed the program to administer placebos to see if the patient experienced discomfort. Apparently there was some fear that someone might try to sneak in and get high for five days for free. Then the doctor would get in trouble. Among the students gathered obediently in a half circle behind him was Renny, the fellow who had been running my mother's ward the evening she committed suicide.

A nurse spoke, indicating the exhibit, me. "He had bad cramps last night, Doctor."

"Well, that sounds like it then." He nodded with satisfaction, turning to the students. They all nodded. I was qualified as a genuine junkie. "Mr. Frank, we have some group therapy sessions that I think you ought to get into." This was spoken in a tone of command.

"I don't really want to go into group therapy."

His head popped back like he'd been slapped. There was a seething pause.

"We've found," he resumed testily, "that for people to have the best chance of not having a relapse of their addiction, is when they go into Group. If you really want to recover, you should really consider it. I would be much happier if I knew you were doing that."

"When I checked in here, they said that group therapy wasn't mandatory."

"We really prefer that *everybody* takes full advantage of the program—and that means getting into Group. That way we know that they have the best chance of succeeding with the program. Hey! Some people like it so much they stay in for months! Why, even some of these students are in group therapy!" He turned his palm upward and gave a halfhearted grin. Grinning looked painful. Behind him the students smiled and nodded.

We continued this sparring over his reluctance to admit that attendance wasn't required. Clearly, he didn't like failing to convince me in front of his audience and was getting more and more blown out with my refusal. Never having been a group-oriented person, I would no sooner appear in Group than climb into a confessional.

"Mr. Frank." He finally stood up, red faced. "You're full of shit!"

The heads of some of the students retreated timidly into their shoulders. Relieved, I gave him my best shit-eating grin. After all, there was only so far he could go. I was the son of a colleague.

But he was right about one thing. I was, in fact, quite full of shit. My steady diet of heroin had left me in the most complete state of constipation, and I hadn't moved my bowels since before entering the hospital. At my request for a laxative the nurses acted as if I'd suggested my own drug therapy. The whole attitude of the place was purely either/or. Either you did drugs and were a lousy addict or you did nothing, not even aspirin or laxatives. Upon checking out they advised me that I'd probably suffer from headaches, maybe for up to six months, but that taking merely an aspirin would be flirting with demons. I don't know which was more ridiculous, the idea that aspirin was a threat to my recovery or the thought that they had any say in how I would live after leaving their clutches. I had a small stash of Valiums back in the room, and I was damned if I was going to throw them away on principle.

Later that afternoon I had a bedside interview with the intern I'd recognized earlier among the students. Renny was his name. We remembered each other from my visit to my mother's ward after her death. Plainly, he was ill at ease in my presence. As he related her last night to me, he spoke softly, often looking down.

"Your mother was really a very, very nice person. You know, the night she died she was really quite upbeat. She was singing along with everyone else, clapping her hands, and the other people really enjoyed having her around." I pictured my mother's horribly gnarled, arthritic hands clapping. Renny folded and unfolded his hands, intertwining long fingers nervously. He had trouble meeting my eye. Actually, I held little animosity toward him for the situation he continued to describe.

"She'd gotten some dry cleaning brought to her during the day, and it was in her room. In that ward we're supposed to keep out anything patients might use to hurt themselves. I knew it was in there, but I thought, 'No, she wouldn't really do anything like that.' I didn't want to embarrass her by taking it. She was quite happy, and all that evening . . . We're told that people who commit suicide are often in high spirits just before they do it, but I just didn't think that . . . I check all the patients throughout the night about every fifteen or twenty minutes, so she must've started just after one of my checks. By the time I got back she'd already stopped breathing with the bag wrapped around her head. . . ."

Renny clearly felt terrible about his part in her suicide, and at one point I found myself in the absurd position of having to comfort him. He had one of those calm, understanding personalities, which, for some reason, always makes me picture how that person would look in a frothing rage.

With that off his chest, he began administering a bunch of verbal response tests to me, designed to gauge my mental clarity. The one I remember best had him reading off lists of single-digit numbers and having me repeat them backward. After reaching fourteen numbers and having me recite them backward correctly, he got the idea that I could think coherently. This surprised him.

"How can you remember so many numbers while you're under the influence of strong narcotics?"

"I just remember them as phone numbers."

Like most social service people who work to cure the "drug problem," he was shockingly uneducated about dope. These people simply cannot imagine drug use and any kind of productive activity as existing together. Often, their idea of getting high is getting dizzy, and, of course, they can't see the point of that. Nor can I. So the next question was no surprise.

"So, Scott, why did you feel the need to do heroin in the first place?"

I knew it was coming. I didn't know from whom, where, or when, but I knew that I could count on hearing it. I had prepared a pat answer, just like for the cut on my finger. In light of who received it, it was ironic.

"I had been dabbling in it a bit before my mother died, but it was nothing big—I wasn't strung out or anything. But after she died I found that it just washed away the pain. It just depressed me so much when I thought about her and how my father acted afterward that I no longer really cared about whether I got strung out or not. I guess that's the danger of fooling around with the stuff; you might end up having something really bad happen for you, and you know that there's something that'll be sure to take the pain away."

Now this was not entirely fiction. But I knew that they'd never buy the real reason: *I had liked doing it.* It had made me feel wonderful! I was not ridden with suppressed feelings of guilt. I did not agree that it was the kind of disease they claimed it was, that is, some kind of convoluted subconscious, Dr. Jekyll/ Mr. Hyde, self-destructive, who-is-this-hidden-ogre-within-me type of bit. It is a metabolic disease. But junk made me feel wonderful, and I enjoyed that. Mentally active. Physically delicious. Serene euphoria. Well-being. I see nothing wrong with feeling any of these things. After I'd been doing it intravenously, and for too long, it no longer provided the same thrill, but by then I couldn't kick it myself. I didn't like doing it anymore, and I heard about a program to help me kick. I steadfastly refuse, to this day, to adopt some guilt-ridden complex over it. How can it be legal in part of the world and the people who use it function in everyday society, and simultaneously be such a source of dread and woe in our part of the world? Because here it's against the law? And somehow, magically, from the law springs a compulsion to get users to confess to feelings of inadequacy, self-punishment, manic-depressive psychosis? Or because it's addictive? Many people, including some doctors, believe that addiction is purely a personal choice. Well, I wasn't buying the party line, but I knew I couldn't express my real feelings. It certainly wouldn't fly in "Group."

Addiction is a physical disease. The psychological effects are most often secondary to the metabolic alteration. This is true for alcoholics as well. As Burroughs points out, treating physical imbalances from a psychological standpoint is as logical as sending a flu victim to group therapy. Alcoholics and other addicts experience relapses and the continuing "need to" because their physical condition remains uncorrected. That's why they call it a fix. When you consider that for the whole time the addict has been putting chemicals into his body, the idea of physical disease becomes logical. Why should we have to endure an unending drug addict and alcoholic crime wave when we can end it by treating the physical basis of the disease?

Renny bought my cover story. Maybe my social worker–father would be embarrassed over my aversion to group therapy, but he could be proud that I had learned the right lines about compulsive, self-defeating behavior!

The rest of the days were rather uneventful. My dose shrank a bit every day, but I still got steady Valiums and sleeping pills. About the only thing of real interest that took place was when Harry, the pregnant miracle boy, gave birth. I beheld him in his bed, straining and getting red faced and sweaty. Then followed a period of great calm. Afterward, he called in the nurses and the doctor to show them his new child. Swaddling it lovingly inside a soft, white blanket and beaming proudly as the world looked on, he displayed a masterfully well-formed turd.

The uproar that this caused was entirely inappropriate to the crime. Harry's offspring was torn with disgust from his arms, and he was thrown into a locked isolation room. I felt painfully poignant amusement as I watched Harry silently yell and pound on the window of the door to that soundproofed, padded cell. Mute pleas made it seem as if he were about to be punitively shot off into the eternity of deepest, blackest space.

The day before I was to leave the ward, my fifth day, a nurse informed me that I had one more dose of methadone coming. I could take it whenever I wished, *but* I couldn't leave the hospital for twenty-four hours after I took it, *so* if I wished to leave early the next day, I'd better take it soon. I agreed to consume it immediately, and she handed me one of the little mustard cups. The nurses always watched carefully whenever administering pills, going so far as to make the patients open their mouths to see if they had really swallowed them. Handily, I stuck the pill into the side of my mouth, took a big gulp of water, and opened up. The nurse saw nothing in there, but she did look at me kind of funny. I had decided on saving the last dose until bedtime. That way I'd stave off whatever discomforts I might feel the next day, and I could combine it with my Valium and sleeping pill. They hadn't allowed me a decent, nodding high since I'd arrived, and I was yenning for one.

After lights-out I surreptitiously swallowed my cocktail, then spent a lovely couple hours sitting up in bed, smoking cigarettes, and feeling good. The high felt a little trashy from the mix, but I was in no position to be picky. I had no trouble falling asleep when I desired to.

My little entertainment did not go unnoticed, for the next morning I was subjected to a grilling. It seemed like I was high last night. Had I saved up some pills and taken them all at once? I was seen sitting up and smoking. Looked like I was enjoying that Marlboro a little too much. We said no discharge until twenty-four hours without medication.

No, no, nothing like that. Just sitting up smoking cigarettes, taking in the atmosphere. They weren't buying it, but there was nothing they could do. After a ripple of resentful shrugs, they chalked up a mark in the probable failure column. How can we help him if he doesn't want to help himself?

Actually, they'd helped me a great deal. They'd helped me get over the Big Hump; I'd finally kicked, and I knew that I didn't want to get back on the stuff. The physical kick was my problem. Psychologically I was ready to stop. Sure, I had longings for the great dreams and feelings of my early days, but whenever I thought about obtaining them I realized that all I could expect from the needle and heroin would be that horrible feeling of a thick coating of lead pouring over me, followed by anxiety. And having to feel it *every day*. Despite all their quizzings, I didn't admit to having the small stash of Valiums back in my room. I didn't buy the "either you stay off everything or you're nothing but a low-down junkie" philosophy. That intractable policy, with its accompanying "all drugs are bad, you sick fool" attitude, has contributed to more people returning to damaging, irresponsible drug use than it can ever hope to keep off.

There was a little inkling of a problem lingering in the back of my mind for my last few days in the hospital, and, on the morning of my discharge, it blossomed into full-fledged panic. I was aghast at the prospect of returning to my shoddy little room. I was broke. And I'd be surrounded by the same crowd in which I'd become enmeshed during my lengthy stay there.

With this in mind I had phoned a friend, Barry, to ask him to pick me up. When they unlocked the doors for me, I must admit that I was happier to be let out than I had been to be let in. That last day another candidate for the methadone treatment arrived. They asked me not to inform him of their little placebo trick. I figured, why should I? It would only cause him worries. I still don't understand why they housed me in a psycho ward. It seemed an inappropriate place to administer the treatment. My rationality had stuck out like a sore thumb.

I waited out in front of the hospital. It was a healthy 109 degrees, and the aftereffects of my previous evening's cocktail caused glare on the sidewalks and walls to shoot behind my eyes like spears. Finally, two hours later, I saw Barry's green, late-model convertible meander up into the driveway.

He'd bought this car by transporting weed, and those cross-country drives were one of the many things we had in common to discuss. I'd known him since the fourth grade. It was I who had administered Barry's first shot of heroin. "I just want to see what all you guys have been raving about," he claimed. He didn't feel it at first, but a few minutes later he declared that he liked it alot. Nevertheless, alcohol remained his true love. He drank fairly steadily—tequila—from late morning after breakfast until late at night. Eventually he developed an alcohol habit so overwhelming that he would arrive at a party stone cold sober and in two hours be passed out, pissing on the mattress and himself.

With the car's top down, the hot breeze tousled our hair. I found the press of the sun on my head unpleasant. My simmering worries threatened to boil over. "Barry! I can't go back to the Geronimo! It'll just be the same fucking thing. I don't know if I can handle it!"

Even with his bald spot Barry had always taken the sun better than I did. Glancing sideways, he noticed my discomfort and started to raise the car's roof. "Why don't you come and stay at my place for a few days? I was thinking you might need something like that."

My sense of relief at not having to see the Geronimo was tremendous. Even though it loomed in the near future, my dread was partially quelled, since it wasn't immediately bearing down on me. Barry had a nice little apartment up in the hills of the Tucson Mountains to the west of town. Always a good host, he offered drinks as soon as I arrived, but I just rolled up a joint, avoiding booze for the first couple days. After that I joined him in a few drinks and some joints, but there was no way I could keep up with him and I didn't try.

Barry was a writer, though he hadn't published anything. I'd always envied his ability to polish off ten or twenty single-spaced typewritten pages at a sitting. "I'm writing the great American novel!" he declared. But his writing was quite uncompelling, merely rehashes of conversations and social situations encountered at bars; for the most part it was boring and unreadable. He didn't appreciate my lack of enthusiasm for his work.

This brief, idyllic vacation ended after five days. Those few days after kicking, when everything looks so bright and wonderful, passed all too quickly. I was finally faced with the inevitable—the return to Room 316 at the Geronimo. Barry laid a twenty on me and dropped me off.

My arrival went quite unnoticed. My absence had probably gone the same way. Nobody had broken into my room while I was gone. What would they have gotten, a hot plate? The halls were just as shadowy and still. I was surprised that the bed was made; I had forgotten doing that. The coolers hummed softly. From down the hall came the faint ringing of a phone. The place was as tomblike as I recalled, and it made me wonder at the extent of the panic I'd felt at the prospect of returning. The respite at Barry's had done me good. Looking out my window, I noticed Nazi Paul's bicycle still chained to the lightpost on the sidewalk below. It had been there before I left and looked untouched. He had stolen it from somewhere.

I had no urges to do any more shots or buy any dope. And not because I was broke. I enjoyed the freedom of not having to hustle around and score, of not feeling high whether I wanted to or not, and of simply having energy to get up off my ass and go outside. Not that there was much to do out there, but having the option felt good. Though the days were boring, somehow they weren't as bleak and flat as I remembered them without junk.

Sitting in my quiet room, I looked back over a long casualty list. Yaqui Jim, Little Bill, Richard, and on and on. I never again heard from that jerk Steve. A couple months later I saw a news blurb mentioning (in about forty words) that he'd become the second knifing fatality of the year up at Florence State Prison. He was always a pushy, disagreeable guy, and I guess he'd pushed someone too far.

About a week after my return I heard chains rattling below my window. Peering down, I spied Nazi Paul trying to sneak his bike away. He was such a bumbler that he of course made noise doing it.

"Hey! Long time no see!" I called down.

He jumped and looked up with a grimace. "You would have to be the one to see me," he grumbled. "Has anybody been here asking for me?"

"Like who? You mean Terry and those guys?"

A painful squint. He put his fingers to his lips. "No," he whispered back up. "I mean somebody else. You know, have any guys *in suits* been asking about me?"

I still didn't get it. "No, no," I called down, still too loudly for him. I lowered my voice at his wince. "You want me to give someone a message?"

After throwing his hands up in disgust, he started wheeling the bike away. "No," he growled. "Don't be giving anyone messages about me. Don't even say that you saw me, okay?" With that he left, and I never saw him again.

A few days later there was a small article in the paper reciting an apprehension for bank robbery at some cheap downtown motel. The FBI had shown a photo to the clerk, and the clerk had pointed out to the pool where Paul was sunning himself. I could picture his scrawny body, ribs casting a shadow on his stomach. He hadn't learned to avoid Tucson motels with his hot money, $9,000 this time. Tucson had been like hitting a brick wall for Paul. He offered no resistance.

I still sometimes spent evenings smoking cigarettes and joints on the third-floor porch, but I no longer greeted the dawn. So it wasn't a problem avoiding the junkies' circle down on the night lawn. When I felt like getting high, beer and weed were my mainstays. Quite reliable.

Gradually my apprehensions subsided. I found that I had restraint against any desires to institute a new habit, and most sellers didn't press me about buying stuff. Settling down to a slow routine based in my room, I sometimes played music with people around the neighborhood, read, visited a few friends. Beer and weed were accepted intoxicants in most college-age circles, as they are today, so I fit right in. Most of the people I visited had no idea that I'd just gotten off heroin. Sometimes I spied Mac, the Vietnam medic; I avoided his gaze. I never did hear from the cops about that jewelry store incident. The only unpleasant experience I had was when I visited a drummer friend of mine and we drank beer and smoked some of his hashish. The white mold on the outside of the hash should have tipped me off, but it wasn't until I'd taken a number of hits that I realized it was mixed with opium. That ended up causing me a couple days' discomfort, but it passed. I was determined to get over it.

My afternoon walks around the crumbling lodges and grounds of the hotel were short. Halfheartedly, I hunted those old ghosts and memories that were the fabric of the Geronimo. They stayed well hidden from the day's stark, white heat. Anyone with any sense would. Parts of the lawn had browned when someone made the mistake of watering it in the daytime. Each droplet of water became a tiny magnifying glass and burned the grass to shit. As I regarded bushes and trees in the courtyard, the sunlight reflecting off leaves was so bright that hundreds of piercing white spots irritated my head. The courtyard was heavy with the cooing of doves. A radio faintly announced that it had hit 111 degrees. Spots of green afterimages swam before me. The buzzing of the cicadas was vibrant, fanatical. Inviting shadows under weathered arches and on porches suggested hints of secret mysteries, but they faded like a mirage when I walked into their shade to cool off. It was sweltering in the shade, too. I stayed in my room during the day, waiting until sunset to venture outside.

During an early-evening twilight walk, with the sun behind the buildings, I ran into Stegman over by the main archway leading into the courtyard. Same green shirt, pens in the pocket. I saw no index cards. His unkempt beard had grown little gray curls at the bottom, and he smelled salty.

"Well, well, young man. Where you been keeping yourself? Haven't seen you around for a bit."

"I've been on a little vacation."

"Someplace nice, I hope. Enjoy yourself?"

"Oh, I had a great time. Boy, I really needed it." I changed the subject to end this charade. "Looks like you've been spending some time in the sun. Your face is all red, especially your nose." That thick, bulbous nose was like a beacon.

"Not me. Never go in the sun, not if I can help it. No, no, that red you see on my face is just high blood pressure. Gotta take pills for that. Guess I just had too much fun in my younger days. Too many hot toddies around the old fireplace."

A portrait formed: Stegman in a plush armchair, feet propped up to a huge stone hearth. In a silk smoking robe and slippers, he held a glass as flames danced off his round, red cheeks.

"Just working on the angles, then?" I asked. He seemed distracted, melancholy.

"Ahh-pih!" He blew out a puff of disgust. "If I were a bit younger I'd have the stamina and patience to work with those young upstarts they have over there." He nodded toward the university. "Time was that you could . . . ahh, just born too late . . . fourteenth century would've done. . . ." He suddenly faced me. "I know what I did. I made history! But"—he sighed—"I guess that'll be a secret between Pythagoras and me . . . and you, too."

I expected him to shake his head sadly, but he stood there regarding me. No judgment, no regret, like he didn't have the time to waste on such frivolities. He looked so firmly at me that there was nothing I could add to the equation. My head gave a small, involuntary jerk before that potent gaze.

He spoke again. "Gonna be taking a vacation of sorts soon myself."

Did he mean death? "Oh, yeah?" I brightened up. "Where you going?"

"Oh, back to Ohio, visit my grandkids, then stay up with my sister. She invited me to move in with them. I'll be checking out of here after all these years. Who knows what these ten years add up to?"

Somewhere behind me the sun peeked out from under a cloud, making the Geronimo's peach pastels flare splendorously. We stood by the archway, the pillars glowing. A gate for initiates into the dynasties of Phoenicia, Alexandria, the Golden Age of Greece. A quivering began in my gut.

"So . . . you're moving out? Well, uh, do you know when, that is, uh, is anyone getting your room up there?" I felt a flutter of excitement.

"You're too late, son. By about a week. It's already spoken for."

I sucked in the side of my mouth. That was the week I'd been kicking. I tried not to show my disappointment. "Gee, Stegman, I'll be sorry to see you go. Listen, let me have an address and I'll drop you a line."

He raised a brow slightly and looked at me like I was some harmless, yapping pup. At loose ends, I blathered on. "Yeah! Maybe I'll come up and visit you up there."

Old Stegman regarded a small pink and gray cloud in the

sunset. He reached to his nose with thumb and forefinger, clamped them firmly together, and deftly tugged a long, gray hair from his nostril.

"We'll probably never see each other again," he declared firmly.

Moisture formed around the rims of his eyes. That nose hair had to have hurt. Then he reverted to his distant, mildly thoughtful gaze, and I realized that the specter of his own death was lulling itself into acceptance in the idling hum of his mind. I wondered again if he'd seen me on the night lawn from up in his tower. Then I knew that it didn't matter.

The days blended into summer haze. I passed them patiently, knowing I was putting time between me and my habit and that would be the real cure. The headaches I'd been warned about developed, but Valiums and aspirins took care of the worst ones. They passed after a few months.

I kept drifting along. Sometimes I'd stay for days with well-to-do friends and eat sumptuously, get a bit of money, then return to the Geronimo and starve. My room rent fell further and further behind, but I didn't worry. Something would come up eventually.

I didn't miss all the tough talk and bluster that I'd heard over the previous year. Nor did I seek out the junk crowd there; we no longer had a common ground. Every once in a while I'd get a packing job or throw together some penny-ante deal, and it would carry me a bit further. That and Seeing the Threads. But I did pine for those long hours of reverie, the private, silent times when I so effortlessly fused with the lingering, subtle spirit of the Geronimo. Those gentle ghosts sometimes seemed to be the reason that the place still stood. Could I and these flophouse residents, I wondered, be just incidental to these grounds, and the shadows, voices, and dreams be the real reasons for the Geronimo? After all, we who paid the rent were just passing through.

I ate. I dreamt. I was honed into just one more element in that crumbling matrix of arches and rooms. My deathlike skull gave up its deep bags and pallor, and I gained weight and color. I stopped fighting the flatness of the days. Borrowing a guitar, I wrote a song:

> *Remember your dreams*
> *And the gifts that they brought.*
> *Forget what you are*
> *And what you're not.*

One morning I awoke toward the first light of dawn. It was so silent and still—I had to remember where I was. Open windows let in fresh, crisp air. The coolest time of day. A breeze caressed me gently, and I heard it rustling in the trees. There's a quality of wind so soothing that it fairly lulls you into mist. My mind's eye saw it blowing through darkened arches, down dimly lit halls. That cool dawn breeze was so relaxing; I just floated in a lovely space between waking and sleep. And I heard the whispers of finer times.

When the world still spun for dreamers. And we thanked them for their dreams. Through the ether they cast new airwaves to this desert, with such strange and simple shows. And the dreams of Tesla, in his tuxedo, holding that ball of cold fire in the palm of his hand.

It was a cool, blue desert dawn of white tuxedos and elegant gowns. Lovers met between the lodges, faint music flowed across the grounds. And they caress beneath a slow dawn glow. Twilight drifts through my curtains; darkness lingers in the corners. It's a gentle, blue, cottony light, just before the sun appears. You know, it's when time takes a breather.

Today I sit in the New Geronimo. It's now a collection of smart little boutiques, bookstores, and hip restaurants. The upper floors have been converted to offices. Richard's old lodge, Number 1, is an espresso shop. No sign remains of the sacking it received from the cops. All Ptolemaic sensations have been exorcised. Nazi Paul's lodge serves sushi. The hotel lobby has been redone. Somewhere behind new false walls stand a dormant fireplace and sealed doors to hidden passages. Foolishly, they did away with the old phone booth. Its polished oak and glass would be the height of chic now. The whole complex is repainted pastel pink, the wooden bordering, blue. At least they didn't tear the thing down.

On the other hand, most of the night lawn has been preserved. The old tower still commands the eye to regard its memories. My trusted haven, the outside, third-floor porch, still exists, overlooking seas of students on their way to and from the university's main gates. Only a practiced eye can glimpse the ghosts and romance that have insisted on staying. And hidden under one of the outside stairs, placed to jump into the mind at a defenseless moment, I've scrawled some graffiti:

Why suffer?